W9-BWM-373

the food of
CHINA

the food of CHINA

Photography by Jason Lowe
Recipes by Deh-Ta Hsiung and Nina Simonds

MURDOCH
BOOKS

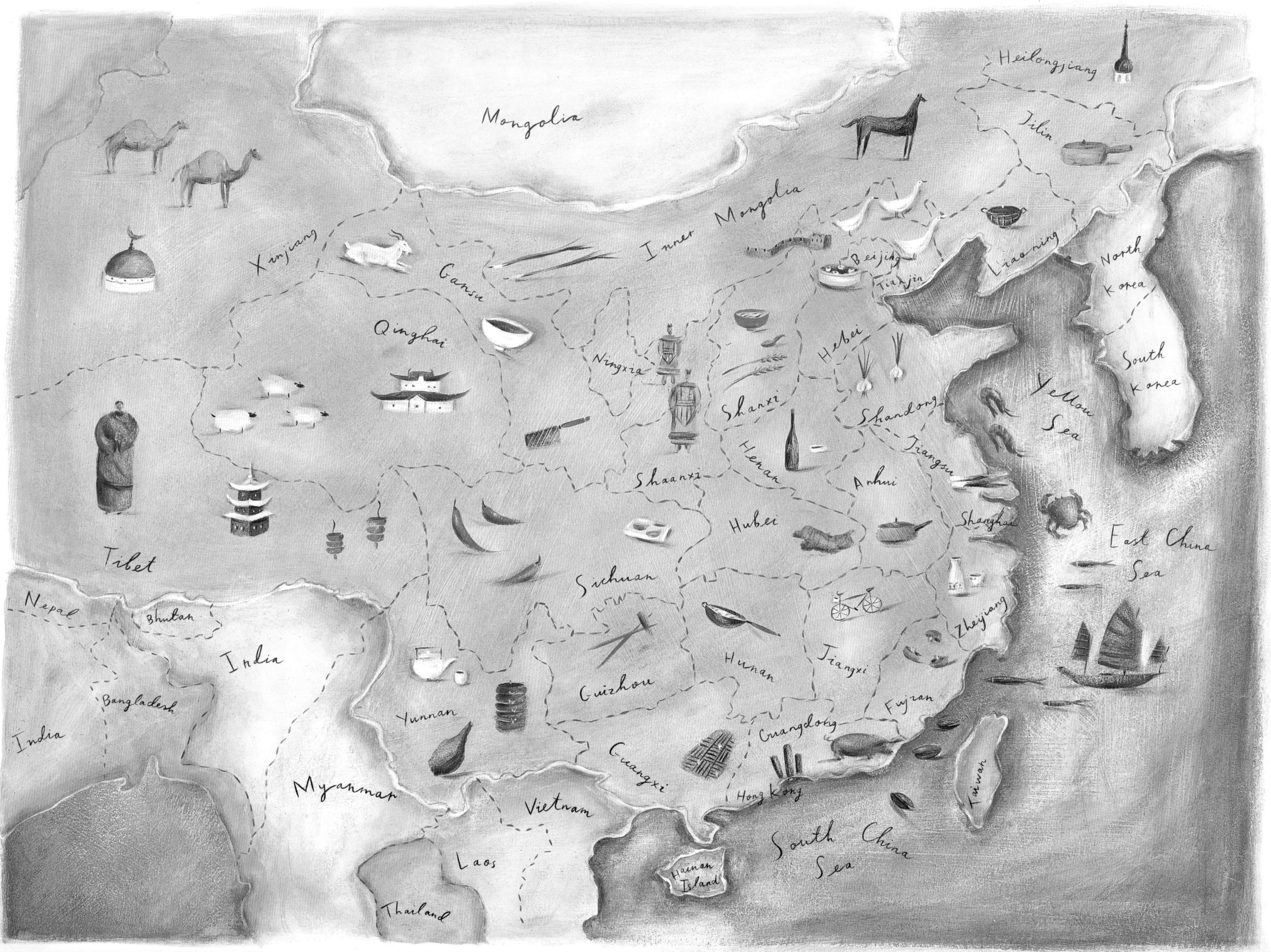
Mongolia
Heilongjiang
Jilin
Inner Mongolia
Liaoning
Xinjiang
Gansu
Beijing
Tianjin
North Korea
South Korea
Qinghai
Ningxia
Hebei
Shanxi
Shandong
Yellow Sea
Henan
Jiangsu
Anhui
Shaanxi
Hubei
Shanghai
East China Sea
Tibet
Sichuan
Zhejiang
Nepal
Bhutan
India
Guizhou
Hunan
Jiangxi
Bangladesh
Yunnan
Fujian
Guangdong
India
Guangxi
Myanmar
Hong Kong
Taiwan
Vietnam
South China Sea
Laos
Hainan Island
Thailand

CONTENTS

the food of CHINA

AN ENORMOUS COUNTRY, WITH A LARGE POPULATION TO FEED AND A DIVERSE GEOGRAPY AND CLIMATE, CHINA HAS ONE OF THE GREAT CUISINES OF THE WORLD AND EATING PLAYS A MAJOR ROLE IN DAILY LIFE AND IN RITUALS AND FESTIVITIES.

Chinese meals are always centered around a staple, or fan, such as rice, wheat, corn or millet. Rice, always white and polished, is the food most associated with China and is usually steamed, while wheat grows well in the harsh climate of the North and is made into breads and noodles. In poorer areas, millet is more common, eaten as porridge. The staple is then accompanied by secondary dishes, or cai, of meat, seafood or vegetables, pickles and condiments. Snacks, from dumplings to spicy bowls of noodles, are eaten all day long, both as sustenance and to satisfy the taste buds.

INGREDIENTS

The most important factor is freshness: poultry and seafood are bought live, and a cook may make more than one trip to the market in a day. Chinese cuisine developed around the foods available—often there was little meat, poultry or fish, so rice and vegetables are particularly important. However, many of the foods we associate with China today, such as chiles, bell peppers, corn and cilantro all came to China via trading routes. The Chinese also incorporate a lot of preserved vegetables and dried foods, particularly seafood, into their diet, which is especially important in areas where the climate and terrain make growing enough food a struggle.

FLAVORS

Chinese cooking tries to reach a balance between tastes: sweet and sour, hot and cold, plain and spicy. At the heart of Chinese food is a trinity of flavors: ginger, scallions and garlic which, though by no means included in all Chinese dishes, contribute to a flavor that is seen as being

Snacking on noodles in the street, or feasting on steamed dumplings in a restaurant, are part of the Chinese enjoyment of food. A new sign goes up in Chengdu and a panda eats breakfast in Sichuan. Bean curd and chives are used in many dishes, while fried fish rolls served at a banquet and fried bread sold in the market, both use the same cooking technique.

In the North, wheat flour is made into staples like noodles, dumplings and breads. New Year is China's most important festival, celebrated with lanterns and food, including these sweet round dumplings. In Guangxi, cormorants are still used to catch fish. All parts of the pig are sold in Chinese markets, and scallions are one of Chinese cooking's most essential ingredients.

quintessentially "Chinese". Soy bean products are another essential flavouring, and fermented bean curd, soy sauce and bean sauces are tastes that define Chinese food, along with vinegars and sesame oil. In the West of the country, chiles and Sichuan pepper add heat to ingredients that are usually more simply cooked.

COOKING STYLES

A wok is without doubt the central item in a Chinese kitchen, and wok cooking, either stir-frying or deep-frying, is at the heart of China's quick style of cooking. Other techniques, such as steaming, poaching and braising, cook food a little slower. Few families own an oven, and foods that need to be oven-roasted, such as roast ducks or char siu, are instead bought from special restaurants. All food is "prepared" in China, salads and raw foods are not eaten, and ingredients are cooked, however briefly, or preserved. A good Chinese meal will include a mix of cooking-styles so all the dishes can be ready at the same time.

EATING

A Chinese meal will also consist of a number of dishes, all made to share, that are fully prepared in the kitchen (not even carving is done at the table) and can be picked up and eaten with chopsticks. Not only must the ingredients be fresh; the finished food must also be fresh. Stir-fried dishes should be served immediately so they still have wok hei or the breath of the wok about them, indicating that they have been cooked at exactly the right heat to exactly the right timing.

BANQUET FOOD

Food eaten at banquets is created to be the very opposite of the everyday diet of grains. The point of a banquet is eating for pleasure, not sustenance, thus rice or noodles are served only at the end, and may be left untouched. Banquet food is often symbolic and as extravagant as can be afforded with dishes such as abalone, shark's fin and whole fish.

MEDICAL

In no other cuisine is the medicinal nature of food so tied to even everyday cooking. Achieving balance at every meal is an essential part of Chinese food. Every ingredient is accorded a nature—hot, warm, cool and neutral—and a flavor—sweet, sour, bitter, salty and pungent—and these are matched to a person's imbalances: a cooling food for a fever, warming food after childbirth. Along with the use of everyday ingredients, are more exotic foods, such as dried lizards, wolf berries and black silky chickens, which are often cooked in special soups and preparations.

THE FOOD OF THE NORTH

The cuisine of the North, centered around Beijing, comes from an area that is generally inhospitable with, apart from Shandong, little fertile land, harsh long winters and short scorching summers. Historically the region has swung between drought and flooding from the Yellow River, "China's Sorrow", though dams and irrigation schemes have improved things in recent years. The main crops have thus always been hardy ones: wheat and millet are eaten as noodles, breads and porridge, while in the winter, vegetables such as turnips and cabbage are supplied to the capital by farmers from neighboring provinces, who drive in trucks to Beijing's markets and live on them until their load of vegetables has been sold. Shandong on the coast is the most fertile area and it has become a source of fruit and vegetables for the capital, as well as providing plentiful seafood.

Flavors are strong, with salty bean pastes and soy sauces, vinegar, scallions and garlic all being important ingredients. Winter vegetables are preserved or pickled, while spicy or piquant condiments are eaten with bowls of steaming noodles or rice when little else is available

The main outside influence on the region has been the Muslim cooking of the Mongol and Manchu invaders who crossed the Great Wall from the North. Mutton and, in spring and summer, lamb, is sold as barbecued skewers on the street and stir-fried and wrapped in wheat pancakes. Steaming Mongolian hotpots and Mongolian barbecues cooked on a grill are seen everywhere.

Peking Duck, however, remains Beijings most famous dish, and is cooked in specialty restaurants all over the city. Beggar's chicken is another local specialty, wrapped in lotus leaves and baked for hours in hot ashes.

In stark contrast to the comforting dumplings and hotpots of Beijing's streets is the imperial cuisine created inside the Forbidden City. The presence of the court not only encouraged a huge diversity of cooking styles in the city from every province in China, but also elevated cooking to a standard probably never seen elsewhere in the world. Food was as important to the myth surrounding the Emperor as his armies, and he employed hundreds if not thousands in his kitchens. This elaborate cuisine is no longer reproduced in its entirety, but is remembered as a set of skills, recipes and flavor combinations important today in both banquet and everyday cooking.

A little girl eats ice cream, old men play Chinese checkers, and visitors climb the steps to the Temple of Heaven despite the cold of a Beijing winter. Steaming hot buns are a staple of the North, along with cabbage, huge winter melons, red carrots and pickled vegetables. Barbecued skewers of lamb and the ubiquitous pot noodles are sold as warming street snacks.

Hangzhou is famous for its serene tea houses, while in Shanghai a woman poses for a photo in front of frantic Yuyuan Gardens, known for its snacks and Heart of the Lake Tea House, where tea comes with an orange and a memento. High-rise Pudong towers over old Shanghai, in whose alleys a woman makes lunch and a man walks under New Year lanterns. Fish and bok choy are sold in markets.

THE FOOD OF THE EAST

Though the huge port city of Shanghai now dominates the East, the city is very much a modern one and it is difficult to talk of a real "Shanghai cuisine." Rather, the city's food reflects that of the agriculturally rich provinces that surround it on the fertile plains of the Yangtze Delta. Together they have given this area the nickname "the land of fish and rice."

With a warmer climate than the North and an all-year-round growing season, the cuisine has been shaped by the variety of available ingredients, from rice and wheat to a whole array of vegetables—bok choy, bamboo, beans and squash, as well as some of China's finest fish—freshwater carp from the tributaries of the Yangtze, Shanghai's infamous hairy crabs and fresh seafood from the coast. Duck, chicken and pork from this region are also considered particularly good and a cured ham from Jinhua rivals that of Yunnan.

The cusine is based on slow-braising rather than steaming or stir-frying, and thus has a reputation for being more oily than other regions. Shaoxing wine, an amber rice wine produced for both drinking and cooking in the city of Shaoxing, flavors many dishes, as does black vinegar from Chinkiang and ginger and garlic. A pinch of sugar is often added to balance these flavors, and it is in this region that sweet-and-sour dishes are most expertly cooked. Much of China's soy sauce is produced in the East, and red-cooking is a favored cooking technique using a soy sauce and rice wine stock to braise the area's fine meat and poultry, which is also presented in the form of a mixed cold platter that begins most formal meals. Though many of the region's flavorings are strong, vegetables, fish and seafood tend to be treated simply.

The area is abundant in regional specialties, including spareribs from Wuxi cooked in soy sauce and rice wine; lion's head meatballs from Yangzhou; pressed ducks from Nanjing; and West-lake carp from Hangzhou, which also grows China's finest green tea, Dragon Well, that is sometimes used as an ingredient. The people of Shanghai love their fish and seafood, particularly the freshwater hairy crabs so associated with the city, and available for little over a month every autumn.

Snacking is an obsession, especially in Shanghai, with jiaozi, steamed buns and noodle dishes found everywhere. While rice is grown in the region, filling wheat-based breads, dumplings and noodles are favored, particularly in winter.

THE FOOD OF THE WEST

The cooking of China's central and western heartlands is dominated by the spice of Sichuan, whose fertile plains are fed by the Yangtze River and its tributaries. It is famous for its hot cuisine and the sheer variety of its cooking-styles, summed up in the phrase "one hundred dishes and one hundred flavors".

Chiles are not indigenous to China, and in fact came to Asia from South America with the Portuguese. It was therefore probably Buddhist traders and missionaries from the West who brought Indian spices and cooking techniques into Sichuan, and also left the legacy of an imaginative Buddhist vegetarian cuisine.

Sichuan pepper is the dominant spice in many dishes. Not related to Western black and white pepper, it is hot and pungent, leaving a numb sensation in the mouth. The use of chile peppers and ginger adds additional layers of heat. Red (chile) oil, sesame oil, various bean pastes and vinegars are common, as are nuts and sesame seeds in dishes like bang bang chicken. These flavors are uniquely Sichuan, and quite different from those in the rest of China.

Cooking styles are also unusual. "Fish flavored" (Yuxiang) sauces are made from ginger, garlic, vinegar, chiles and scallions, usually served with vegetables like eggplant, but never with even a hint of fish present. Other tastes include hot-and-sour (Cuan La), such as in the famous soup, and a numb-chile flavor (Ma La), such as in the beancurd dish ma po dofu with its fiery sauce. Sichuan also has its own version of the hotpot, the Chongqing hot pot, which is heavily flavored by chile and oil and, true to the style of the region, is red-hot.

Chiles are widely used in other areas of the West, particularly in neighboring Hunan and Guangxi, whose Guilin chile sauce is eaten all over China. Guangxi is also a major rice-growing region, with vast stepped terraces covering its hills.

Southwest China has the most varied mix of ethnic minorities in the country, and it is the only area in which dairy products such as goat cheese are used. Muslim influences are also apparent and goat meat and dried beef are available. Yunnan ham is a whole ham cured in a sweet style, and Yunnan specialties include steampot chicken, cooked with medicinal ingredients, and crossing-the-bridge noodles, cooked in a bowl of boiling hot broth.

Modern Chengdu bustles round a statue of Mao, while a Naxi girl represents one of Yunnan's ethnic minorities. Bean curd is sold on the street and used in ma po dofu, and spicy noodles are a familiar snack. Mushrooms from the mountains, red chile bean paste, bamboo shoots and eggplant are all part of a rich diet. Rice grows in Guilin and sheep live under the mountains of Yunnan.

Dried food stores are found all over Hong Kong and sell many kinds of dried seafood, which is also sold fresh in the markets. Dim sum is enjoyed in Hong Kong at old-fashioned tea houses and at the famous Luk Yu Tea House, with its smart waiters, while egg noodles, steamed whole fish, oyster sauce and bowls of freshly steamed rice are all part of the varied Cantonese diet.

THE FOOD OF THE SOUTH

The food of the South, and especially that of Guangdong (Canton), is renowned both within and outside China as the country's finest. Guangdong has a subtropical climate that sustains rice crops and many vegetables and fruit virtually all year round, while an extensive coastline and inland waterways provide the freshest fish and shellfish.

The area also prides itself on its well-trained chefs, whose restaurants have always catered to the rich merchants of Guangzhou and Hong Kong. They insist on high quality ingredients, which they cook in numerous ways: stir-fried, steamed or boiled, but which are usually kept simple and cooked with little oil to enhance the food's fresh flavor.

The flavors of the South are relatively simple, emphasizing the freshness of the food with just a delicate base of ginger, garlic and scallions. Unlike the rest of China, spicy or fragrant condiments are often served with dishes, particularly bean pastes and sauces, so the diner can add their own flavorings. The area is responsible for the invention of oyster, hoisin, black bean and XO sauces.

Guangzhou is known for its wonderful fish and seafood dishes, served in every restaurant. Always fresh, the customer picks from a large fish tank and specifies the cooking technique. The favored meat of the South is without a doubt pork—roasted or babecued (char siu) and bought from the carry-out counters of roast-meat restaurants, who hang up their wares to tempt customers. Ducks are another favorite, bred all over the South and roasted until crispy. Dim sum is a specialty of Guangzhou and Hong Kong and these snacks, served in tea houses or dim sum restaurants, are universally popular.

The Cantonese are also known for eating just about anything—from shark's fin and snakes to monkeys and dogs. The people of this region are certainly knowledgeable and adventerous about food, though many of the more esoteric ingredients are served only at specialized restaurants or are eaten mostly for their medicinal qualities.

As well as the Cantonese cooking of Guangdong, the South is also home to the food of the Hakka people, China's gypsies, whose cooking is an earthier version of Cantonese, and Chiu Chow food from the east coast of the province, with its emphasis on seafood, goose and sauces. There are also specialties from Fujian and Taiwan.

APPETIZERS

JIAOZI

PERHAPS NO OTHER FOOD TYPIFIES THE HEARTY CHARACTERISTICS OF NORTHERN HOME-STYLE COOKING MORE THAN THESE MEAT DUMPLINGS. YOU CAN PURCHASE GOOD-QUALITY DUMPLING WRAPPERS AT ASIAN MARKETS, WHICH MAKES THESE A QUICK, EASY SNACK TO PREPARE.

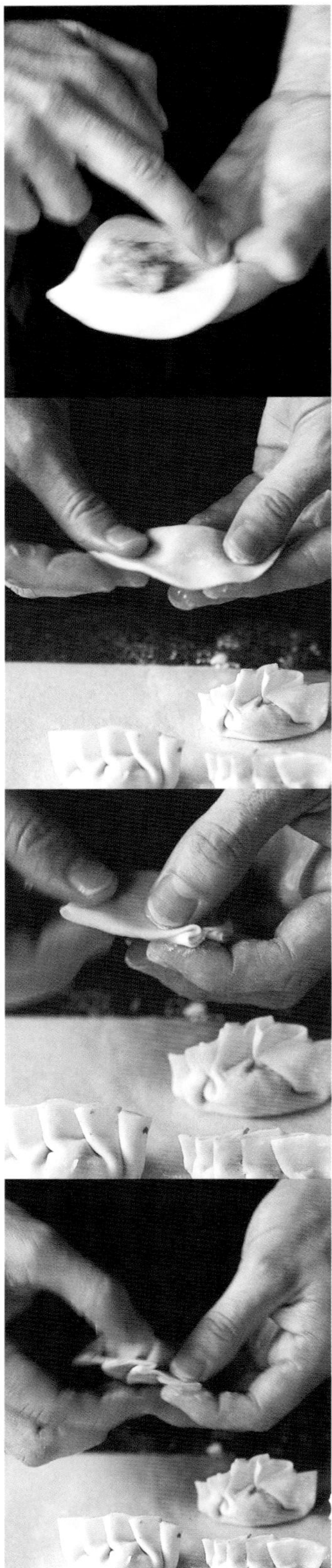

Fold the dumplings as shown, handling the wrappers carefully so they don't tear and making sure they don't get too wet. Squeeze the pleats firmly or they will come undone as they cook.

FILLING
6 cups Chinese (Napa) cabbage, finely chopped
1 teaspoon salt
1 lb ground pork
2 cups Chinese garlic chives, finely chopped
2 1/2 tablespoons light soy sauce
1 tablespoon Shaoxing rice wine
2 tablespoons roasted sesame oil
1 tablespoon finely chopped ginger
1 tablespoon cornstarch

50 round wheat dumpling wrappers
red rice vinegar or a dipping sauce (page 282)

MAKES 50

TO MAKE the filling, put the cabbage and salt in a bowl and toss lightly to combine. Allow to stand for 30 minutes. Squeeze all the water from the cabbage and put the cabbage in a large bowl. Add the pork, garlic chives, soy sauce, rice wine, sesame oil, ginger and cornstarch. Stir until combined and drain off any excess liquid.

PLACE a heaping teaspoon of the filling in the center of each wrapper. Spread a little water along the edge of the wrapper and fold the wrapper over to make a half-moon shape. Use your thumb and index finger to form small pleats along the sealed edge. With the other hand, press the 2 opposite edges together to seal. Place the dumplings on a baking sheet that has been lightly dusted with cornstarch. Do not allow the dumplings to sit for too long or they will go soggy.

BRING a large saucepan of water to a boil. Add half the dumplings, stirring immediately to prevent them from sticking together, and return to a boil. For the traditional method of cooking dumplings, add 1 cup cold water and continue cooking over high heat until the water boils. Add another 3 cups cold water and cook until the water boils again. Alternatively, cook the dumplings in the boiling water for 8–9 minutes. Remove the saucepan from the heat and drain the dumplings. Repeat with the remaining dumplings.

THE DUMPLINGS can also be fried. Heat 1 tablespoon oil in a frying pan, add a single layer of dumplings and cook for 2 minutes, shaking the pan to make sure they don't stick. Add 1/3 cup water, cover and steam for 2 minutes, then uncover and cook until the water has evaporated. Repeat with the remaining dumplings.

SERVE with red rice vinegar or a dipping sauce.

SPRING ROLLS

THE FAT, SOLID SPRING ROLLS FOUND IN MANY WESTERN RESTAURANTS ARE QUITE DIFFERENT FROM THE SLENDER AND REFINED SPRING ROLLS THAT ARE TRADITIONALLY MADE TO CELEBRATE CHINESE NEW YEAR. HERE'S AN EASY RENDITION OF THE CLASSIC.

FILLING
5 tablespoons light soy sauce
2 teaspoons roasted sesame oil
3 1/2 tablespoons Shaoxing rice wine
1 1/2 teaspoons cornstarch
1 lb center-cut pork loin, trimmed and cut into very thin strips
6 dried Chinese mushrooms
1/2 teaspoon freshly ground black pepper
4 tablespoons oil
1 tablespoon finely chopped ginger
3 garlic cloves, finely chopped
3 cups Chinese (Napa) cabbage, finely shredded
1 cup carrots, finely shredded
2/3 cup Chinese garlic chives, cut into 1 inch pieces
2 cups bean sprouts

1 egg yolk
2 tablespoons all-purpose flour
20 square spring roll wrappers
oil for deep-frying
hoisin sauce

MAKES 20

TO MAKE the filling, combine 2 tablespoons of the soy sauce and half the sesame oil with 1 1/2 tablespoons of the rice wine and 1 teaspoon of the cornstarch. Add the pork and toss to coat. Marinate in the fridge for 20 minutes. Meanwhile, soak the dried mushrooms in boiling water for 30 minutes, then drain and squeeze out any excess water. Remove and discard the stems and shred the caps. Combine the remaining soy sauce, sesame oil and cornstarch with the black pepper.

HEAT a wok over high heat, add half the oil and heat until very hot. Add the pork mixture and stir-fry for 2 minutes, or until cooked. Remove and drain. Wipe out the wok.

REHEAT the wok over high heat, add the remaining oil and heat until very hot. Stir-fry the mushrooms, ginger and garlic for 15 seconds. Add the cabbage and carrots and toss lightly. Pour in the remaining rice wine, then stir-fry for 1 minute. Add the garlic chives and bean sprouts and stir-fry for 1 minute, or until the sprouts are limp. Add the pork mixture and soy sauce mixture and cook until thickened. Transfer to a colander and drain for 5 minutes, tossing occasionally to remove the excess liquid.

COMBINE the egg yolk, flour and 3 tablespoons water. Place 2 tablespoons of filling on the corner of a wrapper, leaving the corner itself free. Spread some of the yolk mixture on the opposite corner. Fold over one corner and start rolling, but not too tightly. Fold in the other corners, roll up and press to secure. Repeat with the remaining wrappers.

FILL a wok one quarter full with oil. Heat the oil to 375°F, or until a piece of bread fries golden brown in 10 seconds when dropped in the oil. Cook the spring rolls in 2 batches, turning constantly, for 5 minutes, or until golden. Remove and drain on paper towels. Serve with hoisin sauce.

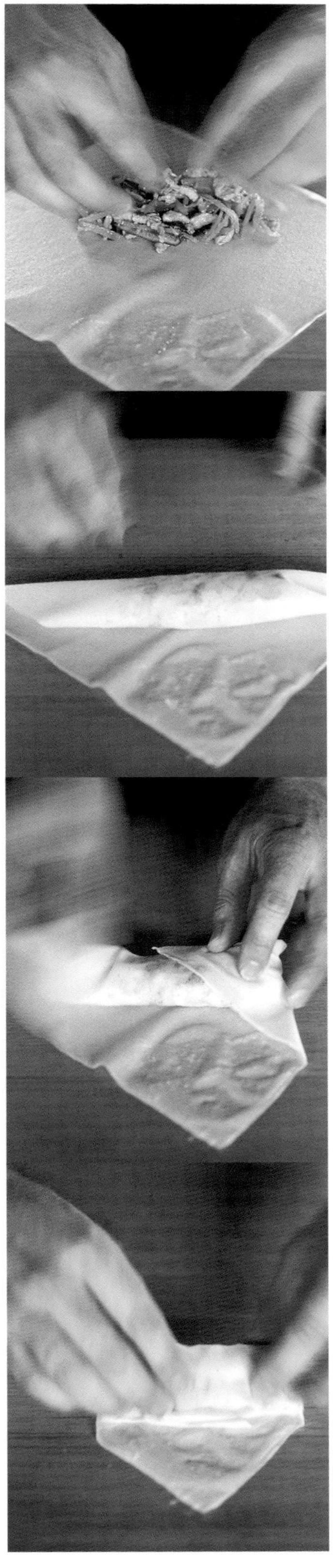

Spring rolls should look elegant rather than chunky, so use a small amount of filling in each and roll them neatly. Don't roll them too tightly or they may burst open as they cook.

Luk Yu Tea House, Hong Kong

CHAR SIU BAU

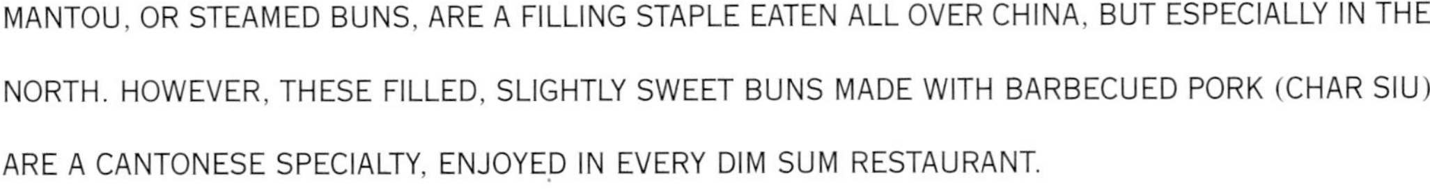

MANTOU, OR STEAMED BUNS, ARE A FILLING STAPLE EATEN ALL OVER CHINA, BUT ESPECIALLY IN THE NORTH. HOWEVER, THESE FILLED, SLIGHTLY SWEET BUNS MADE WITH BARBECUED PORK (CHAR SIU) ARE A CANTONESE SPECIALTY, ENJOYED IN EVERY DIM SUM RESTAURANT.

1 teaspoon oil
8 oz barbecued pork (char siu), diced
3 teaspoons Shaoxing rice wine
1 teaspoon roasted sesame oil
2 tablespoons oyster sauce
2 teaspoons light soy sauce
3 teaspoons sugar
1 quantity basic yeast dough (page 278)
chili sauce

MAKES 12 LARGE OR 24 SMALL BUNS

HEAT the oil in a wok. Add the pork, rice wine, sesame oil, oyster sauce, soy sauce and sugar and cook for 1 minute. Allow to cool.

DIVIDE the dough into 12 or 24 portions, depending on how large you want the buns to be, and cover with a kitchen towel. Working with 1 portion at a time, press the dough into circles with the edges thinner than the center. Place 1 teaspoon of filling on the dough for a small bun or 3 teaspoons for a large bun. Draw the sides in to enclose the filling. Pinch the top together and put each bun on a square of waxed paper. When you get more proficient at making these, you may be able to get more filling into the buns, which will make them less doughy. Ensure that you seal them properly. The buns can also be turned over, then cooked the other way up so they look like round balls.

ARRANGE the buns well spaced in 3 steamers. Cover and steam over simmering water in a wok, reversing the steamers halfway through, for 15 minutes, or until the buns are well risen and a skewer inserted into the centre comes out hot. Serve with some chili sauce.

Gather in the tops of the buns as neatly as you can to make round balls. Bear in mind that they will open slightly as they cook to show their filling.

麵好湯濃肉大塊

荷叶糯米团

STEAMED GLUTINOUS RICE IN LOTUS LEAVES

LOR MAI GAI ARE A DIM SUM CLASSIC THAT ALSO MAKE GOOD SNACKS. WHEN STEAMED, THE RICE TAKES ON THE FLAVORS OF THE OTHER INGREDIENTS AND OF THE LOTUS LEAVES THEMSELVES. THE PACKAGES CAN BE MADE AHEAD AND FROZEN, THEN STEAMED FOR 40 MINUTES.

1 1/4 lb glutinous rice
4 large lotus leaves

FILLING
2 tablespoons dried shrimp
4 dried Chinese mushrooms
2 tablespoons oil
12 oz skinned, boneless chicken breasts, cut into 1/2 inch cubes
1 garlic clove, crushed
2 Chinese sausages (lap cheong), thinly sliced
2 scallions, thinly sliced
1 tablespoon oyster sauce
3 teaspoons light soy sauce
3 teaspoons sugar
1 teaspoon roasted sesame oil
1 tablespoon cornstarch
chili sauce

MAKES 8

PLACE the rice in a bowl, cover with cold water and allow to soak overnight. Drain in a colander and place the rice in a bamboo steamer lined with a kitchen towel. Steam, covered, over simmering water in a wok for 30–40 minutes, or until the rice is cooked. Cool slightly before using.

SOAK the lotus leaves in boiling water for 1 hour, or until softened. Shake dry and cut the leaves in half to give 8 equal pieces.

TO MAKE the filling, soak the dried shrimp in boiling water for 1 hour, then drain. Soak the dried mushrooms in boiling water for 30 minutes, then drain and squeeze out any excess water. Remove and discard the stems and finely chop the caps.

HEAT a wok over high heat, add half the oil and heat until very hot. Stir-fry the chicken for 2–3 minutes, or until browned. Add the shrimp, mushrooms, garlic, sausage and scallions. Stir-fry for another 1–2 minutes, or until aromatic. Add the oyster sauce, soy sauce, sugar and sesame oil and toss well. Combine the cornstarch with 3/4 cup water, add to the sauce and simmer until thickened.

WITH WET hands, divide the rice into 16 balls. Place the lotus leaves on a work surface, put a ball of rice in the center of each leaf and flatten the ball slightly, making a slight indentation in the middle. Spoon one eighth of the filling onto each rice ball, top with another slightly flattened rice ball and smooth into one ball. Wrap up firmly by folding the leaves over to form an envelope.

PLACE the packages in 3 steamers. Cover and steam over simmering water in a wok, reversing the steamers halfway through, for 30 minutes. To serve, open up each leaf and eat straight from the leaf while hot with some chili sauce.

Enclose the filling in the rice as much as possible, then neatly fold over the leaves. The leaves seal in the flavor and hold the rice in shape while cooking.

Rock sugar is sold loose in a market in Sichuan.

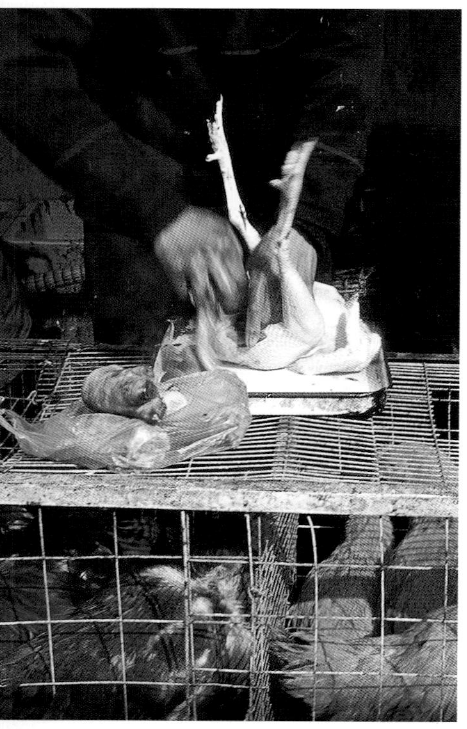

Chickens are bought live and prepared on the spot in Beijing market to make sure they are really fresh.

BRAISED CHICKEN WINGS

THESE DEEP-FRIED, CRISP WINGS ARE A FAVORITE SNACK FOR THE CHINESE. THIS RECIPE IS A SIMPLE ONE THAT MAKES A GOOD SNACK OR FIRST COURSE. YOU'LL NEED TO HAND OUT FINGER BOWLS FOR YOUR GUESTS.

24 chicken wings
2 tablespoons rock sugar
1 tablespoon dark soy sauce
1 tablespoon light soy sauce
1 tablespoon Shaoxing rice wine
oil for deep-frying
2 teaspoons finely chopped ginger
1 scallion, finely chopped
2 tablespoons hoisin sauce
1/2 cup chicken stock (page 281)

SERVES 6

DISCARD the tip of each chicken wing. Cut each wing into 2 pieces through the joint. Put the wing pieces in a bowl.

PUT the rock sugar, dark soy sauce, light soy sauce and rice wine in a small pitcher or bowl. Mix until combined, breaking the sugar down as much as you can. Pour the mixture over the chicken wings. Marinate in the fridge for at least 1 hour, or overnight.

DRAIN the chicken wings, reserving the marinade. Fill a wok one quarter full of oil. Heat the oil to 350°F, or until a piece of bread fries golden brown in 15 seconds when dropped in the oil. Cook the chicken wings in batches for 2–3 minutes, or until they are well browned. Drain on paper towels.

CAREFULLY POUR the oil from the wok, reserving 1 tablespoon. Reheat the wok over high heat, add the reserved oil and heat until very hot. Stir-fry the ginger and scallion for 1 minute. Add the hoisin sauce, reserved marinade and chicken wings and cook for 1 minute, then add the stock and bring to a boil. Reduce the heat, cover the wok and cook gently for 8–10 minutes, or until the chicken wings are cooked through and tender.

INCREASE the heat and bring the sauce to a boil, uncovered. Cook until the sauce reduces to a sticky coating.

Traveling by truck in Yunnan.

STEAMED RICE NOODLE ROLLS

A DIM SUM FAVORITE, THESE SILKY RICE NOODLES CAN BE FILLED WITH BARBECUED PORK (CHAR SIU), SHRIMP OR VEGETABLES. THE NOODLES ARE SOLD AS A LONG SHEET FOLDED INTO A ROLL. DO NOT REFRIGERATE THEM—THEY MUST BE USED AT ROOM TEMPERATURE OR THEY WILL BREAK.

PORK FILLING
11 oz Chinese barbecued pork (char siu), chopped
3 scallions, finely chopped
2 tablespoons chopped cilantro

OR

SHRIMP FILLING
8 oz shrimp
1 tablespoon oil
3 scallions, finely chopped
2 tablespoons finely chopped cilantro

OR

VEGETABLE FILLING
1 bunch (about 3/4 lb) Chinese broccoli (gai lan)
1 teaspoon light soy sauce
1 teaspoon roasted sesame oil
2 scallions, finely chopped

4 fresh rice noodle rolls
oyster sauce

MAKES 4

TO MAKE the pork filling, combine the pork with the scallions and cilantro.

TO MAKE the shrimp filling, peel and devein the shrimp. Heat a wok over high heat, add the oil and heat until very hot. Stir-fry the shrimp for 1 minute, or until they are pink and cooked through. Season with salt and white pepper. Add the scallions and cilantro and mix well.

TO MAKE the vegetable filling, wash the Chinese broccoli well. Discard any tough-looking stems and chop the rest of the stems. Put on a plate in a steamer, cover and steam over simmering water in a wok for 3 minutes, or until all the and leaves are just tender. Combine the broccoli with the soy sauce, sesame oil and scallions.

CAREFULLY UNROLL the rice noodle rolls (don't worry if they crack or tear a little at the sides). Trim each one into a neat rectangle 6 x 7 inches (you may be able to get 2 rectangles out of 1 roll if they are very large). Divide the filling among the rolls, then reroll the noodles. Put the rolls on a plate in a large steamer, cover and steam over simmering water in a wok for 5 minutes. Serve the rolls cut into pieces and drizzled with the oyster sauce.

Put the filling on the piece of noodle roll closest to you. Roll up carefully so you don't tear it, keeping the filling tucked inside.

A cleaver is the only knife heavy enough to easily cut through the bones of spareribs.

香辣椒盐排骨

SPICY SALT AND PEPPER SPARERIBS

2 lb Chinese-style pork spareribs
1 egg, beaten
2–3 tablespoons all-purpose flour
oil for deep-frying
2 scallions, finely chopped
2 small red chiles, finely chopped

MARINADE
1/2 teaspoon ground Sichuan peppercorns
1/2 teaspoon five-spice powder
1/2 teaspoon salt
1 tablespoon light soy sauce
1 tablespoon Shaoxing rice wine
1/4 teaspoon roasted sesame oil

SERVES 4

ASK the butcher to cut the slab of spareribs crosswise into thirds that measure 1 1/2–2 inch in length, or use a cleaver to do so yourself. Cut the ribs between the bones to separate them.

TO MAKE the marinade, combine the ingredients in a bowl. Add the ribs and toss lightly. Marinate in the fridge for at least 3 hours, or overnight.

MIX the egg, flour and a little water to form a smooth batter with the consistency of heavy cream. Fill a wok one quarter full of oil. Heat the oil to 350°F, or until a piece of bread fries golden brown in 15 seconds when dropped in the oil. Dip the ribs in the batter and fry in batches for 5 minutes until they are crisp and golden, stirring to separate them, then remove and drain. Reheat the oil and fry the ribs for 1 minute to darken their color. Remove and drain on paper towels.

SOAK the scallions and chiles in the hot oil (with the heat off) for 2 minutes. Remove with a wire strainer or slotted spoon and place on top of the ribs.

BARBECUED SPARERIBS

BARBECUED SPARERIBS

3 lb Chinese-style pork spareribs

MARINADE
1/2 cup hoisin sauce
3 tablespoons light soy sauce
3 tablespoons Shaoxing rice wine
2 tablespoons sugar
3 tablespoons tomato ketchup
4 garlic cloves, finely chopped
3 tablespoons finely chopped ginger

SERVES 6

ASK the butcher to cut the slab of spareribs crosswise into thirds that measure 1 1/2–2 inch in length, or use a cleaver to do so yourself.

PLACE the spareribs in a large clay pot, braising pan or saucepan and cover with water. Bring to a boil, then reduce the heat to a simmer. Cook for 20 minutes, drain and allow the ribs to cool. Cut the ribs between the bones to separate them.

TO MAKE the marinade, combine the ingredients in a bowl. Add the ribs and toss lightly. Marinate in the fridge for at least 3 hours, or overnight.

PREHEAT the oven to 350°F. Put the ribs and marinade on a baking sheet lined with aluminium foil. Bake for 45 minutes, turning once, until golden.

HAR GAU

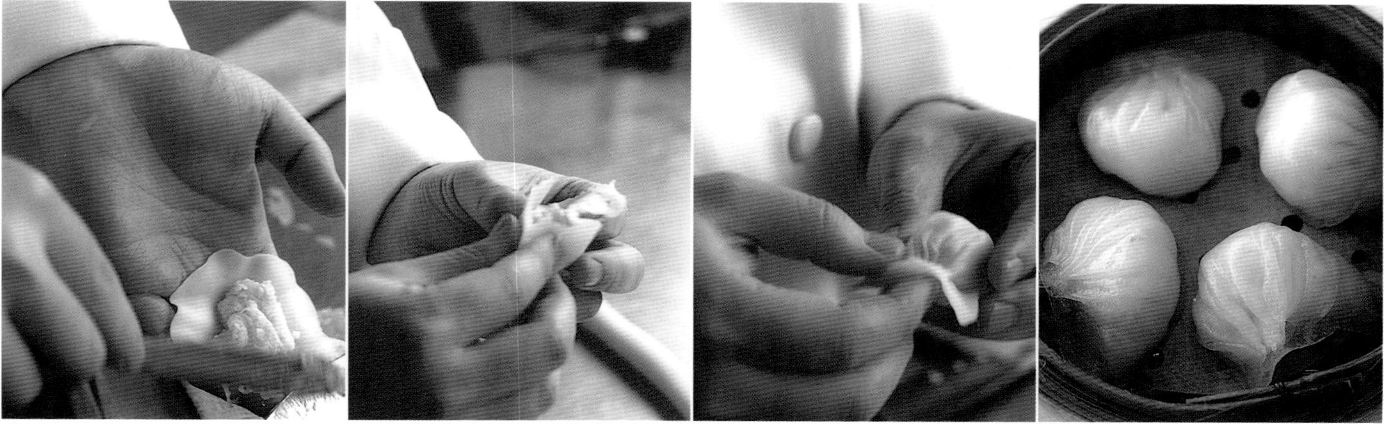

HAR GAU are the benchmark dim sum for any restaurant. The filling of prawns and minced water chestnuts or bamboo is folded into wrappers made from wheat starch. Each wrapper is filled as it is made because the pastry is hard to handle. The wrapper is then pleated, sealed and the dim sum placed in a steamer. As the har gau cook they turn from an opaque white to translucent, showing the filling inside.

SIU MAI

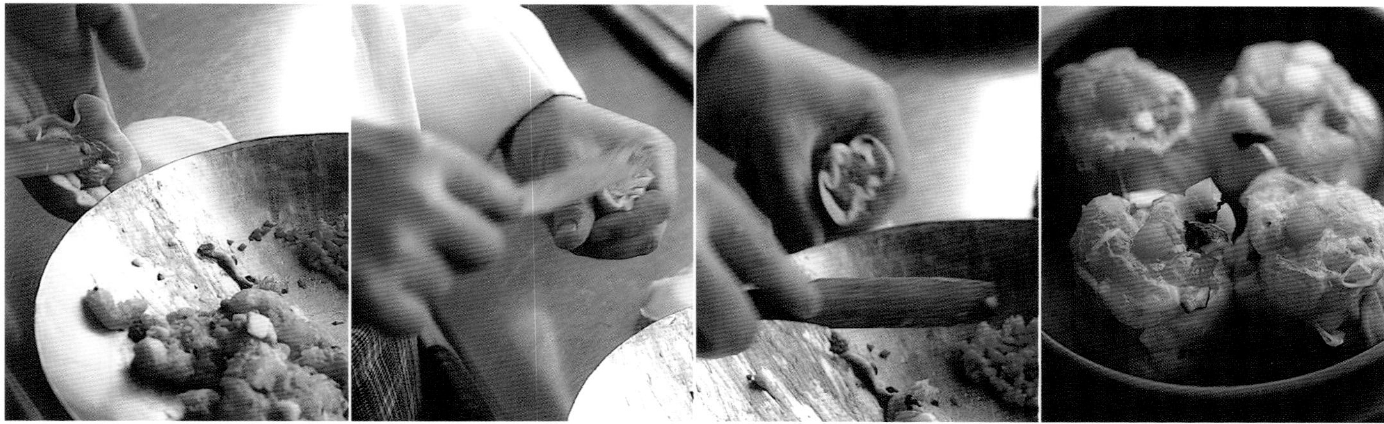

SIU MAI means 'cook and sell' because of their unsurpassed popularity. Egg noodle wrappers are filled with a mixture of pork, prawns and Chinese mushrooms or water chestnuts. The round wrapper is held in one hand and the filling is placed in the middle. The wrapper is then squeezed up around the filling and the top levelled off. Siu mai are usually dotted with a small blob of duck egg yolk or crab roe.

SWEET DIM SUM

BO LOH BAU sweet yellow cream pastries encased in a glazed yeast dough and baked.

LIN YUNG BAU sweet chewy buns filled with lotus seed paste. The red dot indicates it is sweet.

DAN TA these rich, golden egg custard tarts are set in a flaky pastry and are served warm.

LAI WONG restaurants often invent their own 'signature' dim sum, like these sweet rabbits.

CITY HALL CHINESE RESTAURANT is one of Hong Kong's busiest dim sum restaurants, appealing to the building's civil servants during the week and long queues of families at the weekends. The dim sum are stacked on trolleys that are wheeled from table to table, and are also found at 'stations' throughout the room, such as the one above frying turnip cake and noodles to order.

DIM SUM

DIM SUM ARE SNACKS AND DUMPLINGS THAT 'TOUCH THE HEART' AND ARE CENTRAL TO THE CANTONESE TEA HOUSE TRADITION OF YUM CHA. YUM CHA MEANS SIMPLY 'TO DRINK TEA', BUT EATING DIM SUM, READING NEWSPAPERS AND CATCHING UP WITH FRIENDS AND FAMILY ARE ALL PART OF THE EXPERIENCE.

The Chinese love to snack and each region has its favourites, from mantou and jiaozi in the North to little spicy Sichuan dishes. But it is in Guangzhou and Hong Kong's tea houses that dim sum—China's most famous snacks—are found.

TEA HOUSES

Traditional tea houses are almost like a pub. Regulars, mostly older men, spend their early mornings sipping tea, eating just a few dim sum and reading the newspapers. In a few tea houses, the men are accompanied by their song birds, whose cages are hung up around the room. Today, most tea houses are bright, dim sum palaces. Often huge, multi-level restaurants, they work at a frantic, noisy pace, with office workers or families eating a whole meal of dim sum.

EATING DIM SUM

Dim sum is usually eaten mid-morning, but it can be found at any time, and even enjoyed as a midnight snack in busy Hong Kong. The meal begins by choosing a tea, usually pu-er (a black tea), jasmine or chrysanthemum. In fact, yum cha is the only meal where the tea is drunk with the food rather than before or afterwards. Anyone from the table can top up

THIS TRADITIONAL TEA HOUSE in Sham Shui Po, Hong Kong, opens as early as 5 o'clock in the morning for its regulars, almost all of whom are men. The dim sum are brought around in trays hung from the server's neck and are mostly large and filling. Just one or two items are chosen to supplement the important business of tea drinking, gossiping and catching up on the racing form.

the tea cups during the meal, and they are thanked by tapping your fingers on the table, expressing gratitude even when mouths are full. To get the pot refilled, the lid is lifted to the side so the waiters can see that it is empty.

Sometimes dim sum is ordered from a menu, but in the most busy places it is usually taken around the tables in trays or trolleys hot from the kitchen. Servers shout out the name of the dishes they have and people lift up the lids to peak at what is on offer. There may also be 'stations' where noodles are fried and vegetables cooked. Dim sum mostly come in small steamers or dishes, usually three servings to a portion.

Dim sum are rarely made at home and restaurants prize their chefs, who make everything by hand. These chefs undergo an apprenticeship of 3 years, and take another 5 years on average to become fully qualified dim sum chefs.

THE BILL for a dim sum meal is calculated from a card kept on each table. Each time a dish is ordered, the server marks the card with a stamp called a chop.

NGAU YUK KAO beef balls shaped from minced beef, seasoned with coriander and soy sauce and steamed. They may also contain pork and are served on thin bean curd sheets.

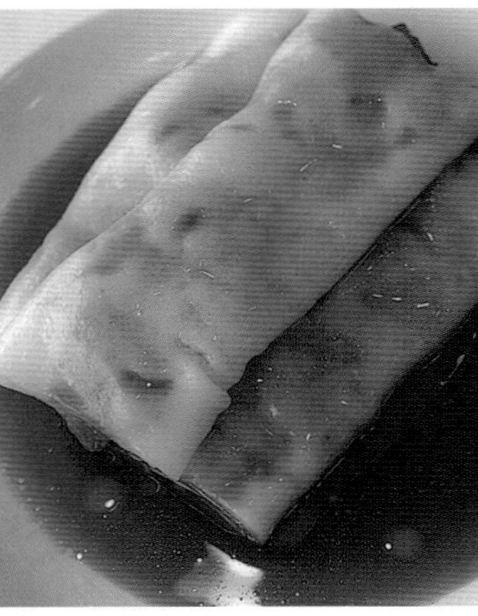

CHEUNG FAN sheets of silky rice noodles wrapped around a filling such as barbecue pork or prawns, then steamed. A soy and sesame oil sauce is poured over just before serving.

PAI GWAT meaning 'fat ribs', these are spareribs, usually pork, which are fried and then steamed, often with a black bean or chilli sauce.

WU GOK a mashed taro pastry wrapped around a filling such as prawn or pork and deep-fried. The pastry flakes up to give a crispy appearance.

LOH BAK GOH a turnip cake made from grated Chinese turnip, a sort of daikon radish, flavoured with Chinese bacon or sausage, steamed, cut in slices and fried to order until crispy.

FUNG JAU meaning 'phoenix claws', these are in fact chickens' feet, steamed in a black bean or soy chilli sauce. The feet are eaten whole, the flavour sucked out, and the bones spat out.

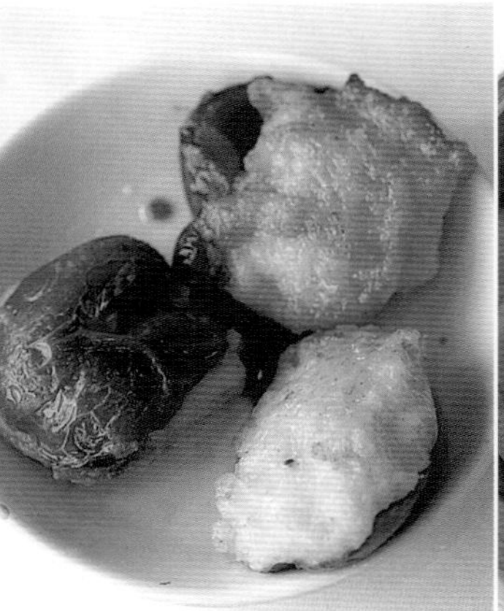

NIANG QING JIAO green peppers stuffed with a minced fish or shrimp stuffing and then deep-fried. Aubergine pieces are treated in a similar way.

JAI GAU glutinous rice wrappers with a vegetarian filling such as garlic chives, ginger and spinach. The dumplings are steamed until the wrappers turn translucent and their filling shows through.

LUO MAI GAI parcels of sticky rice mixed with dried shrimp, Chinese sausage and cubed chicken, wrapped in lotus leaves and steamed. The leaves add flavour, but are not eaten.

HOM SUI GOK these sticky torpedo-shaped dumplings are made from a rice dough filled with a mixture of dried shrimp, pork and Chinese mushrooms. The dumplings are deep-fried.

CHAR SIU BAU steamed buns made from a slightly sweet yeast dough filled with barbecue pork, oyster and soy sauces. The best crack open a little at the top to reveal the filling.

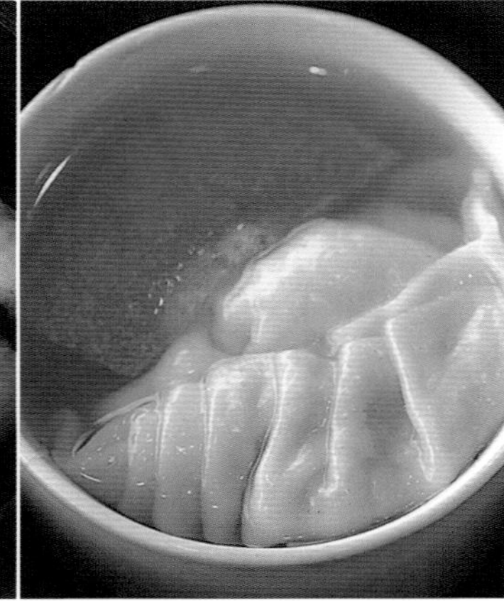

YU CHI GAU a large dumpling filled with shark's fin and served in a broth. The dumpling can contain other fillings and the whole dish is steamed.

虾饺

HAR GAU

HAR GAU ARE THE BENCHMARK DIM SUM BY WHICH RESTAURANTS ARE MEASURED AND THEY ARE NOT EASY TO MAKE. THE WHEAT STARCH DOUGH IS HARD TO HANDLE AND NEEDS TO BE KEPT WARM WHILE YOU WORK WITH IT, BUT THE RESULTS ARE VERY SATISFYING.

FILLING
- 1 lb shrimp
- 1 1/2 oz pork or bacon fat (rind removed), finely chopped
- 1/4 cup fresh or canned bamboo shoots, rinsed, drained and finely chopped
- 1 scallion, finely chopped
- 1 teaspoon sugar
- 3 teaspoons light soy sauce
- 1/2 teaspoon roasted sesame oil
- 1 egg white, lightly beaten
- 1 teaspoon salt
- 1 tablespoon cornstarch

WRAPPER DOUGH
- 1 1/2 cups wheat starch
- 3 teaspoons cornstarch
- 2 teaspoons oil

soy sauce, chili sauce or a dipping sauce (page 282)

MAKES 24

TO MAKE the filling, peel and devein the shrimp and cut half of them into 1/2 inch chunks. Chop the remaining shrimp very finely. Combine all the shrimp in a large bowl. Add the pork or bacon fat, bamboo shoots, scallion, sugar, soy sauce, sesame oil, egg white, salt and cornstarch. Mix well and drain off any excess liquid.

TO MAKE the dough, put the wheat starch, cornstarch and oil in a small bowl. Add 1 cup boiling water and mix until well combined. Add a little extra wheat starch if the dough is too sticky.

ROLL the dough into a long cylinder, divide it into 24 pieces and cover with a hot damp kitchen towel. Working with 1 portion at a time, roll out the dough using a rolling pin or a well-oiled cleaver. If using a rolling pin, roll the dough into a 3 1/2–4 inch round between 2 pieces of greased plastic wrap. If using a cleaver, place the blade facing away from you and gently press down on the flat side of the blade with your palm, squashing the dough while twisting the handle at the same time to form a round shape. Fill each wrapper as you make it.

PLACE a heaping teaspoon of the filling in the center of each wrapper. Spread a little water along the wrapper edge and fold the wrapper over to make a half-moon shape. Use your thumb and index finger to form small pleats along the top edge. With the other hand, press the 2 opposite edges together. Place in 4 steamers lined with waxed paper punched with holes. Cover the har gau as you make them.

COVER AND steam the har gau over simmering water in a wok, reversing the steamers halfway through, for 6–8 minutes, or until the wrappers are translucent. Serve with soy sauce, chili sauce or a dipping sauce.

Har gau pastry is more delicate to handle than noodle-type wrappers. To make it easier, keep the pastry warm and pliable while you are working with it.

TURNIP CAKE

ONE OF THE MORE COMMON DIM SUM, TURNIP CAKE IS SOLD BY WOMEN PUSHING HOT PLATES ON CARTS. EACH PORTION OF THE TURNIP CAKE IS FRESHLY FRIED TO ORDER. SERVE WITH LIGHT SOY SAUCE OR A CHILI SAUCE FOR DIPPING.

2 lb Chinese turnip, grated
1 oz dried shrimp
$1\frac{1}{3}$ cups dried Chinese mushrooms
5 oz Chinese sausage (lap cheong)
1 tablespoon oil
3 scallions, thinly sliced
3 teaspoons sugar
3 teaspoons Shaoxing rice wine
$\frac{1}{4}$ teaspoon freshly ground white pepper
2 tablespoons finely chopped cilantro
$1\frac{2}{3}$ cups rice flour
oil for frying

MAKES 6

PLACE the turnip in a large bowl and cover with boiling water for 5 minutes. Drain, reserving any liquid, then allow the turnip to drain in a colander. When it is cool enough to handle, squeeze out any excess liquid. Place in a large bowl.

SOAK the dried shrimp in boiling water for 1 hour, then drain, adding any soaking liquid to the reserved turnip liquid.

SOAK the dried mushrooms in boiling water for 30 minutes, then drain, adding any soaking liquid to the reserved turnip liquid. Squeeze out any excess water from the mushrooms. Remove and discard the stems and finely dice the caps.

PLACE the sausage on a plate in a steamer. Cover and steam over simmering water in a wok for 10 minutes, then finely dice it.

HEAT a wok over high heat, add the oil and heat until very hot. Stir-fry the sausage for 1 minute, then add the shrimp and mushrooms and stir-fry for 2 minutes, or until fragrant. Add the scallions, sugar, rice wine and pepper, then add the turnip, cilantro and rice flour and toss to combine. Pour in 2 cups of the reserved liquid and mix well.

PLACE the mixture in a greased and lined 10 inch square cake pan (or in 2 smaller dishes if your steamers are small). Place the pan in a steamer. Cover and steam over simmering water in a wok for $1\frac{1}{4}$–$1\frac{1}{2}$ hours, or until firm, replenishing with boiling water during cooking. Remove the pan and cool in the fridge overnight. Take the cake from the pan and cut into 2 inch squares that are $\frac{1}{2}$ inch thick.

HEAT a wok over high heat, add 2 tablespoons of the oil and heat until very hot. Cook the turnip cakes in batches, adding more oil between batches if necessary, until golden and crispy.

In dim sum restaurants, turnip cake is always fried to order.

SCALLION PANCAKES

ONE OF THE MOST POPULAR SNACKS IN NORTHERN CHINA IS CRISP SCALLION PANCAKES EATEN STRAIGHT FROM THE HOT OIL. SOME RESTAURANTS ALSO MAKE BIG, THICK PANCAKES THAT THEY CUT INTO WEDGES AND SERVE AS AN ACCOMPANIMENT TO A MEAL.

2 cups all-purpose flour
1/2 teaspoon salt
1 tablespoon oil
3 tablespoons roasted sesame oil
2 scallions, green part only, finely chopped
oil for frying

MAKES 24

PLACE the flour and salt in a mixing bowl and stir to combine. Add the oil and 3/4 cup boiling water and, using a wooden spoon, mix to a rough dough. Turn the dough out onto a lightly floured surface and knead for 5 minutes, or until smooth and elastic. If the dough is very sticky, knead in a little more flour. Cover the dough with a cloth and let it rest for 20 minutes.

ON a lightly floured surface, use your hands to roll the dough into a long cylinder. Divide the dough into 24 pieces. Working with 1 portion of dough at a time, place the dough, cut edge down, on the work surface. Using a small rolling pin, roll it out to a 4 inch circle. Brush the surface generously with the sesame oil and sprinkle with some scallion. Starting with the edge closest to you, roll up the dough and pinch the ends to seal in the scallion and sesame oil. Lightly flatten the roll, then roll it up again from one end like a snail, pinching the end to seal it. Repeat with the remaining dough, sesame oil and scallion. Let the cylinders rest for 20 minutes.

PLACE EACH roll flat on the work surface and press down with the palm of your hand. Roll out to a 4 inch circle and place on a lightly floured baking sheet. Stack the pancakes between lightly floured sheets of waxed paper and allow to rest for 20 minutes.

HEAT a frying pan over medium heat, brush the surface with oil, and add 2 or 3 of the pancakes at a time. Cook for 2–3 minutes on each side, turning once, until the pancakes are light golden brown and crisp. Remove and drain on paper towels. Serve immediately.

YOU CAN reheat the pancakes, wrapped in aluminium foil, in a 350°F oven for 15 minutes.

Spread the scallion through the dough by first rolling up the pancake and scallion, then rolling this into a snail shape, and finally by rolling the snail into a pancake shape again.

Folding sesame oil into the dough means that when the breads are steamed, the layers will spring open.

Steaming mantou being sold in the streets in Beijing.

蒸馒头

STEAMED BREADS

THE BASIC YEAST DOUGH CAN BE USED TO MAKE LOTS OF DIFFERENT STEAMED BUNS, CALLED "MANTOU" IN CHINA. FLOWER ROLLS ARE ONE OF THE SIMPLEST SHAPES, WHILE SILVER THREAD ROLLS REQUIRE MORE DEXTERITY. THESE BREADS ARE DELICIOUS WITH MEATS INSTEAD OF RICE.

1 quantity basic yeast dough (page 278)
3 tablespoons roasted sesame oil

MAKES 12 FLOWER ROLLS
OR 6 SILVER THREAD LOAVES

CUT the dough in half and, on a lightly floured surface, roll out each half to form a 12 x 4 inch rectangle. Brush the surface of the rectangles liberally with the sesame oil. Place one rectangle directly on top of the other, with both oiled surfaces facing up. Starting with one of the long edges, roll up the dough jelly-roll style. Pinch the 2 ends to seal in the sesame oil.

LIGHTLY FLATTEN the roll with the heel of your hand and cut the roll into 2 inch pieces. Using a chopstick, press down on the center of each roll, holding the chopstick parallel to the cut edges. (This will cause the ends to "flower" when they are steamed.) Arrange the shaped rolls well spaced in 4 steamers lined with waxed paper punched with holes. Cover and let rise for 15 minutes.

COVER AND steam each steamer separately over simmering water in a wok for 15 minutes, or until the rolls are light and springy. Keep the rolls covered until you are about to eat them to make sure they stay soft.

THE DOUGH can also be shaped in other ways, one of the most popular being silver thread bread. Divide the dough in half and roll each half into a sausage about 1 1/4 inches in diameter, then cut each sausage into 6 pieces. Roll 6 of the pieces into rectangles 8 x 4 inches and set aside. Roll the remaining pieces into rectangles 8 x 4 inches, brush each with a little sesame oil and fold in half to a 4 inch square. Brush with more sesame oil and fold in half again. Cut into thin strips crosswise. Place one of the rectangles on the work surface and stretch the strips so they fit down the center. Fold the ends and sides in to completely enclose the strips. Repeat with the remaining dough until you have 6 loaves. Steam as for the flower rolls for 20–25 minutes.

茶叶蛋

TEA EGGS

TEA EGGS, BRAISED IN A FRAGRANT TEA AND SOY SAUCE MIXTURE, ARE EASY TO MAKE AND GREAT FOR SNACKS—THEY CAN BE REHEATED AND TASTE EQUALLY GOOD HOT OR COLD. IN CHINA, THEY ARE FOUND IN TEA HOUSES AND ROADSIDE STANDS, OFTEN BUBBLING AWAY IN VATS FULL OF HOT TEA.

10 very fresh eggs or 20 quail eggs

TEA COOKING MIXTURE
3 tablespoons light soy sauce
3 tablespoons Shaoxing rice wine
1 star anise
1 tablespoon sugar
1 cinnamon stick
3 slices ginger, smashed with the flat side of a cleaver
3 tablespoons Chinese black tea leaves

MAKES 10 EGGS OR 20 QUAIL EGGS

PLACE the eggs in a saucepan with enough cold water to cover. Bring the water to a boil, then reduce the heat to low and let the eggs simmer for 10 minutes, or until they are hard-boiled. Refresh the eggs in cold water. Drain the eggs and lightly tap and roll the shells on a hard surface to crack them. Do not remove the shells.

PUT the tea cooking mixture ingredients in a heavy-bottomed clay pot, braising pan or saucepan with 4 cups water and heat until boiling. Reduce the heat to low and simmer for 20 minutes. Add the cooked eggs and simmer for another 45 minutes. Turn off the heat and let the eggs sit in the tea mixture until cool enough to handle. Remove the shells and serve the eggs warm or cold, cut into wedges, with some of the cooking mixture on top.

Tea eggs sold warm as a snack.

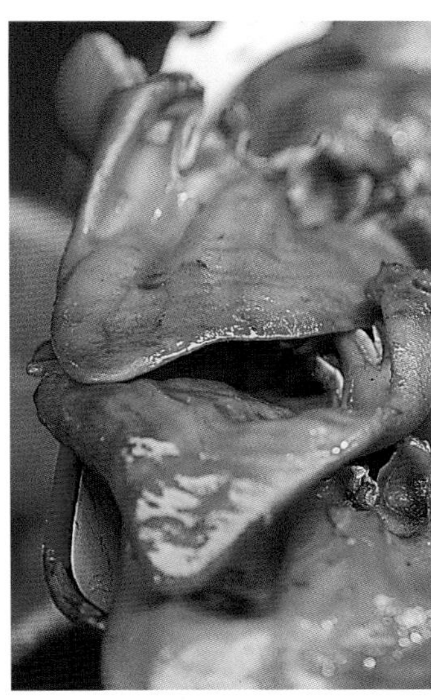

脆皮猪耳沙律

CRISPY FRIED PIG'S EAR

EVERY PART OF THE PIG IS USED IN ONE WAY OR ANOTHER IN CHINESE COOKING. HERE PIG'S EARS ARE SLOW-COOKED WHOLE TO BRING OUT THEIR MELTING, GELATINOUS QUALITIES, THEN SHREDDED AND FRIED TO GIVE THEM A CRISP COATING. EAT AS A SNACK WITH DRINKS OR AS AN APPETIZER.

1 pig's ear
1 tablespoon Shaoxing rice wine
1 tablespoon oil
2 garlic cloves, crushed
4 scallions, thinly sliced
2 tablespoons light soy sauce
1/2 teaspoon salt
2 teaspoons chili oil
2 teaspoons roasted sesame oil

SERVES 4 AS A SNACK

SCRAPE the pig's ear to get rid of any bristles and rinse. Put it in a clay pot, braising pan or saucepan, cover with water, add the rice wine and bring to the boil. Reduce the heat and simmer for 40 minutes, or until tender. Drain and allow to cool.

SLICE the ear diagonally into thin strips and finely shred the strips. Heat a wok over high heat, add the oil and heat until very hot. Cook the strips until very crisp. Add the garlic and scallions and toss together. Add the soy sauce, salt and chili and sesame oils and toss together. Serve immediately.

CRISPY FRIED PIG'S EAR

四川腌黄瓜

SICHUAN PICKLED CUCUMBER

THE COMPLEXITY OF FLAVORS IN THIS SIMPLE PICKLE IS UNUSUAL. THE SEASONINGS COMBINE TO CREATE A TASTE THAT IS SIMULTANEOUSLY SWEET, SOUR, HOT AND NUMBING.

A wide variety of hot pickles are sold in the markets in Sichuan.

1/2 lb cucumbers
1/2 teaspoon salt
1 1/2 tablespoons finely shredded ginger
1/2 small red chile, seeded and finely shredded
3 tablespoons roasted sesame oil
1/2 teaspoon Sichuan peppercorns
6 dried chiles, seeded and cut into 1/4 inch pieces
1 1/2 tablespoons clear rice vinegar
1 1/2 tablespoons sugar

SERVES 6 AS A SNACK

CUT the cucumbers in half lengthwise, remove the seeds, and cut into 2 1/2 inch long, 3/4 inch thick slices. Place in a bowl, add the salt, toss lightly and allow to sit for 30 minutes. Place the ginger in a bowl and soak in cold water for 20 minutes.

POUR OFF any water that has accumulated with the cucumbers, rinse the cucumbers lightly, then drain thoroughly and pat dry. Place the cucumber in a bowl with the drained ginger and chiles.

HEAT a wok over high heat, add the sesame oil and heat until very hot. Add the peppercorns and stir-fry for 15 seconds until fragrant. Add the dried chiles and stir-fry for 15 seconds, or until dark. Pour into the bowl with the cucumbers, toss lightly and allow to cool. Add the vinegar and sugar, toss to coat, then keep in the fridge for at least 6 hours or overnight. Serve cold or at room temperature.

CANTONESE PICKLED VEGETABLES

广东腌菜

CANTONESE PICKLED VEGETABLES

VARIATIONS OF PICKLED VEGETABLE SALADS ARE FOUND ALL OVER CHINA. THIS SWEET-AND-SOUR VERSION FROM THE SOUTH IS GOOD ALONE OR WITH SWEET-AND-SOUR SHRIMP OR PORK.

1/2 lb Chinese turnip, peeled
2 carrots
1 cucumber
1/2 teaspoon salt
1/3 cup sugar
1/3 cup clear rice vinegar
5 thin slices ginger, smashed with the flat side of a cleaver

SERVES 6 AS A SNACK

CUT the turnip in half lengthwise, then cut lengthwise into thirds and diagonally cut into 3/4 inch pieces. Diagonally cut the carrots into 3/4 inch pieces. Cut the cucumber in half lengthwise, remove any seeds and cut lengthwise into thirds. Diagonally cut into 3/4 inch pieces. Place the vegetables in a bowl, add the salt, toss lightly, and allow to sit for 1 hour. Dry thoroughly.

COMBINE the sugar and vinegar and stir until the sugar has dissolved. Add to the vegetables with the ginger and toss lightly to coat. Keep in the fridge for at least 6 hours, or overnight.

盐水蚕豆

SALTED SOY BEAN PODS

3/4 lb fresh soy bean pods
1 tablespoon coarse sea salt
4 star anise

SERVES 4 AS A SNACK

TRIM both ends of the soy bean pods, then place in a bowl with the salt and rub some of the fuzz off the skin. Rinse the pods. Place in a saucepan of salted water with the star anise and bring to a boil. Reduce the heat and simmer for 20 minutes, or until tender. Drain and allow to cool.

TO EAT, suck the beans out of the pods and throw the pods away. Serve as a snack.

SALTED SOY BEAN PODS

油炸花生米

FRIED PEANUTS

1 tablespoon Sichuan peppercorns
4 star anise
1 tablespoon sugar
1 teaspoon salt
2 lb shelled peanuts with skins on
3 tablespoons roasted sesame oil

SERVES 8 AS A SNACK

PUT 3 cups water in a saucepan with the spices, sugar and salt and bring to a boil. Add the peanuts and simmer for 5 minutes. Turn off the heat and allow the peanuts to cool in the liquid.

DRAIN and dry the peanuts, removing the whole spices. Heat the sesame oil in a wok and fry the peanuts until brown. Serve warm or cold as a snack.

FRIED PEANUTS

密饯核桃仁

CANDIED WALNUTS

1 cup sugar
4 1/2 cups shelled walnut halves
oil for deep-frying

SERVES 8 AS A SNACK

DISSOLVE the sugar in 1/2 cup water, then bring to a boil and cook for 2 minutes.

BLANCH the walnuts in a saucepan of boiling water briefly, then drain. Put immediately into the syrup, stirring to coat. Cool for 5 minutes; drain.

FILL a wok one quarter full of oil. Heat the oil to 375°F, or until a piece of bread fries golden brown in 10 seconds when dropped in the oil. Add the walnuts in batches, stirring to brown evenly. As soon as they brown, remove with a wire strainer or slotted spoon and lay on some aluminium foil, making sure they are well spaced. Do not touch as they will be hot. When cool, drain on paper towels. Serve as a snack or at the start of a meal.

CANDIED WALNUTS

SOUPS

港式玉米汤

CANTONESE CORN SOUP

THIS DELECTABLE SOUP IS A CANTONESE CLASSIC. YOU NEED TO USE A GOOD-QUALITY CAN OF CREAMED CORN WITH A SMOOTH TEXTURE, OR ALTERNATIVELY, IF IT IS QUITE COARSE, QUICKLY BLEND A CAN OF CREAMED CORN IN A BLENDER OR FOOD PROCESSOR TO MAKE IT EXTRA SMOOTH.

Stripping corn cobs in Yunnan.

- 1 lb skinned boneless chicken breasts, ground
- 1/2 cup Shaoxing rice wine
- 1 2/3 cups canned creamed corn
- 6 cups chicken stock (page 281)
- 1 teaspoon salt
- 2 1/2 tablespoons cornstarch
- 2 egg whites, lightly beaten
- 1 teaspoon roasted sesame oil

SERVES 6

PLACE the chicken in a bowl, add 3 tablespoons of the rice wine and stir to combine. In a large clay pot or saucepan, combine the creamed corn, stock, remaining rice wine and salt. Bring to a boil, stirring. Add the chicken and stir to separate the meat. Return to a boil and skim any impurities from the surface.

COMBINE the cornstarch with enough water to make a paste, add to the soup and simmer until thickened. Remove from the heat. Mix 2 tablespoons water into the egg white, then slowly add to the clay pot or saucepan in a thin stream around the edge of the saucepan. Stir once or twice, then add the sesame oil. Check the seasoning, adding more salt if necessary. Serve immediately.

CHICKEN AND MUSHROOM SOUP

蘑菇鸡汤

CHICKEN AND MUSHROOM SOUP

FOR THIS SOUP YOU CAN USE EITHER BUTTON OR CHINESE MUSHROOMS. CHINESE MUSHROOMS ARE USUALLY LABELLED SHIITAKE (THE JAPANESE NAME FOR THEM) WHEN FRESH AND WILL ADD MORE FLAVOR TO THE FINISHED SOUP.

- 2 tablespoons cornstarch
- 3–4 egg whites, beaten
- 4 oz skinned, boneless chicken breasts, thinly sliced
- 3 cups chicken and meat stock (page 281)
- 1/4 lb fresh button or Chinese mushrooms, thinly sliced
- 1 teaspoon roasted sesame oil
- chopped scallion

SERVES 4

COMBINE the cornstarch with enough water to make a paste. Mix 1 teaspoon each of the egg white and cornstarch paste and a pinch of salt with the chicken. Blend the remaining egg white and cornstarch mixture to a smooth paste.

BRING the stock to a rolling boil in a large clay pot or saucepan. Add the chicken and return to a boil, then add the mushrooms and salt. Return to the boil then, very slowly, pour in the egg white and cornstarch mixture, stirring constantly. As soon as the soup has thickened, add the sesame oil. Serve sprinkled with the chopped scallion.

鱼翅汤

SHARK'S FIN SOUP

ONE OF THE MOST EXPENSIVE AND PRIZED OF ALL CHINESE DELICACIES, SHARK'S FIN IS SERVED ON SPECIAL OCCASIONS AND AT BANQUETS. IF POSSIBLE, MAKE THE STOCK A DAY IN ADVANCE AND STORE IN THE FRIDGE. THIS WILL IMPROVE THE FLAVORS AND ALLOW ANY FAT TO EASILY BE SKIMMED OFF.

10 oz prepackaged shark's fin
13 oz bacon or ham bones
1 lb chicken bones
1 lb beef bones
4 slices ginger
10 oz skinned boneless chicken breasts, ground
1 egg white, lightly beaten
4 tablespoons cornstarch
1 tablespoon light soy sauce
red rice vinegar

SERVES 6

PLACE the shark's fin in a large bowl and cover with cold water. Allow to soak overnight. Strain the shark's fin and rinse gently to remove any remaining sand and sediment. Bring a stockpot of water to a boil. Add the shark's fin, reduce the heat and simmer, covered, for 1 hour. Strain and set aside.

PLACE the bacon or ham bones, chicken bones and beef bones in a large stockpot with the ginger slices and 8 cups water. Bring to a boil, then reduce the heat and simmer, covered, for 2 hours. Skim off any impurities and fat during cooking. Strain the stock, discarding the bones. Measure the stock—you will need 6–7 cups. If you have more, return the stock to the stockpot and reduce it further until you have the correct amount.

COMBINE the chicken, egg white and 1 tablespoon of the cornstarch. Set aside in the fridge.

PUT the prepared shark's fin and stock in a large braising pan or saucepan and simmer, covered, for 30 minutes. Add the chicken mixture and stir to separate the meat. Simmer for 10 minutes, or until the chicken is cooked.

SEASON the soup with the soy sauce and some salt and white pepper. Combine the remaining cornstarch with 1/2 cup water, add to the soup and simmer until thickened.

SERVE the soup with some red rice vinegar, which can be added to the soup to taste.

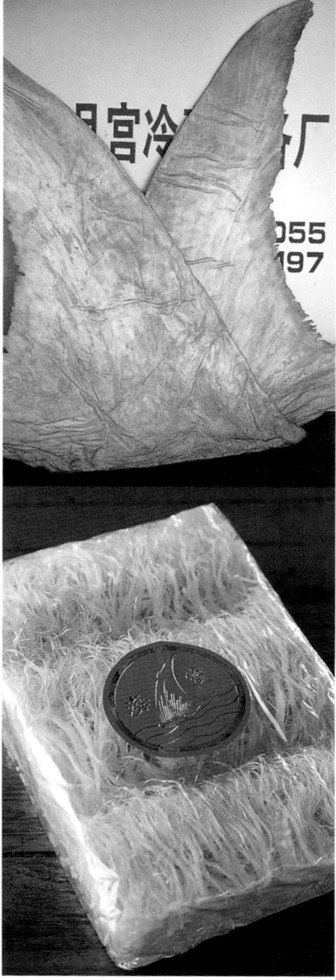

Shark's fin comes prepackaged, usually compressed and shrink-wrapped. It needs to be soaked and simmered to soften it before you use it.

To see if they have been fertilized, eggs are checked at the market by placing them above a light.

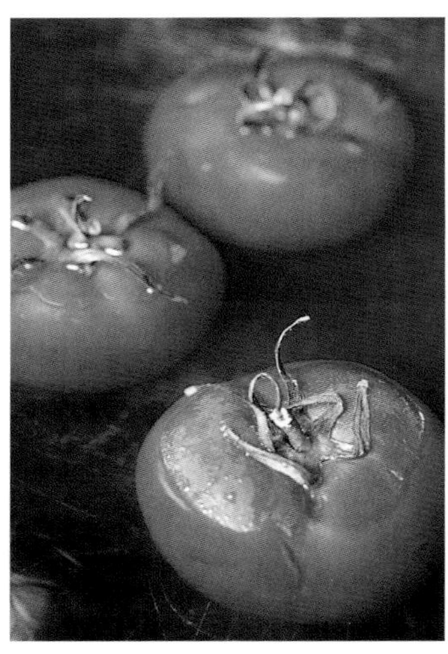

Scalding the tomatoes in boiling water makes it very easy to peel off their skins.

TOMATO AND EGG SOUP

THIS DELICIOUS AND NUTRITIOUS SOUP IS SIMPLICITY ITSELF AND IS SOMETIMES KNOWN AS EGG DROP SOUP BECAUSE THE EGG IS SLOWLY POURED IN NEAR THE END OF COOKING. MAKE SURE YOU USE RIPE TOMATOES OR BOTH THE COLOR AND FLAVOR WILL BE INSIPID.

1 lb firm ripe tomatoes
2 eggs
1 scallion, finely chopped
1 tablespoon oil
4 cups vegetable or chicken and meat stock (page 281)
1 tablespoon light soy sauce
1 tablespoon cornstarch

SERVES 4

SCORE a cross in the bottom of each tomato. Plunge into boiling water for 20 seconds, then drain and peel the skin away from the cross. Cut into slices or thin wedges, trimming off the core. Beat the eggs with a pinch of salt and a few pieces of scallion.

HEAT a wok over high heat, add the oil and heat until very hot. Stir-fry the scallion for a few seconds to flavor the oil, then pour in the stock and bring to a boil. Add the tomatoes and return to a boil. Add the soy sauce and very slowly pour in the beaten eggs, stirring as you pour. Return to a boil.

COMBINE the cornstarch with enough water to make a paste, add to the soup and simmer until thickened.

TOMATO AND EGG SOUP

豆腐菠菜汤

BEAN CURD AND SPINACH SOUP

THIS SIMPLE BUT BEAUTIFUL SOUP IS ALSO KNOWN AS "EMERALD AND WHITE JADE SOUP" IN CHINESE. IT IS A CLEAR SOUP, WHICH REQUIRES A VERY GOOD STOCK FOR FLAVOR, WHILE PIECES OF SOFT BEAN CURD ADD TEXTURE AND THE SPINACH ADDS COLOR AND FLAVOR.

1/4 lb soft bean curd, drained
2 cups baby spinach leaves
4 cups chicken and meat stock (page 281)
1 tablespoon light soy sauce

SERVES 4

CUT the bean curd into small slices about 1/4 inch thick. Chop the baby spinach leaves roughly if they are large.

BRING the stock to a rolling boil in a large clay pot or saucepan, then add the bean curd slices and soy sauce. Return to a boil, then reduce the heat and simmer gently for 2 minutes. Skim any impurities from the surface. Add the spinach and cook for 1–2 minutes. Season with salt and white pepper. Serve hot.

BEAN CURD AND SPINACH SOUP

冬瓜火腿汤

WINTER MELON AND HAM SOUP

ALTHOUGH IT LOOKS LIKE A WATERMELON, A WINTER MELON IS REALLY A MARROW OR WAX GOURD. IT IS SAID THAT WINTER MELONS WITH A GOOD COVERING OF WHITE POWDER ARE BEST. THE DELICATE FLESH BECOMES ALMOST TRANSLUCENT WHEN COOKED AND TASTES A LITTLE LIKE MARROW.

1 tablespoon dried shrimp
1/2 lb winter melon, rind and seeds removed
3 cups chicken and meat stock (page 281)
5 oz Chinese ham or prosciutto, chopped

SERVES 4

SOAK the dried shrimp in boiling water for 1 hour, then drain. Cut the winter melon into small pieces.

BRING the stock to a rolling boil in a large clay pot or saucepan. Add the shrimp, winter melon and ham. Return to a boil, then reduce the heat and simmer for 2 minutes. Season with salt and white pepper. Serve hot.

什锦菜汤

MIXED VEGETABLE SOUP

ALMOST ANY TYPE OF VEGETABLE CAN BE USED FOR THIS SOUP. CHOOSE THREE OR FOUR DIFFERENT ITEMS FROM THE INGREDIENTS LIST DEPENDING ON WHAT'S IN SEASON, BEARING IN MIND THAT THEY SHOULD CREATE A HARMONY OF COLOR AND TEXTURES.

1 lb mixed vegetables, such as carrots, baby corn, bamboo shoots, Chinese (shiitake) or button mushrooms, asparagus, spinach leaves, lettuce, cucumber, Chinese (Napa) cabbage or tomatoes
1/4 lb soft bean curd, drained
3 cups vegetable or chicken stock (page 281)
1 tablespoon light soy sauce
1/2 teaspoon roasted sesame oil
chopped scallion or chives

SERVES 4

CUT YOUR selection of vegetables and the bean curd into a roughly uniform shape and size. You can cut into shreds, cubes or slices, but the pieces should be small enough for a spoonful of soup to include several at once, giving a balance of flavors.

BRING the stock to a rolling boil in a large clay pot or saucepan. Add your selection of the carrots, corn, bamboo shoots and mushrooms first and cook for 2–3 minutes, then add any other vegetables and the bean curd and cook for 1 minute. Do not overcook the vegetables or they will become soggy and lose their crispness and delicate flavor.

SEASON WITH salt and white pepper. Add the soy sauce, drizzle with the sesame oil and sprinkle with the chopped scallion or chives.

WINTER MELON AND HAM SOUP

MIXED VEGETABLE SOUP

Using a cornstarch mixture to coat seafood before cooking is called "velveting." The coating adds a silky texture to the cooked food while protecting it and keeping it moist.

鱼片香菜汤

SLICED FISH AND CILANTRO SOUP

THE CHINESE OFTEN USE A CHICKEN AND MEAT STOCK WHEN COOKING SEAFOOD. HOWEVER, IF YOU PREFER, YOU CAN USE A VEGETABLE OR FISH STOCK FOR THIS RECIPE.

- 1/2 lb firm white fish fillets, such as cod, halibut or monkfish, skin removed
- 2 teaspoons egg white, beaten
- 1 teaspoon Shaoxing rice wine
- 2 teaspoons cornstarch
- 3 cups chicken and meat stock (page 281)
- 1 tablespoon light soy sauce
- 1 1/3 cups cilantro leaves

SERVES 4

CUT the fish into 3/4 x 1 1/4 inch slices. Blend the egg white, rice wine and cornstarch to make a smooth paste, and use it to coat each fish slice.

BRING the stock to a rolling boil in a large clay pot or saucepan. Add the fish slices one by one, stir gently and return to a boil. Reduce the heat and simmer for 1 minute, then add the soy sauce and cilantro leaves. Return to a boil, season with salt and white pepper and serve immediately.

西湖牛肉汤

WEST LAKE BEEF SOUP

THERE IS A WEST LAKE (AND OFTEN A NORTH, SOUTH OR EAST LAKE) IN MOST CITIES IN CHINA, SO THIS SOUP IS MORE LIKELY NAMED AFTER A LAKE IN ITS PROVINCE OF ORIGIN, GUANGZHOU, THAN THE FAMOUS WEST LAKE OF HANGZHOU.

- 5 oz beef top round steak
- 1 teaspoon salt
- 1 teaspoon sugar
- 1 tablespoon light soy sauce
- 1 tablespoon Shaoxing rice wine
- 2 tablespoons cornstarch
- 1/2 teaspoon roasted sesame oil
- 3 cups chicken and meat stock (page 281)
- 3/4 cup peas, fresh or frozen
- 1 egg, lightly beaten
- chopped scallion

SERVES 4

TRIM the fat off the steak and cut the steak into small pieces, about the size of the peas. Combine the beef with a pinch of the salt, about half the sugar, 1 teaspoon each of the soy sauce, rice wine and cornstarch and the sesame oil. Marinate in the fridge for at least 20 minutes.

BRING the stock to a rolling boil in a large clay pot or saucepan. Add the beef and stir to separate the meat, then add the peas and the remaining salt, sugar, soy sauce and rice wine. Return to a boil, then stir in the egg. Combine the remaining cornstarch with enough water to make a paste, add to the soup and simmer until thickened. Garnish with the chopped scallion.

WEST LAKE BEEF SOUP

十宝炖汤

TEN-TREASURE SOUP

THIS MEAL-IN-ONE SOUP IS ALMOST A KIND OF STEW, WHERE THE INGREDIENTS SIMMER TOGETHER SO THAT THE FLAVORS MIX. TRADITIONALLY THIS SOUP HAS TEN MAIN INGREDIENTS, BUT THE EXACT NUMBER DOES NOT MATTER AND YOU CAN VARY THE INGREDIENTS DEPENDING ON WHAT'S AVAILABLE.

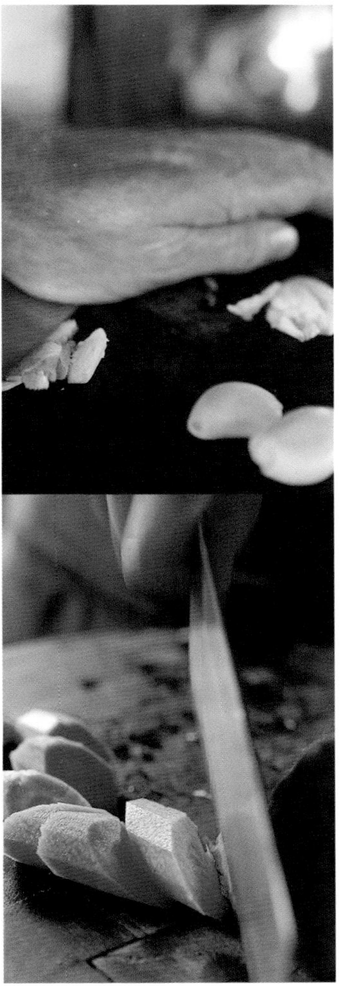

Use the flat side of a cleaver to smash the garlic cloves and the blade for cutting the carrots.

9 cups Chinese (Napa) cabbage
2 tablespoons oil
4 garlic cloves, smashed with the flat side of a cleaver
1/2 cup Shaoxing rice wine
6 cups chicken stock (page 281)
1 teaspoon salt
1/2 lb center-cut pork loin, trimmed
2 teaspoons light soy sauce
1/2 teaspoon roasted sesame oil
1 lb shrimp
3 slices ginger, smashed with the flat side of a cleaver
1 oz bean thread noodles
6 dried Chinese mushrooms
1 lb firm bean curd, drained and cut into 1 inch squares
2 carrots, cut into 3/4 inch pieces
4 1/2 cups baby spinach leaves
3 scallions, green part only, cut diagonally into 1/2 inch pieces

SERVES 6

REMOVE the stems from the cabbage and cut the leaves into 2 inch squares. Separate the hard cabbage pieces from the leafy ones. Heat a wok over high heat, add the oil and heat until very hot. Add the hard cabbage pieces and the garlic. Toss lightly over high heat, adding 1 tablespoon of the rice wine. Stir-fry for several minutes, then add the leafy cabbage pieces. Stir-fry for 1 minute, then add 4 tablespoons of the rice wine, the stock and half of the salt. Bring to a boil, then reduce the heat to low and cook for 30 minutes. Transfer to a clay pot or saucepan.

CUT the pork against the grain into slices about 1/8 inch thick. Place the pork in a bowl, add the soy sauce and sesame oil, and toss lightly. Marinate in the fridge for 20 minutes.

PEEL and devein the shrimps, then place in a bowl with the ginger, remaining rice wine and salt and toss lightly. Marinate in the fridge for 20 minutes. Remove and discard the ginger.

SOAK the bean thread noodles in hot water for 10 minutes, then drain and cut into 6 inch pieces. Soak the dried mushrooms in boiling water for 30 minutes, then drain and squeeze out any excess water. Remove and discard the stems.

ARRANGE the pork slices, bean curd, mushrooms, noodles and carrots in separate piles on top of the cabbage in the casserole, leaving some space in the center for the shrimps and spinach. Cover and cook over medium heat for 20 minutes. Arrange the shrimps and spinach in the center and sprinkle with the scallions. Cover and cook for 5 minutes, or until the shrimp are pink and cooked through. Season with salt if necessary. Serve directly from the clay pot.

酸辣汤

HOT-AND-SOUR SOUP

THIS SOUP SHOULD NOT CONTAIN HOT CHILES—THE HOTNESS COMES FROM GROUND WHITE PEPPER, WHICH, IN ORDER TO GET A GOOD FLAVOR, MUST BE VERY FRESHLY GROUND.

Adding the egg to the hot soup forms egg drops. Pour it in in an even stream.

4 dried Chinese mushrooms
2 tablespoons dried black fungus (wood ears)
4 oz lean pork, thinly shredded
1 tablespoon cornstarch
4 oz firm bean curd, drained
1/4 cup fresh or canned bamboo shoots, rinsed and drained
4 cups chicken and meat stock (page 281)
1 teaspoon salt
1 tablespoon Shaoxing rice wine
2 tablespoons light soy sauce
1–2 tablespoons Chinese black rice vinegar
2 eggs, beaten
1–2 teaspoons freshly ground white pepper
chopped scallion

SERVES 4

SOAK the dried mushrooms in boiling water for 30 minutes, then drain and squeeze out any excess water. Remove and discard the stems and shred the caps. Soak the dried black fungus in cold water for 20 minutes, then drain and squeeze out any excess water. Shred the black fungus.

COMBINE the pork, a pinch of salt and 1 teaspoon of the cornstarch. Thinly shred the bean curd and bamboo shoots to the same size as the pork.

BRING the stock to a boil in a large clay pot or saucepan. Add the pork and stir to separate the meat, then add the mushrooms, bean curd and bamboo. Return to a boil and add the salt, rice wine, soy sauce and vinegar. Slowly pour in the egg, whisking to form thin threads, and cook for 1 minute. Combine the remaining cornstarch with enough water to make a paste, add to the soup and simmer until thick. Put the pepper in a bowl, pour in the soup and stir. Garnish with scallion.

LAMB AND CUCUMBER SOUP

羊肉黄瓜汤

LAMB AND CUCUMBER SOUP

1/2 lb lamb steak
1 tablespoon Shaoxing rice wine
1 tablespoon light soy sauce
1 teaspoon roasted sesame oil
1/2 cucumber
3 cups chicken and meat stock (page 281)
2 teaspoons Chinese black rice vinegar, or to taste
cilantro leaves

SERVES 4

CUT the lamb into very thin slices and combine with the rice wine, soy sauce and sesame oil. Marinate in the fridge for at least 15 minutes. Halve the cucumber lengthwise, discarding the seeds, and cut it into thin slices.

BRING the stock to a rolling boil in a large clay pot or saucepan. Add the lamb and stir to separate the meat. Return to a boil, then add the cucumber and rice vinegar, and season with salt and white pepper. Return to a boil. Serve garnished with the cilantro leaves.

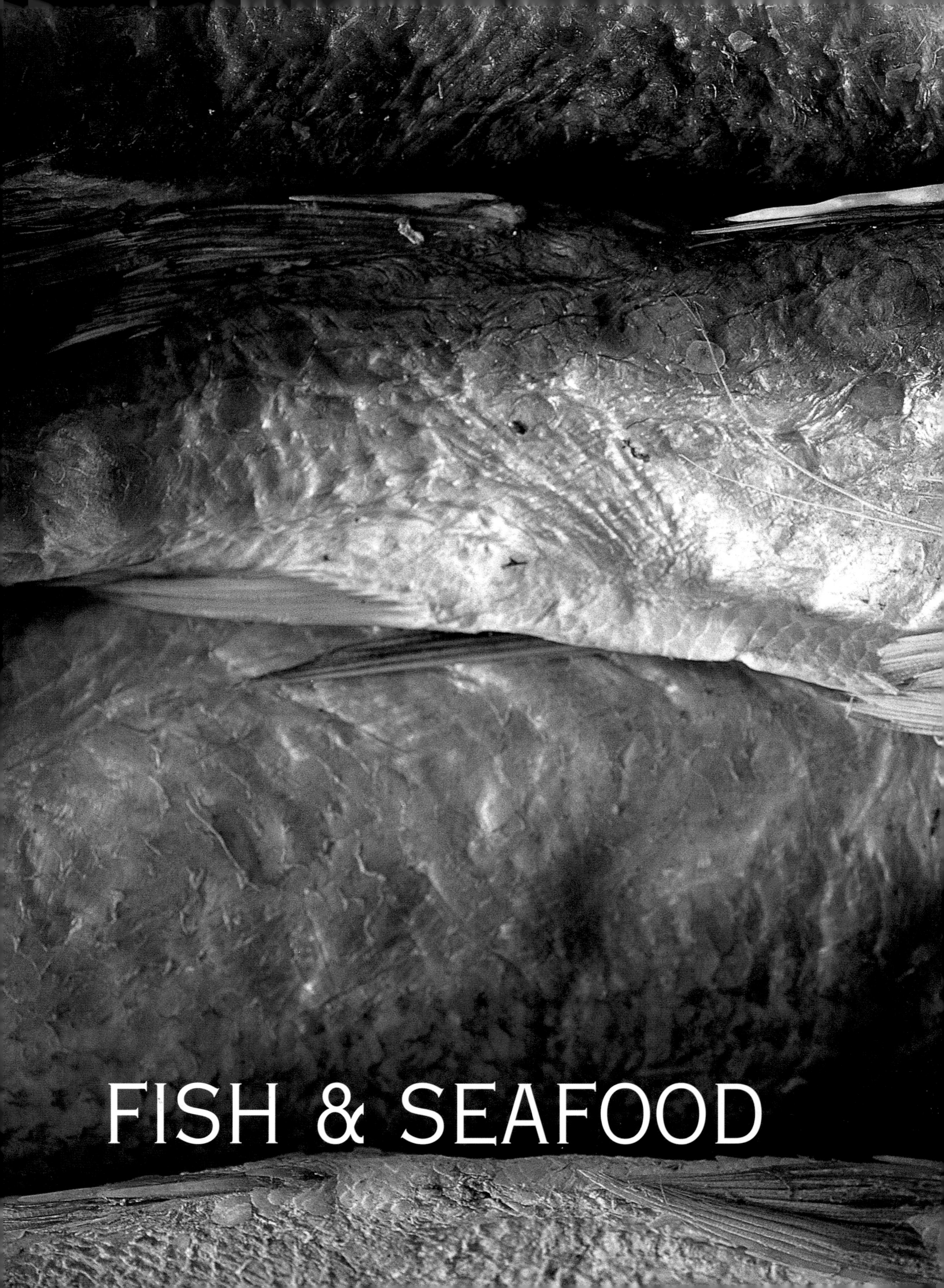

FISH & SEAFOOD

极品海鲜（鲍鱼、焖荷兰豆和凤尾菇）

ABALONE, SNOW PEAS AND OYSTER MUSHROOMS

ABALONE IS EATEN IN CHINA AT FESTIVAL TIMES, ESPECIALLY AT NEW YEAR AS THE CHINESE NAME FOR ABALONE, "BAU YU," SOUNDS JUST LIKE THE WORDS FOR "GUARANTEED WEALTH." DRIED ABALONE IS OFTEN USED IN CHINA, BUT FRESH OR TINNED ABALONE IS MUCH EASIER TO PREPARE.

Remove the meat from the abalone by severing the muscle that holds it to the shell. Trim off any hard patches.

New Year fireworks over Beijing.

2 3/4 lb fresh abalone (1 lb prepared weight) or 1 lb canned abalone
3/4 lb snow peas, ends trimmed
1/4 lb oyster mushrooms
2 tablespoons oil
2 garlic cloves, finely chopped
2 teaspoons finely chopped ginger
2 tablespoons oyster sauce
2 teaspoons light soy sauce
1 teaspoon sugar
3 teaspoons cornstarch

SERVES 4

PREPARE the fresh abalone by removing the meat from the shell using a sharp knife. Wash the meat under cold running water, rubbing well to remove any dark-colored slime. Trim off any hard outer edges and the mouth as well as any hard patches on the bottom of the foot. Pound the meat with a mallet for 1 minute to tenderize it, but be careful not to break the flesh.

PLACE the fresh abalone in a saucepan of simmering water and cook, covered, for 2 hours, or until the meat is tender (test it by seeing if a fork will pierce the meat easily). Drain the abalone and, when it is cool enough to handle, cut it into thin slices.

IF YOU are using canned abalone, simply drain, reserving the juice, and cut into thin slices.

CUT any large snow peas in half diagonally. Halve any large oyster mushrooms.

HEAT a wok over medium heat, add the oil and heat until hot. Stir-fry the snow peas and mushrooms for 1 minute. Add the garlic and ginger and stir for 1 minute, or until aromatic.

REDUCE the heat slightly and add the oyster sauce, soy sauce, sugar and the sliced abalone. Stir well to combine. Combine the cornstarch with enough water (or the reserved abalone juice if using canned abalone) to make a paste, add to the sauce and simmer until thickened.

CANTONESE-STYLE STEAMED FISH

ALL CHINESE COOKS, BUT PARTICULARLY THE CANTONESE, DEMAND THE FRESHEST INGREDIENTS. THE LUSH LAND OF GUANGZHOU PROVIDES FRESH VEGETABLES, AND SINCE THE REGION IS BORDERED BY THE SEA AND HAS MANY RIVERS AND LAKES, FISH IS SOLD LIVE AND KILLED JUST BEFORE COOKING.

1 1/2–2 lb whole fish, such as carp, porgy, grouper or sea bass
2 tablespoons Shaoxing rice wine
1 1/2 tablespoons light soy sauce
1 tablespoon finely chopped ginger
1 teaspoon roasted sesame oil
2 tablespoons oil
2 scallions, finely shredded
3 tablespoons finely shredded ginger
1/4 teaspoon freshly ground black pepper

SERVES 4

IF YOU do manage to buy a live fish, then ask the fishmonger to gut it through the gills. This is harder than gutting through the stomach, but leaves the fish looking whole. If you are gutting the fish yourself, make a cut from the throat to the tail and pull out the guts through the stomach. Remove any scales with a fish scaler or the back of a knife. Check that the gills have been cut out, then rinse the fish under cold, running water and drain thoroughly in a colander.

PLACE the fish in a large bowl. Add the rice wine, soy sauce, chopped ginger and sesame oil, and toss lightly to coat. Cover with plastic wrap and allow to marinate in the fridge for 10 minutes.

ARRANGE the fish on a flameproof plate, with the marinade, and place in a steamer. Steam over simmering water in a covered wok for 5–8 minutes, or until the fish flakes when the skin is pressed firmly or the dorsal fin pulls out easily. Remove the fish from the steamer and place on a flameproof platter.

HEAT a wok over high heat, add the oil and heat until smoking. Sprinkle the steamed fish with the shredded scallions, shredded ginger and pepper, and slowly pour the hot oil over the fish. This will cause the skin to crisp, and cook the garnish.

Test if the flesh of the fish is cooked by pressing it to see if it feels or looks flaky—you can use either a pair of chopsticks or your fingers.

Scrub off any barnacles from the mussels, then remove the beards (byssus) by tugging on them firmly.

豆豉蒸蚌

STEAMED MUSSELS WITH BLACK BEAN SAUCE

MUSSELS ARE NOT EATEN AS MUCH IN CHINA AS CLAMS, HOWEVER, THEY ARE ENJOYED IN SEASIDE AREAS. THIS RECIPE WORKS EQUALLY WELL WITH CLAMS IF YOU PREFER.

2 lb mussels
1 tablespoon oil
1 garlic clove, finely chopped
1/2 teaspoon finely chopped ginger
2 scallions, finely chopped
1 red chile, chopped
1 tablespoon light soy sauce
1 tablespoon Shaoxing rice wine
1 tablespoon salted, fermented black beans, rinsed and mashed
2 tablespoons chicken and meat stock (page 281)
few drops of roasted sesame oil

SERVES 4

SCRUB the mussels, remove any beards, and throw away any that do not close when tapped on the work surface.

PLACE the mussels in a large dish in a steamer. Steam over simmering water in a covered wok for 4 minutes, discarding any that do not open after this time.

MEANWHILE, HEAT the oil in a small saucepan. Add the garlic, ginger, scallions and chile and cook, stirring, for 30 seconds. Add the remaining ingredients, and blend well. Bring to a boil, then reduce the heat and simmer for 1 minute.

TO SERVE, remove and discard the top shell of each mussel, pour 2 teaspoons of the sauce into each mussel and serve on the shell.

CLAMS IN YELLOW BEAN SAUCE

豆酱焖蛤

CLAMS IN YELLOW BEAN SAUCE

CLAMS ARE IMMENSELY POPULAR IN CHINA AND ARE SEEN AS A SYMBOL OF GOOD FORTUNE AS THEIR SHELLS ARE SAID TO LOOK LIKE COINS. THIS IS A VERY SIMPLE RECIPE FOR THEM.

3 lb hard-shelled clams
1 tablespoon oil
2 garlic cloves, crushed
1 tablespoon grated ginger
2 tablespoons yellow bean sauce
1/2 cup chicken stock (page 281)
1 scallion, sliced

SERVES 4

WASH the clams in several changes of cold water, leaving them for a few minutes each time to remove any grit. Scrub the clams well, discarding any that remain open. Drain well.

HEAT a wok over high heat, add the oil and heat until very hot. Stir-fry the garlic and ginger for 30 seconds, then add the bean sauce and clams and toss together. Add the stock and stir for 3 minutes until the clams have opened, discarding any that do not open after this time. Season with salt and white pepper. Transfer the clams to a plate and sprinkle with the scallion.

The Li River in Guangxi.

Fishermen on the Li River use tame cormorants to catch fish.

熏鱼

SMOKED FISH

IN FACT, THE FISH IN THIS DISH IS NOT SMOKED AT ALL. INSTEAD IT ACQUIRES A SMOKY FLAVOR FROM BEING MARINATED AND BRAISED IN A SPICY SAUCE, THEN BEING DEEP-FRIED AND MARINATED IN THE SAUCE ONCE MORE BEFORE SERVING.

2 tablespoons light soy sauce
1 tablespoon dark soy sauce
3 tablespoons Shaoxing rice wine
2 tablespoons rock sugar
2 teaspoons five-spice powder
1 scallion, finely chopped
2 teaspoons finely chopped ginger
1 lb firm white fish fillets, such as monkfish, rock cod or sea bass, with skin
1 1/4 cups chicken and meat stock (page 281)
oil for deep-frying
cilantro leaves

SERVES 6

MIX together the soy sauces, rice wine, sugar, five-spice powder, scallion and ginger. Pat dry the fish and leave in the marinade for 1 hour. Transfer the fish and marinade to a clay pot or saucepan. Add the stock and bring to a boil. Reduce the heat and simmer gently for 10 minutes, or until the fish is cooked through, then drain the fish, reserving the marinade.

FILL a wok one quarter full of oil. Heat the oil to 375°F, or until a piece of bread fries golden brown in 10 seconds when dropped in the oil. Carefully cook the fish in batches for 3–4 minutes, or until golden and crisp (it will spit a little). Remove the fish from the oil and return it to the marinade. Allow to cool for 2–3 hours.

REMOVE the fish from the marinade and allow to dry for a few minutes. Cut the fish into thin slices and serve cold, sprinkled with cilantro leaves.

THE MARINADE can be reused as a "Master Sauce" (see page 290).

油炸椒盐苏东

DEEP-FRIED SQUID FLOWERS WITH SPICY SALT

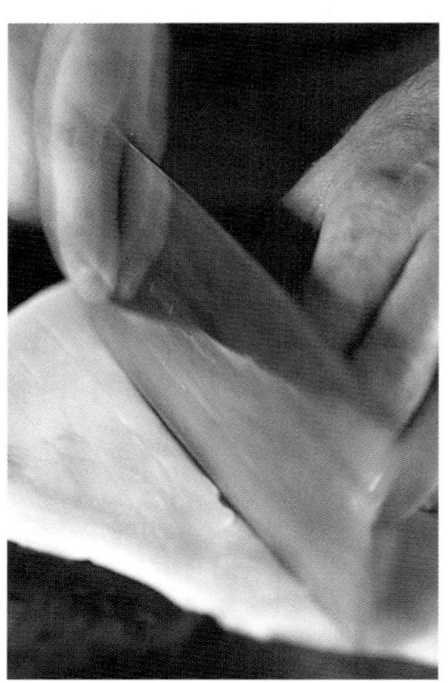

Score the inside of the squid with fine lines in a crisscross pattern before cutting into pieces.

1 lb squid bodies
1 teaspoon ginger juice (page 285)
1 tablespoon Shaoxing rice wine
oil for deep-frying
2 teaspoons spicy salt and pepper (page 285)
cilantro leaves

SERVES 4

OPEN UP the squid bodies and scrub off any soft jelly-like substance, then score the inside of the flesh with a fine crisscross pattern, making sure you do not cut all the way through. Cut the squid into 1¼ x 2 inch pieces.

BLANCH the squid in a saucepan of boiling water for 25–30 seconds—each piece will curl up and the crisscross pattern will open out, hence the name "squid flower." Remove, refresh in cold water, then drain and dry. Marinate in the ginger juice and the rice wine for 25–30 minutes.

FILL a wok one quarter full of oil. Heat the oil to 350°F, or until a piece of bread fries golden brown in 15 seconds when dropped into the oil. Cook the squid for 35–40 seconds, then carefully remove and drain well. Sprinkle with the spicy salt and pepper and toss to coat. Serve sprinkled with the cilantro.

辣椒炒苏东

STIR-FRIED SQUID FLOWERS WITH PEPPERS

STIR-FRIED SQUID FLOWERS WITH PEPPERS

13 oz squid bodies
3 tablespoons oil
2 tablespoons salted, fermented black beans, rinsed and mashed
1 small onion, cut into small cubes
1 small green pepper, cut into small cubes
3–4 small slices ginger
1 scallion, cut into short lengths
1 small red chile, chopped
1 tablespoon Shaoxing rice wine
½ teaspoon roasted sesame oil

SERVES 4

OPEN UP the squid bodies and scrub off any soft jelly-like substance, then score the inside of the flesh with a fine crisscross pattern, making sure you do not cut all the way through. Cut the squid into 1¼ x 2 inch pieces.

BLANCH the squid in a saucepan of boiling water for 25–30 seconds—each piece will curl up and the crisscross pattern will open out, hence the name "squid flower." Remove and refresh in cold water, then drain and dry well.

HEAT a wok over high heat, add the oil and heat until very hot. Stir-fry the black beans, onion, green pepper, ginger, scallion and chile for 1 minute. Add the squid and rice wine, mix together and stir for 1 minute. Sprinkle with the sesame oil.

西湖鱼

WEST LAKE FISH

HANGZHOU IN THE EAST OF CHINA IS FAMOUS FOR ITS REFINED CUISINE AND EXQUISITE SCENERY. A SPECIALTY OF THIS REGION IS WEST LAKE FISH MADE WITH FRESHWATER CARP. THE POACHING METHOD IS UNIQUE AND QUITE INGENIOUS AS THE FISH IS COOKED OFF THE HEAT.

- 3 1/2 lb whole fish, such as carp, porgy, grouper or sea bass
- 4 tablespoons Shaoxing rice wine
- 2 teaspoons salt
- 4 slices ginger, smashed with the flat side of a cleaver
- 4 scallions, sliced and smashed with the flat side of a cleaver
- 1 tablespoon oil
- 2 tablespoons finely shredded ginger
- 1 scallion, finely shredded
- 1 red chile, seeded and finely shredded
- 1/2 teaspoon freshly ground white pepper
- 2 1/2 tablespoons light soy sauce
- 2 tablespoons sugar
- 2 tablespoons Chinese black rice vinegar
- 1 tablespoon cornstarch

SERVES 6

IF YOU do manage to buy a live fish, then ask the fishmonger to gut it through the gills. This is harder than gutting through the stomach, but leaves the fish looking whole. If you are gutting the fish yourself, make a cut from the throat to the tail and pull out the guts through the stomach. Remove any scales with a fish scaler or the back of a knife. Check that the gills have been cut out, then rinse the fish under cold, running water and drain thoroughly in a colander.

DIAGONALLY score both sides of the fish, cutting through as far as the bone at intervals of 3/4 inch.

COMBINE 1 tablespoon of the rice wine, 1 teaspoon of the salt, the ginger slices and smashed scallions. Pinch the ginger slices and the scallions in the marinade repeatedly for several minutes to impart their flavors into the marinade. Rub the marinade all over the outside of the fish and into the slits. Allow the fish to marinate in the refrigerator for 30 minutes.

BRING 16 cups water to a boil in a wok with the oil and remaining rice wine. Gently lower the fish into the poaching liquid and return to a boil. Turn off the heat, cover, and allow to sit for 20 minutes, or until the fish flakes when the skin is pressed firmly or the dorsal fin pulls out easily. If the fish is not cooked through, cook over low heat for 5 minutes. Using slotted spoons, carefully transfer the fish to a platter. Reserve 1 1/2 cups of the poaching liquid. Sprinkle the ginger, shredded scallion, chile and white pepper over the fish.

ADD the soy sauce, remaining salt, sugar and black vinegar to the liquid. Heat the wok over high heat, add the liquid and bring to a boil. Combine the cornstarch with enough water to make a paste, add to the sauce and simmer until thickened. Pour the sauce over the fish.

Rinse the fish thoroughly, making sure that all the scales are washed off—scales left on will be hard and unpalatable. Marinating the fish not only adds flavor but also makes it aromatic and less "fishy" tasting.

青菜炒干贝

STIR-FRIED SCALLOPS WITH CHINESE GREENS

THIS DISH EMPHASIZES THE FRESHNESS AND DELICATE SEASONING THAT GIVE CANTONESE CUISINE ITS REPUTATION, WHILE A HIGH HEAT AND SHORT COOKING TIME ARE ALSO ESSENTIAL TO ITS SUCCESS. CHINESE BROCCOLI OR BOK CHOY IS TRADITIONALLY USED, BUT YOU COULD USE REGULAR BROCCOLI.

Slice the white muscle off the side of each scallop—these will be hard and rubbery if left on and cooked. Stir-fry the scallops in the sauce for only a few seconds just to heat them through; if they overcook they can be tough.

11 oz scallops, roe removed
2 tablespoons Shaoxing rice wine
1 tablespoon roasted sesame oil
1 teaspoon finely chopped ginger
1/2 scallion, finely chopped
1 bunch (about 1/2 lb) Chinese broccoli (gai lan) or bok choy
1/3 cup chicken stock (page 281)
1/2 teaspoon salt
1/4 teaspoon sugar
1/4 teaspoon freshly ground white pepper
1 teaspoon cornstarch
1 tablespoon oil
1 tablespoon finely shredded ginger
1 scallion, finely shredded
1 garlic clove, very thinly sliced

SERVES 6

SLICE the small, hard white muscle off the side of each scallop and pull off any membrane. Rinse the scallops and drain. Holding a knife blade parallel to the cutting surface, slice each scallop in half horizontally. Place the scallops in a bowl with 1 tablespoon of the rice wine, 1/4 teaspoon of the sesame oil and the chopped ginger and scallion. Toss lightly, then leave to marinate for 20 minutes.

WASH the broccoli well. Discard any tough-looking stems and diagonally cut into 3/4 inch pieces through the stem and the leaf. Blanch the Chinese broccoli in a pan of boiling water for 2 minutes, or until the stems and leaves are just tender, then refresh in cold water and dry thoroughly.

COMBINE the chicken stock, salt, sugar, white pepper, cornstarch and the remaining rice wine and sesame oil.

HEAT a wok over high heat, add the oil and heat until very hot. Add the scallops and stir-fry for 30 seconds, then remove. Add the shredded ginger, shredded scallion and garlic and stir-fry for 10 seconds. Add the stock mixture and cook, stirring constantly, until the sauce thickens. Add the Chinese broccoli and scallops. Toss lightly to coat with the sauce.

A fresh produce market in Sichuan.

Bottles of condiments and sauces for sale in a grocery shop in Beijing.

酸甜素菜拌虾

SWEET-AND-SOUR SHRIMP WITH VEGETABLES

SWEET AND SOUR IS PROBABLY ONE OF THE MOST ABUSED CHINESE DISHES, BUT WHEN WELL DONE IT CAN BE ONE OF THE MOST PLEASING. THE KEY IS THE SAUCE, WHICH HAS EQUAL AMOUNTS OF RICE VINEGAR AND SUGAR TO GIVE IT ITS SWEET-AND-SOUR FLAVOR.

1 1/2 lb shrimp
2 tablespoons Shaoxing rice wine
2 slices ginger, smashed with the flat side of a cleaver
3 teaspoons roasted sesame oil
1 1/2 tablespoons cornstarch
1/2 cup oil
2 scallions, white part only, finely chopped
1 tablespoon finely chopped ginger
2 garlic cloves, finely chopped
1 red pepper, diced
1 green pepper, diced
2 1/2 tablespoons tomato ketchup
2 tablespoons clear rice vinegar
2 tablespoons sugar
1 teaspoon light soy sauce
1/2 teaspoon salt

SERVES 6

PEEL the shrimp, score each one along the length of the back so the shrimp will "butterfly" when cooked, and devein them. Place the shrimp in a bowl and add the rice wine, ginger, 2 teaspoons of the sesame oil and 1 tablespoon of the cornstarch. Pinch the ginger slices in the marinade repeatedly for several minutes to impart the flavor into the marinade. Toss lightly, then allow to marinate for 20 minutes. Discard the ginger slices and drain the shrimp.

HEAT a wok over high heat, add 2 tablespoons of the oil and heat until very hot. Add half the shrimp and toss lightly over high heat for about 1 1/2 minutes, or until the shrimp turn pink and curl up. Remove with a wire strainer or slotted spoon and drain. Repeat with another 2 tablespoons of the oil and the remaining shrimp. Pour out the oil and wipe out the wok.

REHEAT the wok over high heat, add the remaining oil and heat until very hot. Add the scallion, ginger and garlic and stir-fry for 15 seconds, or until fragrant. Add the red and green pepper and stir-fry for 1 minute. Combine the tomato ketchup, rice vinegar, sugar, soy sauce, salt and the remaining sesame oil and cornstarch with 1/2 cup water, add to the sauce and simmer until thickened. Add the shrimp and toss lightly to coat.

芙蓉龙虾

LOBSTER FU RONG

THE WORDS "FU RONG" MEAN EGG WHITES AND IN RECIPES DENOTE A CLASSIC CANTONESE COOKING METHOD, THOUGH THE TERM IS OFTEN ASSOCIATED WITH THE QUITE DIFFERENT EGG FOO YOUNG OF WESTERN CHINESE RESTAURANTS. THIS DISH CAN BE MADE WITH ANY KIND OF SEAFOOD.

1 lb lobster meat
3 tablespoons Shaoxing rice wine
3 teaspoons finely chopped ginger
1 1/2 teaspoons salt
12 egg whites
1/2 teaspoon cream of tartar
oil for deep-frying
1/2 cup chicken stock (page 281)
1/4 teaspoon freshly ground white pepper
1 teaspoon roasted sesame oil
1 teaspoon cornstarch
2 scallions, finely chopped
2 scallions, green part only, sliced

SERVES 6

CUT the lobster meat into pieces, put in a bowl with 1 tablespoon of the rice wine, 1 teaspoon of the ginger and 1/2 teaspoon of the salt and toss lightly to coat. Beat the egg whites and cream of tartar using a hand whisk or electric mixer until stiff. Fold the lobster into the egg white mixture.

FILL a wok one quarter full of oil. Heat the oil to 375°F, or until a piece of bread fries golden brown in 10 seconds when dropped in the oil. Pour the lobster into the wok in batches—do not stir, otherwise it will scatter, but gently stir the oil from the bottom of the wok so that the "fu rong" rises to the surface. Remove each batch as soon as it is set, without letting it go too brown, and drain well. Pour the oil out, reserving 2 tablespoons.

COMBINE the chicken stock, remaining rice wine and salt, white pepper, sesame oil and cornstarch.

REHEAT the reserved oil over high heat until very hot and stir-fry the finely chopped scallion and the remaining ginger for 10 seconds, or until fragrant. Add the stock mixture and cook, stirring constantly to prevent lumps, until thickened. Add the cooked lobster mixture and carefully toss it in the sauce. Transfer to a serving platter, sprinkle with the sliced scallions and serve.

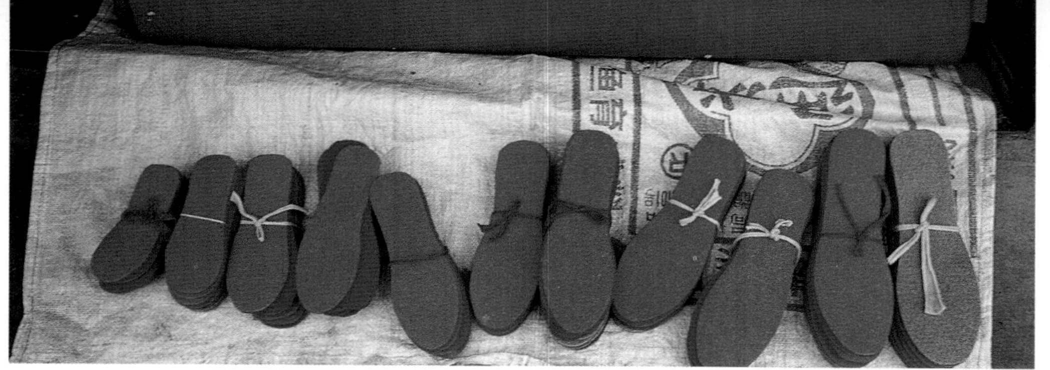

JELLYFISH AND CHICKEN SALAD

JELLYFISH ARE ONLY EVER EATEN ONCE THEY HAVE BEEN PRESERVED AND DRIED. THEY HAVE A CRUNCHY TEXTURE AND ARE NOT LIKE JELLY. YOU CAN BUY THEM DRIED, CUT INTO STRIPS OR WHOLE, AND ALSO ALREADY RECONSTITUTED IN VACUUM PACKS. THE LATTER ARE MUCH EASIER TO USE.

12 oz dried or prepackaged jellyfish
2¾ lb chicken
2 celery stalks, cut into 2 inch pieces and finely shredded
1 carrot, cut into 2 inch pieces and finely shredded
1 tablespoon oyster sauce
2 teaspoons light soy sauce
2 teaspoons roasted sesame oil
¾ cup cilantro leaves
3 teaspoons sesame seeds

DRESSING
¾ cup clear rice vinegar
¼ cup sugar
1 tablespoon finely chopped ginger
3 scallions, thinly sliced

SERVES 8

TO PREPARE dried jellyfish, remove from the package, cover with tepid water and soak overnight. Drain, then rinse to remove any sand and sediment. Drain well. Cut into strands using a pair of scissors, then cut any long strands into shorter pieces. If you are using vacuum-packed jellyfish, remove it from the package and rinse.

RINSE the chicken, drain, and remove any fat from the cavity opening and around the neck. Cut off and discard the tail. Bring a large saucepan of water to a boil. Add the chicken and bring the water to a gentle simmer. Cook, covered, for 25–30 minutes, or until the chicken is cooked through. Remove the chicken from the saucepan and plunge into cold water. When cool enough to handle, remove the skin and bones from the chicken and finely shred the meat.

PLACE the chicken in a large bowl and add the jellyfish, celery, carrot, oyster sauce, soy sauce, sesame oil and cilantro. Mix well to combine.

TO MAKE the dressing, place the vinegar and sugar in a bowl and stir until dissolved. Stir in the ginger and scallions.

TOAST the sesame seeds by dry-frying in a pan until brown and popping. Sprinkle the salad with the sesame seeds and serve cold with the dressing on the side.

It is easiest to cut the jellyfish using a pair of scissors. Make sure you keep the strands roughly the same width.

Cut the last 2 joints off all the crab legs as these don't contain much meat.

辣椒螃蟹

CHILI CRAB

- 4 x 1/2 lb live crabs
- 3 tablespoons oil
- 1 tablespoon Guilin chili sauce
- 2 tablespoons light soy sauce
- 3 teaspoons clear rice vinegar
- 4 tablespoons Shaoxing rice wine
- 1/2 teaspoon salt
- 2 tablespoons sugar
- 2 tablespoons chicken stock (page 281)
- 1 tablespoon grated ginger
- 2 garlic cloves, crushed
- 2 scallions, finely chopped

SERVES 4

TO KILL the crabs humanely, put them in the freezer for 1 hour. Bring a large saucepan of water to a boil. Plunge the crabs into boiling water for about 1 minute, then rinse them in cold water. Twist off and discard the upper shell, and remove and discard the spongy grey gill tissue from inside the crab. Rinse the bodies and drain well. Cut away the last two hairy joints of the legs. Cut each crab into 4 to 6 pieces, cutting so that a portion of the body is attached to 1 or 2 legs. Crack the crab claws using crab crackers or the back edge of a cleaver—this will help the flavoring penetrate the crab meat.

HEAT a wok over high heat, add 1 tablespoon of the oil and heat until very hot. Add half the crab and fry for several minutes to cook the meat right through. Remove and drain. Repeat with another tablespoon of the oil and the remaining crab.

COMBINE the chili sauce, soy sauce, rice vinegar, rice wine, salt, sugar and stock.

REHEAT the wok over high heat, add the remaining oil and heat until very hot. Stir-fry the ginger, garlic and scallions for 10 seconds. Add the sauce mixture to the wok and cook briefly. Add the crab pieces and toss lightly to coat with the sauce. Cook, covered, for 5 minutes, then serve immediately.

CRAB IS best eaten with your hands, so supply finger bowls as well as special picks to help remove the meat from the crab claws.

AT A WEDDING BANQUET food is often presented in pairs, like these dumplings and wrapped lettuce parcels, to symbolize marriage. Ducks represent fidelity in Chinese culture because mandarin ducks live in couples for their whole lives. They are used to symbolize a pair that is not identical but belongs together. Here two egg white ducks float on top of a soup.

BANQUET

FOOD PLAYS AN IMPORTANT PART IN THE CHINESE FESTIVALS THAT MARK THE PASSING OF THE YEAR AND LIFE ITSELF, FROM CHINESE NEW YEAR TO THE MOON FESTIVAL, AND FROM BIRTH THROUGH TO MARRIAGE AND EVEN DEATH.

A banquet can be a social or commercial event to celebrate anything from a graduation to a successful business deal. Dishes are chosen carefully as different foods symbolize instantly recognizable meanings to the guests, while the number of courses and even the colour of the food (red and yellow are particularly lucky colours) are important.

Banquets can consist of 10 to 15 courses or even more, though often eight dishes are served as in Chinese the word 'eight' sounds like the word for prosperity and success, or sometimes nine as this word sounds like long-lasting. As each course is served, the host respectfully offers the choice pieces to the honoured guest or perhaps the eldest. The banquet traditionally starts with a beautifully arranged cold platter of sliced meats, seafood and nuts, to be picked at during the toasts. This is followed by some deep-fried, steamed or stir-fried dishes, then shark's fin or another special soup. Next come the main dishes featuring the most expensive and prestigious ingredients: poultry, usually whole, or possibly a roast suckling pig. At New Year, a fish course will be served last so that some may remain on the table for the start of the next year. Simple rice and noodle dishes come at the end to fill up any gaps. Finally fresh fruit, a sweet soup or the equivalent of petits fours are served.

THE LUNAR NEW YEAR is welcomed in with a huge family feast—each dish promising good luck and happiness for the year to come. Shops and homes are decorated in red and yellow and on New Year's Day, envelopes of lucky money and tangerines are exchanged with family and friends. The Lantern Festival marks the end of the festivities, with tiny dumplings and fireworks.

BIRTHDAYS AND MARRIAGES

A child's first celebration occurs at a month old and is a big family affair, with healing dishes of chicken and pig's trotters for the mother. Birthdays are then only celebrated enthusiastically after the age of 60 and every decade thereafter. A marriage is usually an extravagant affair, with a banquet following the ceremony that may involve hundreds of guests. The couple traditionally perform a tea ceremony for their parents.

FESTIVALS

The New Year is the most important festival: houses are cleaned, debts paid and special food prepared. The New Year's Eve meal is a family affair at home, after which the festival continues with 2 weeks of visiting family and friends and eating. The Qing Ming and Hungry Ghosts Festivals honour the dead, offering food to placate the spirits, and moon cakes, pastries filled with egg yolk, are eaten at the Moon Festival.

DURING CHINESE NEW YEAR gods are pasted on the doors of houses along with sayings that wish for happiness, wealth, longevity and fertility, the most longed-for states.

A market stall in Sichuan.

Loosen the shrimp's dark, vein-like digestive tract with the point of some scissors, then gently pull it out.

川式焖虾

SICHUAN-STYLE BRAISED SHRIMP

ALSO KNOWN AS CHILI OR SPICY SHRIMP, THIS IS ONE OF THE MOST POPULAR DISHES IN CHINESE RESTAURANTS. USE UNCOOKED, UNPEELED SHRIMP WITH THEIR HEADS AND TAILS STILL ATTACHED FOR THE BEST RESULTS, AS THE SHELLS ADD FLAVOR TO THE SAUCE.

16 large prawns
oil for deep-frying
1 tablespoon oil, extra
1 garlic clove, finely chopped
1/2 teaspoon finely chopped ginger
1 tablespoon light soy sauce
1 tablespoon Shaoxing rice wine
1 tablespoon chile bean paste (toban jiang)
1 teaspoon sugar
3–4 tablespoons chicken and meat stock (page 281)
1 teaspoon clear rice vinegar
1 scallion, finely chopped
2 red chiles, finely chopped
1/4 teaspoon roasted sesame oil
2 teaspoons cornstarch
cilantro leaves

SERVES 4

PULL OFF the legs from the shrimp, but leave the body shells on. Using a pair of scissors, cut each shrimp along the back to devein it.

FILL a wok one quarter full of oil. Heat the oil to 375°F, or until a piece of bread fries golden brown in 10 seconds when dropped in the oil. Cook the shrimp in batches for 2 minutes, or until they turn bright orange. Remove and drain. It is important to keep the oil hot for each batch or the shells with not turn crisp. Pour out the oil and wipe out the wok.

REHEAT the wok over high heat, add the extra oil and heat until very hot. Cook the garlic and ginger for a few seconds to flavor the oil. Add the soy sauce, rice wine, chile bean paste, sugar and stock. Stir to combine, then bring to a boil. Add the shrimp and cook for 1 minute, then add the rice vinegar, scallion, chiles and sesame oil, stirring constantly. Combine the cornstarch with enough water to make a paste, add to the sauce and simmer until thickened. Serve sprinkled with the cilantro leaves, and provide finger bowls.

The Oriental Pearl Tower in Pudong, Shanghai.

上海式五柳鱼

SHANGHAI-STYLE FIVE-WILLOW FISH

THIS IS A VARIATION ON THE CLASSIC SWEET-AND-SOUR FISH (SEE PAGE 117). THE "FIVE-WILLOW" REFERS TO THE FIVE SHREDDED VEGETABLES USED FOR THE SAUCE, WHILE THE AROMATICS TRADITIONALLY REMOVED ANY "FISHY" TASTE FROM THE FRESHWATER FISH.

3–4 dried Chinese mushrooms
1 1/2–2 lb whole fish, such as carp, porgy, grouper or sea bass
1 teaspoon salt
oil for deep-frying
2 tablespoons oil, extra
1 tablespoon shredded ginger
2 scallions, shredded
1/2 small carrot, shredded
1/2 small green pepper, shredded
1/2 celery stalk, shredded
2 red chiles, seeded and finely shredded
2 tablespoons light soy sauce
3 tablespoons sugar
3 tablespoons Chinese black rice vinegar
1 tablespoon Shaoxing rice wine
1/2 cup chicken and meat stock (page 281)
1 tablespoon cornstarch
1/2 teaspoon roasted sesame oil

SERVES 4

SOAK the dried mushrooms in boiling water for 30 minutes, then drain and squeeze out any excess water. Remove and discard the stems. Finely shred the caps.

IF YOU do manage to buy a live fish, then ask the fishmonger to gut it through the gills. This is harder than gutting through the stomach, but leaves the fish looking whole. If you are gutting the fish yourself, make a cut from the throat to the tail and pull out the guts through the stomach. Remove any scales with a fish scaler or the back of a knife. Check that the gills have been cut out, then rinse the fish under cold, running water and drain thoroughly in a colander.

DIAGONALLY score both sides of the fish, cutting through as far as the bone at intervals of 3/4 inch. Rub the salt all over the inside and outside of the fish and into the slits.

FILL a wok one quarter full of oil. Heat the oil to 375°F, or until a piece of bread fries golden brown in 10 seconds when dropped in the oil. Holding the fish by its tail, gently and carefully lower it into the oil. Cook the fish for 3–4 minutes on each side, or until the fish flakes when the skin is pressed firmly or the dorsal fin pulls out easily. Remove from the wok and drain on paper towels, then place on a dish and keep warm in a low oven. Pour out the oil and wipe out the wok.

REHEAT the wok over high heat, add the extra oil and heat until very hot. Stir-fry the mushrooms, ginger, scallion, carrot, green pepper, celery and chiles for 1 1/2 minutes. Add the soy sauce, sugar, rice vinegar, rice wine and stock, and bring to a boil. Combine the cornstarch with enough water to make a paste, add to the sauce and simmer until thickened. Add the sesame oil, blend well and spoon over the fish.

SEA CUCUMBER WITH MUSHROOMS

SEA CUCUMBER, OR BECHE-DE-MER, IS SOLD DRIED OR RECONSTITUTED. THE DRIED TYPE NEEDS A LOT OF SOAKING TO REHYDRATE AND BECOMES GELATINOUS IN TEXTURE. SEA CUCUMBER HAS NO FLAVOR OF ITS OWN, BUT ABSORBS FLAVORS FROM WHATEVER IT IS COOKED WITH.

- 3 dried or reconstituted sea cucumbers
- 24 dried Chinese mushrooms
- 4 tablespoons oil
- 1 skinned, boneless chicken breast, cut into 3/4 inch cubes
- 1 egg white
- 3–4 tablespoons cornstarch
- 1 tablespoon light soy sauce
- 3 tablespoons oyster sauce
- 3 teaspoons sugar
- 2 scallions, cut into 3/4 inch pieces

SERVES 4

TO PREPARE the dried sea cucumbers, allow up to 4 days for them to rehydrate. On the first day, soak the cucumbers in water overnight. Drain and cook in a saucepan of simmering water for 1 hour, then drain again. Re-soak overnight and repeat the cooking and soaking process at least 3 times to allow the sea cucumbers to soften. Once softened, cut the sea cucumbers in half lengthwise, scrape out and discard the insides and cut into chunks. If you are using reconstituted sea cucumbers, they only need to be rinsed, drained and have the insides discarded before cutting into chunks.

PLACE the dried mushrooms in a saucepan and add 2 cups water and half the oil. Cover, bring to a boil, then reduce the heat and simmer for 1 hour. Drain the mushrooms, reserving 1 cup of the liquid. Remove and discard the stems.

COMBINE the chicken with the egg white and 1 tablespoon of the cornstarch until it is completely coated. Heat a wok over high heat, add the remaining oil and heat until very hot. Stir-fry the chicken pieces in batches for 3 minutes, or until browned. Return all the chicken to the wok and add the sea cucumber, mushrooms, reserved liquid, soy sauce, oyster sauce, sugar and scallions. Stir to combine, then cook for 2 minutes.

COMBINE the remaining cornstarch with enough water to make a paste, add to the sauce and simmer until thickened.

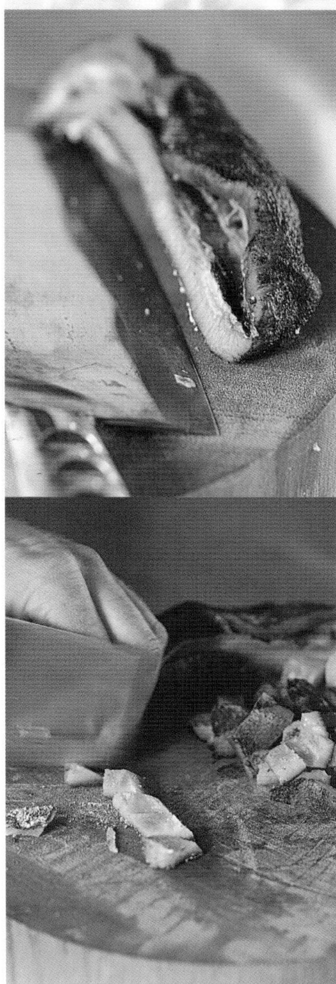

Slice the sea cucumber in half and scrape out the insides, leaving the cavity clean. Cut the sea cucumber into chunks.

鸳鸯大虾

LOVE BIRDS SHRIMP

A theatrical wedding in progress in Hangzhou.

THE CHINESE NAME FOR THIS DISH, YUAN YANG XIA, REFERS TO MANDARIN DUCKS KNOWN AS "LOVE BIRDS" BECAUSE THEY ARE ALWAYS SEEN TOGETHER, SYMBOLIZING AFFECTION AND HAPPINESS. DISHES WITH ONE MAIN INGREDIENT PRESENTED IN TWO WAYS OFTEN REPRESENT THIS IN CHINESE COOKING.

1 1/4 lb large shrimp
1 tablespoon cornstarch
1/2 egg white, beaten
oil for deep-frying
1/4 lb snow peas, ends trimmed
1/2 teaspoon salt
1/2 teaspoon sugar
1 scallion, finely chopped
1 teaspoon finely chopped ginger
1 tablespoon light soy sauce
1 tablespoon Shaoxing rice wine
1/2 teaspoon roasted sesame oil
1 tablespoon chile bean paste (toban jiang)
1 tablespoon tomato paste

SERVES 4

PEEL and devein the shrimp, leaving the tails intact. Combine the cornstarch with enough water to make a paste. Stir in the egg white and a pinch of salt, then stir in the shrimp.

FILL a wok one quarter full of oil. Heat the oil to 350°F, or until a piece of bread fries golden brown in 15 seconds when dropped in the oil. Cook the shrimp for 1 minute, stirring to separate them. Remove the shrimp from the wok with a wire strainer or slotted spoon as soon as the color changes, then drain. Pour the oil out, reserving 1 tablespoon.

REHEAT the reserved oil over high heat until very hot and stir-fry the snow peas with the salt and sugar for 1 1/2 minutes. Remove and place in the center of a serving platter.

REHEAT the wok again and stir-fry the scallion and ginger for a few seconds. Add the shrimps, soy sauce and rice wine, blend well and stir-fry for about 30 seconds, then add the sesame oil. Transfer about half of the shrimp to one end of the serving platter.

ADD the chile bean paste and tomato purée to the remaining shrimps, blend well, tossing to coat the shrimp, then transfer the shrimp to the other end of the platter.

酸甜鱼片

SWEET-AND-SOUR FISH FILLETS

THIS SWEET-AND-SOUR DISH IS SUBTLY VINEGARY AND HAS JUST A FAINT TOUCH OF SWEETNESS. SWEET-AND-SOUR FISH IS EATEN ALL OVER CHINA, OFTEN USING A WHOLE DEEP-FRIED FISH, BUT THIS RECIPE COMES FROM THE SOUTH-EAST AND IS A GREAT WAY TO COOK FISH FILLETS.

1 lb firm white fish fillets, such as monkfish, rock cod or sea bass, skin removed
1/2 teaspoon salt
1 1/2 tablespoons Shaoxing rice wine
1 egg, beaten
3–4 tablespoons all-purpose flour
oil for deep-frying
1/2 teaspoon chopped ginger
1 scallion, finely chopped
1/3 cup chicken and meat stock (page 281)
2 tablespoons light soy sauce
1 tablespoon sugar
2 tablespoons clear rice vinegar
1 red chile, finely chopped (optional)
1 tablespoon cornstarch
1/2 teaspoon roasted sesame oil
cilantro leaves

SERVES 4

PAT DRY the fish, cut into 1 1/4 inch cubes and marinate with the salt and 2 teaspoons of the rice wine for about 15–20 minutes.

MEANWHILE, blend the egg and flour with a little water to form a smooth batter with the consistency of heavy cream. Coat the fish cubes with the batter.

FILL a wok one quarter full of oil. Heat the oil to 350°F, or until a piece of bread fries golden brown in 15 seconds when dropped in the oil. Carefully lower the pieces of fish, one by one, into the hot oil and stir gently to make sure they do not stick together. Cook for about 3 minutes, or until golden. Remove and drain well on crumpled paper towels. Pour out the oil, reserving 1 tablespoon, and wipe out the wok.

REHEAT the reserved oil over high heat until very hot and add the ginger, scallion, stock, soy sauce, remaining rice wine, sugar and half the rice vinegar. Bring to a boil, then reduce the heat and simmer for 30 seconds. Add the fish pieces and cook for 2 minutes. Add the chile, if using, and the remaining rice vinegar. Combine the cornstarch with enough water to make a paste, add to the sauce and simmer until thickened.

SPRINKLE the fish with the sesame oil and the cilantro leaves to serve.

You can use your wok for deep-frying, but make sure that it is really steady on the wok burner. A wire strainer drains away more oil than a slotted spoon and leaves the batter less greasy.

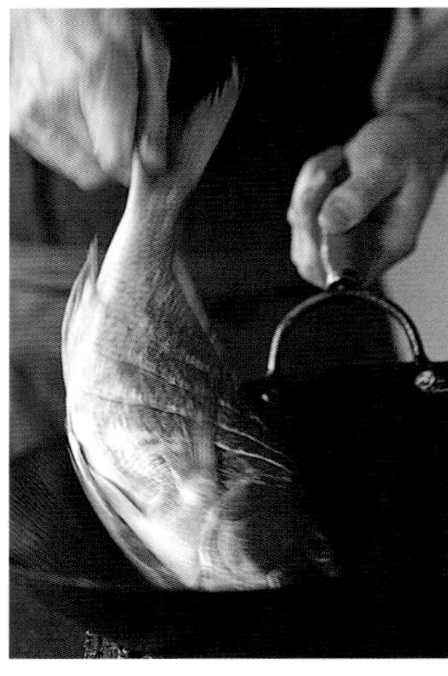

Carefully lower the whole fish into the hot oil. If you like you can gently hold the fish open with a fish lifter so the oil can get inside the cavity easily.

A girl in a traditional headdress in Dali, Yunnan.

Dried fish in the market in Guangzhou.

豆酱金目鲈

WHOLE FISH WITH YELLOW BEAN SAUCE

- $1\frac{1}{2}$–2 lb whole fish, such as carp, porgy, grouper or sea bass
- 1 tablespoon light soy sauce
- 1 tablespoon Shaoxing rice wine
- oil for deep-frying
- 1 tablespoon shredded ginger
- 2 scallions, thinly shredded
- 1 teaspoon sugar
- 1 tablespoon dark soy sauce
- 2 tablespoons yellow bean sauce
- $\frac{1}{2}$ cup chicken and meat stock (page 281)
- $\frac{1}{2}$ teaspoon roasted sesame oil

SERVES 4

IF YOU do manage to buy a live fish, then ask the fishmonger to gut it through the gills. This is harder than gutting through the stomach, but leaves the fish looking whole. If you are gutting the fish yourself, make a cut from the throat to the tail and pull out the guts through the stomach. Remove any scales with a fish scaler or the back of a knife. Check that the gills have been cut out, then rinse the fish under cold, running water and drain thoroughly in a colander.

DIAGONALLY score both sides of the fish, cutting through as far as the bone at intervals of $\frac{3}{4}$ inch. Place the fish in a shallow dish with the light soy sauce and rice wine and allow to marinate for 10–15 minutes, then drain off any liquid, reserving the marinade.

FILL a wok one quarter full of oil. Heat the oil to 375°F, or until a piece of bread fries golden brown in 10 seconds when dropped in the oil. Holding the fish by its tail, gently and carefully lower it into the oil, bending the body so that the cuts open up. Cook for 5 minutes, or until golden brown, tilting the wok so that the entire fish is cooked in the oil. Remove and drain on crumpled paper towels and keep warm in a low oven. Pour the oil from the wok, leaving $1\frac{1}{2}$ tablespoons.

REHEAT the reserved oil over high heat until very hot. Add the ginger, scallions, sugar, dark soy sauce, yellow bean sauce and reserved marinade. Stir for a few seconds, add the stock, bring to a boil and add the fish. Cook for 4–5 minutes, basting constantly and turning the fish once after 2 minutes.

TURN the fish over and sprinkle with the sesame oil. Serve with the sauce poured over.

蒸虾奶油羹

STEAMED SHRIMP CUSTARDS

4 eggs
1 1/4 cups chicken stock (page 281)
16 shrimp
1 scallion, finely chopped
1 tablespoon light soy sauce
1 tablespoon oil

SERVES 4

BEAT the eggs and chicken stock together and season with salt and white pepper. Peel and devein the shrimp, then roughly chop the shrimp meat.

DIVIDE the shrimp among 4 small flameproof bowls. Pour the egg and stock mixture over the shrimp. Put the bowls in a steamer, and steam over simmering water in a covered wok for 10 minutes. The custards should be just set. Shake them gently to see if the center is set. If you overcook them they will be rubbery.

SPRINKLE the custards with the scallion and soy sauce. Heat the oil in a wok until very hot and pour a little over each custard (it will spit as it hits the surface). Serve immediately.

酱油蒸蚌

STEAMED MUSSEL CUSTARDS

STEAMED MUSSEL CUSTARDS

1 lb mussels
2 tablespoons Shaoxing rice wine
1 tablespoon finely chopped ginger
6 eggs
1 teaspoon salt

SERVES 6

SCRUB the mussels, remove any beards, and throw away any that do not close when tapped on the work surface. Put the mussels in a wok with 1 cup water, the rice wine and ginger. Cook, covered, over high heat for 1 minute, or until the mixture is boiling. Reduce the heat to low and cook, covered, for 2 minutes, or until the mussels have opened, shaking the pan so that they cook evenly. Discard any that do not open after 2 minutes.

REMOVE the mussels with a wire strainer or slotted spoon, reserving the liquid, and allow to cool. Remove the mussels from their shells and divide among 6 small flameproof bowls. Lightly beat the eggs, salt and 250 ml of the reserved liquid, then pour over the mussels.

PUT the bowls in a steamer and steam over simmering water in a covered wok for 10 minutes. The custards should be just set. Shake them gently to see if the center is set. If you overcook them they will be rubbery. Serve immediately.

STEAMED SHRIMP CUSTARDS

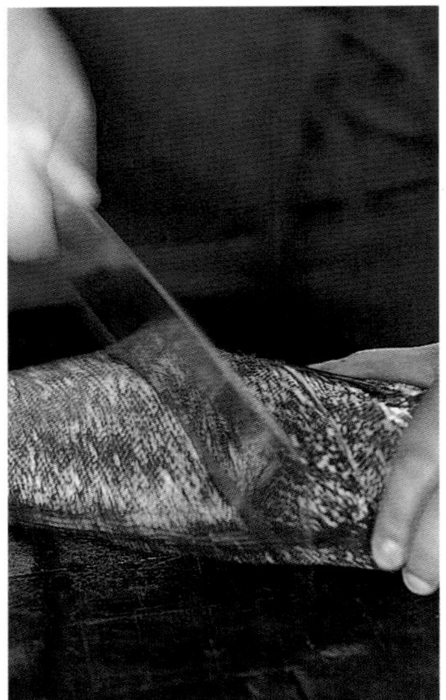

Scoring the fish through the flesh allows the heat to penetrate much more easily.

Renmin Park in Chengdu.

川式辣焖鱼

SICHUANESE BRAISED FISH IN SPICY SAUCE

- 1 x 3 1/2 lb whole fish, such as carp, porgy, grouper or sea bass
- 2 1/2 tablespoons Shaoxing rice wine
- 2 1/2 tablespoons finely chopped ginger
- 1/2 teaspoon salt
- 1/2 oz dried black fungus (wood ears)
- oil for deep-frying
- 2 scallions, finely chopped
- 4 garlic cloves, finely chopped
- 1 1/2 teaspoons chile bean paste (toban jiang)
- 2 cups chicken stock (page 281)
- 1 1/2 tablespoons light soy sauce
- 2 teaspoons sugar
- 1 tablespoon Chinese black vinegar
- 1 tablespoon cornstarch
- 2 scallions, green part only, finely chopped

SERVES 6

IF YOU do manage to buy a live fish, then ask the fishmonger to gut it through the gills. This is harder than gutting through the stomach, but leaves the fish looking whole. If you are gutting the fish yourself, make a cut from the throat to the tail and pull out the guts through the stomach. Remove any scales with a fish scaler or the back of a knife. Check that the gills have been cut out, then rinse the fish under cold, running water and drain thoroughly in a colander.

DIAGONALLY score both sides of the fish, cutting through as far as the bone at intervals of 3/4 inch. Combine 1 tablespoon of rice wine, 2 teaspoons of ginger and the salt. Place the fish in a dish and rub the mixture all over the outside of the fish and into the slits. Marinate for 30 minutes, then drain.

SOAK the dried fungus in cold water for 20 minutes, drain, squeeze out any excess water, and shred.

FILL a wok one quarter full of oil. Heat the oil to 375°F, or until a piece of bread fries golden brown in 10 seconds when dropped in the oil. Holding the fish by its tail, gently and carefully lower it into the oil, bending the body so that the cuts open up. Cook for 5 minutes, or until golden brown, tilting the wok so that the entire fish is cooked in the oil. Remove and drain on crumpled paper towels and keep warm in a low oven. Pour the oil from the wok, leaving 1 1/2 tablespoons.

REHEAT the reserved oil over high heat until very hot and stir-fry the scallions, remaining ginger, garlic and chile bean paste for 10 seconds. Toss in the fungus, then the remaining rice wine, stock, soy sauce, sugar and vinegar and bring to a boil. Add the fish, return to a boil, then reduce the heat and cook, covered, for 12 minutes, or until the fish flakes when the skin is pressed firmly or the dorsal fins pulls out easily. Remove the fish.

SKIM ANY impurities from the sauce and bring to a boil. Combine the cornstarch with enough water to make a paste, add to the sauce and simmer until thickened. Pour over the fish with the scallions.

椒盐软壳蟹

SALT AND PEPPER SOFT-SHELL CRABS

THESE CRABS ARE A DELIGHT TO EAT AS YOU CAN DEVOUR THE ENTIRE CREATURE—SHELLS AND ALL. THEY ARE EATEN WHEN THEY HAVE JUST SHED THEIR OLD SHELL AND BEFORE A NEW SHELL HARDENS.

4 soft-shell crabs
1 teaspoon spicy salt and pepper (page 285)
1 tablespoon Shaoxing rice wine
1 egg, beaten
1 tablespoon all-purpose flour
oil for deep-frying
1 scallion, chopped
2 small red chiles, chopped

SERVES 4

TO KILL the crabs humanely, put them in the freezer for 1 hour. Bring a large saucepan of water to a boil. Plunge the crabs into boiling water for about 1 minute, then rinse them in cold water. Marinate in the spicy salt and pepper and rice wine for 10–15 minutes, then coat with the egg and dust with the flour.

FILL a wok one quarter full of oil. Heat the oil to 375°F, or until a piece of bread fries golden brown in 10 seconds when dropped in the oil. Cook the crabs for 3–4 minutes, or until golden. Remove and drain, reserving the oil. Cut each crab in half and arrange on a serving plate.

SOAK the scallion and chiles in the hot oil (with the heat turned off) for 2 minutes. Remove with a wire strainer or slotted spoon and sprinkle over the crabs.

芙蓉蟹肉

CRABMEAT FU RONG

CRABMEAT FU RONG

1/2 lb crabmeat, picked over
1/2 teaspoon salt
4 egg whites, beaten
1 tablespoon cornstarch
4 tablespoons milk
oil for deep-frying
1/2 cup chicken and meat stock (page 281)
1/2 scallion, finely chopped
1/2 teaspoon grated ginger
2 tablespoons peas
1 teaspoon Shaoxing rice wine
1/4 teaspoon roasted sesame oil
cilantro leaves

SERVES 4

FLAKE the crabmeat and mix with the salt, egg white, cornstarch and milk. Blend well.

FILL a wok one quarter full of oil and heat to 375°F, or until a piece of bread fries golden brown in 10 seconds when dropped in the oil. Pour the crabmeat into the wok in batches—do not stir, otherwise it will scatter, but gently stir the oil from the bottom of the wok so that the “fu rong” rises to the surface. Remove each batch as soon as it is set, without letting it go too brown, and drain. Pour out the oil and wipe out the wok.

REHEAT the wok over high heat until very hot, add the stock, bring to a boil and add the scallion, ginger, peas and rice wine. Add the sesame oil. Pour over the fu rong and sprinkle with cilantro.

SALT AND PEPPER SOFT-SHELL CRABS

酱油炒干贝

SCALLOPS WITH BLACK BEAN SAUCE

2 lb large scallops
2 tablespoons salted, fermented black beans, rinsed and mashed
2 garlic cloves, crushed
3 teaspoons finely chopped ginger
2 teaspoons sugar
2 teaspoons light soy sauce
2 tablespoons oyster sauce
2 tablespoons oil
2 scallions, cut into 3/4 inch pieces

SERVES 6

SLICE the small, hard white muscle off the side of each scallop and pull off any membrane. Rinse the scallops and drain.

PLACE the black beans, garlic, ginger, sugar, and soy and oyster sauces in a bowl and mix together.

HEAT a wok over high heat, add the oil and heat until very hot. Stir-fry the scallops and roes for 2 minutes, or until the scallops are cooked through and opaque. Just before the scallops are cooked, add the scallions. Drain the mixture in a strainer.

REHEAT the wok over medium heat. Stir-fry the black bean mixture for 1–2 minutes, or until aromatic. Return the scallops and scallions to the wok and toss together to combine.

SCALLOPS WITH BLACK BEAN SAUCE

海鲜沙锅

SEAFOOD CLAY POT

8 scallops
12 shrimp
12 hard-shelled clams
8 oysters, shucked
4 slices ginger
2 tablespoons Shaoxing rice wine
1 teaspoon roasted sesame oil
4 1/2 oz bean thread noodles
1 small head (about 1/4 lb) Chinese (Napa) cabbage
1 scallion, thinly sliced
1 1/4 cups chicken stock (page 281)
cilantro sprigs

SERVES 4

SLICE the small, hard white muscle off the side of each scallop and pull off any membrane. Rinse the scallops and drain. Peel and devein the shrimp. Wash the clams in several changes of cold water, leaving them for a few minutes each time to remove any grit. Scrub the clams well, discarding any that remain open. Drain well.

PUT the scallops, shrimp, clams and oysters in a bowl with the ginger, rice wine and sesame oil. Marinate for 30 minutes. Soak the bean thread noodles in hot water for 10 minutes, then drain.

CUT the cabbage into small squares, put in a clay pot or flameproof casserole with the scallion and place the noodles on top. Remove the ginger from the marinade and put the seafood and marinade on top of the noodles. Pour the stock over. Slowly bring to a boil, then simmer, covered, for 10 minutes. Stir once, season and cook for 8 minutes. Serve from the dish, sprinkled with cilantro.

SEAFOOD CLAY POT

酸甜鲤鱼

SWEET-AND-SOUR FISH

PEOPLE TEND TO THINK THAT SWEET-AND-SOUR DISHES ARE CANTONESE, BUT IN FACT COOKS IN THE YELLOW RIVER VALLEY INVENTED THEM TO SUPPRESS THE MUDDY TASTE OF CARP FROM THE YELLOW RIVER. THIS RECIPE REPRESENTS WHAT MAY BE THE ORIGINAL "SWEET-AND-SOUR SAUCE".

1 1/2–2 lb whole fish, such as sea bass, carp, grouper or porgy
1 teaspoon salt
2 tablespoons all-purpose flour
3/4 oz dried black fungus (wood ears)
3–4 peeled water chestnuts
oil for deep-frying
2 tablespoons oil, extra
1/2 teaspoon chopped garlic
1 tablespoon shredded ginger
2 scallions, shredded
1/4 cup fresh or canned bamboo shoots, rinsed and drained, shredded
3 tablespoons rice vinegar
1/2 cup chicken and meat stock (page 281)
3 tablespoons sugar
2 tablespoons light soy sauce
2 tablespoons Shaoxing rice wine
2 teaspoons cornstarch
cilantro leaves

SERVES 4

IF YOU do manage to buy a live fish, then ask the fishmonger to gut it through the gills. This is harder than gutting through the stomach, but leaves the fish looking whole. If you are gutting the fish yourself, make a cut from the throat to the tail and pull out the guts through the stomach. Remove any scales with a fish scaler or the back of a knife. Check that the gills have been cut out, then rinse the fish under cold, running water and drain thoroughly in a colander.

DIAGONALLY score both sides of the fish, cutting through as far as the bone at intervals of 3/4 inch. Rub a little salt, then a little flour, all over the outside of the fish and into the slits. Put the remaining flour in a dish and coat the whole fish, from head to tail on both sides, with flour. Soak the dried black fungus in cold water for 20 minutes then drain, squeeze out any excess water, and shred. Blanch the water chestnuts in a pan of boiling water for 1 minute, then refresh in cold water. Drain, pat dry and roughly chop them.

FILL a wok one quarter full of oil. Heat the oil to 375°F, or until a piece of bread fries golden brown in 10 seconds when dropped in the oil. Holding the fish by the tail, carefully lower it into the oil, bending the body so that the cuts open up. Cook the fish for 5 minutes, or until golden brown. Remove and drain on crumpled paper towels and keep warm in a low oven. Pour off the oil and wipe out the wok.

REHEAT the wok over high heat, add the extra oil and heat until very hot. Stir-fry the garlic, ginger, scallions, bamboo shoots, water chestnuts and black fungus for 30 seconds, then add the vinegar, stock, sugar, soy sauce and rice wine. Combine the cornstarch with enough water to make a paste, add to the sauce and simmer until thickened. Pour over the fish and sprinkle with cilantro.

Peeling water chestnuts with a cleaver requires some dexterity.

Coating the fish in flour soaks up any moisture and gives it a very crisp surface when fried.

A rice wine store in Beijing.

Posters of the gods are pasted on front doors over the New Year period to bring good luck and good fortune.

米酒蘑菇蒸比目鱼

SOLE WITH MUSHROOMS AND RICE WINE

THIS DISH IS SURPRISINGLY SIMILAR TO THE FRENCH SOLE BONNE FEMME (SOLE WITH MUSHROOMS AND WINE SAUCE), THOUGH THE CHINESE VERSION IS MUCH SIMPLER TO MAKE. YOU COULD USE ANY WHITE FISH INSTEAD OF THE FLAT FISH.

1 lb flat fish fillets, such as sole, plaice, flounder or brill
1 egg white, beaten
1 tablespoon cornstarch
1/2 lb button mushrooms
oil for deep-frying
1 garlic clove, thinly shredded
2 scallions, thinly shredded
1 teaspoon shredded ginger
1 teaspoon salt
1 teaspoon sugar
1 tablespoon light soy sauce
2 tablespoons Shaoxing rice wine
1 tablespoon Chinese spirit (Mou Tai) or brandy
1/2 cup chicken and meat stock (page 281)
1/2 teaspoon roasted sesame oil
cilantro leaves

SERVES 4

TRIM the soft bones along the edges of the fish, but leave the skin on. Cut each fillet into 3 or 4 slices if large, 2 or 3 if small. Mix the egg white with half the cornstarch and 1 teaspoon of water. Add the fish slices and toss to coat thoroughly. Thinly slice the mushrooms.

FILL a wok one quarter full of oil. Heat the oil to 350°F, or until a piece of bread fries golden brown in 15 seconds when dropped in the oil. Cook the fish slices for 1 minute, or until golden brown. Stir gently to make sure the slices do not stick together. Remove and drain on paper towels and keep warm in a low oven. Pour the oil out, reserving 2 tablespoons.

REHEAT the reserved oil over high heat until very hot and stir-fry the garlic, scallions, ginger and mushrooms for 1 minute. Add the salt, sugar, soy sauce, wine, Chinese spirit and stock, and bring to a boil. Return the fish slices to the sauce, blend well and simmer for 1 minute.

COMBINE the remaining cornstarch with enough water to make a paste, add to the sauce and simmer until thickened. Sprinkle the fish with the sesame oil and cilantro leaves.

POULTRY

云南气锅鸡

YUNNAN POT CHICKEN

A YUNNAN POT IS AN EARTHENWARE SOUP POT WITH A CHIMNEY. THE POT COOKS FOOD BY "CLOSED STEAMING," WHICH GIVES A CLEARER, MORE INTENSELY FLAVORED STOCK THAN ORDINARY STEAMING. INSTEAD OF A YUNNAN POT, YOU CAN USE A CLAY POT OR BRAISING PAN INSIDE A STEAMER.

Dried jujubes, or Chinese dates.

Chopping ginger outside a shop in Chengdu.

25 jujubes (dried Chinese dates)
3 lb chicken
6 wafer-thin slices dang gui (dried angelica)
6 slices ginger, smashed with the flat side of a cleaver
6 scallions, ends trimmed, smashed with the flat side of a cleaver
1/4 cup Shaoxing rice wine
1/2 teaspoon salt

SERVES 6

SOAK the jujubes in hot water for 20 minutes, then drain and remove the pits.

RINSE the chicken, drain, and remove any fat from the cavity opening and around the neck. Cut off and discard the tail. Using a cleaver, cut the chicken through the bones into square 1 1/2 inch pieces. Blanch the chicken pieces in a saucepan of boiling water for 1 minute, then refresh in cold water and drain thoroughly.

ARRANGE the chicken pieces, jujubes, dang gui, ginger and scallions in a clay pot or braising pan about 10 inches in diameter. Pour the rice wine and 4 cups boiling water over the top and add the salt. Cover the clay pot or casserole tightly, adding a layer of wet cheesecloth, if necessary, between the pot and lid to form a good seal, then place it in a steamer.

STEAM over simmering water in a covered wok for about 2 hours, replenishing with boiling water during cooking.

REMOVE the pot from the steamer and skim any fat from the surface of the liquid. Discard the dang gui, ginger and scallions. Taste and season if necessary. Serve directly from the pot.

香菜炒乳鸽

STIR-FRIED SQUAB IN LETTUCE LEAVES

THIS DISH IS A CANTONESE CLASSIC, SOMETIMES CALLED SAN CHOY BAU, AND THE LITTLE PACKAGES, WITH THE CONTRAST BETWEEN THEIR WARM FILLING AND THE COLD LETTUCE, ARE WONDERFUL. IF SQUAB IS UNAVAILABLE, CHICKEN MAY BE USED INSTEAD.

12 soft lettuce leaves, such as butterhead lettuce
8 oz squab meat
1 lb center-cut pork loin, trimmed
1/3 cup light soy sauce
3 1/2 tablespoons Shaoxing rice wine
2 1/2 teaspoons roasted sesame oil
8 dried Chinese mushrooms
1 1/2 cups peeled water chestnuts
1/2 cup oil
2 scallions, finely chopped
2 tablespoons finely chopped ginger
1 teaspoon salt
1 teaspoon sugar
1 teaspoon cornstarch

SERVES 6

RINSE the lettuce and separate the leaves. Drain thoroughly, then lightly pound each leaf with the flat side of a cleaver. Arrange the flattened leaves in a basket or on a platter and set aside.

GRIND the squab meat in a food processor or chop very finely with a sharp knife. Grind the pork to the same size as the squab. Place the squab and pork in a bowl with 2 tablespoons of the soy sauce, 1 1/2 tablespoons of the rice wine and 1 teaspoon of the sesame oil, and toss lightly. Marinate in the fridge for 20 minutes.

SOAK the dried mushrooms in boiling water for 30 minutes, then drain and squeeze out any excess water. Remove and discard the stems and chop the caps. Blanch the water chestnuts in a saucepan of boiling water for 1 minute, then refresh in cold water. Drain, pat dry and roughly chop them.

HEAT a wok over high heat, add 3 tablespoons of the oil and heat until very hot. Stir-fry the meat mixture, mashing and separating the pieces, until browned. Remove and drain. Reheat the wok, add 3 tablespoons more of the oil and heat until very hot. Stir-fry the scallions and ginger, turning constantly, for 10 seconds, or until fragrant. Add the mushrooms and stir-fry for 5 seconds, turning constantly. Add the water chestnuts and stir-fry for 15 seconds, or until heated through. Add the remaining soy sauce, rice wine and sesame oil with the salt, sugar, cornstarch and 1/2 cup water. Stir-fry, stirring constantly, until thickened. Add the cooked meat mixture and toss lightly.

TO SERVE, place some of the stir-fried meat in a lettuce leaf, roll up and eat.

Like all poultry, pigeons are sold live in the markets so there is no doubt as to how fresh they are.

A restaurant in Beijing.

香菇蒸鸡

STEAMED CHICKEN WITH MUSHROOMS

Preparing scallions in a kitchen in Beijing.

THIS DISH IS TRADITIONALLY COOKED USING PIECES OF CHICKEN WITH BOTH THE BONE AND SKIN STILL ATTACHED, BUT YOU CAN ALSO USE CHICKEN FILLET, IN WHICH CASE THE THIGH MEAT HAS MORE FLAVOR THAN BREAST MEAT.

1 lb skinned, boneless chicken thighs or 3 lb chicken
1 teaspoon salt
1/2 teaspoon sugar
1 tablespoon Shaoxing rice wine
1 teaspoon cornstarch
3–4 dried Chinese mushrooms
1 tablespoon shredded ginger
a pinch of ground Sichuan peppercorns
1 teaspoon roasted sesame oil

SERVES 4

CUT the chicken thighs into bite-size pieces. If using a whole chicken, rinse, drain, and remove any fat from the cavity opening and around the neck. Cut off and discard the tail. Using a cleaver, cut the chicken through the bones into square 1 1/2 inch pieces. Combine with the salt, sugar, rice wine and cornstarch.

SOAK the dried mushrooms in boiling water for 30 minutes, then drain and squeeze out excess water. Discard the stems and shred the caps.

GREASE a shallow flameproof dish and place the chicken pieces on the plate with the mushrooms, ginger, Sichuan peppercorns and sesame oil on top. Put the plate in a steamer. Steam over simmering water in a covered wok for 20 minutes.

Selling vegetables in Yunnan.

芹菜炒鸡丝

SHREDDED CHICKEN WITH CELERY

8 oz skinned, boneless chicken breasts
1/4 egg white, beaten
2 teaspoons cornstarch
3 Chinese celery or celery stalks
1 2/3 cups oil
1 tablespoon shredded ginger
2 scallions, shredded
1 red chile, shredded (optional)
1 teaspoon salt
1/2 teaspoon sugar
1 tablespoon light soy sauce
1 tablespoon Shaoxing rice wine
2 tablespoons chicken and meat stock (page 281)
1/4 teaspoon roasted sesame oil

SERVES 4

CUT the chicken into matchstick-size shreds. Combine with a pinch of salt, the egg white and cornstarch. Shred the celery.

HEAT a wok over high heat. Add the oil and heat until hot, then turn off the heat. Blanch the chicken in the oil for 1 minute. Stir to separate the shreds, then remove and drain. Pour the oil from the wok, leaving 2 tablespoons.

REHEAT the reserved oil over high heat until very hot and stir-fry the ginger, scallion, celery and chile for 1 minute. Add the salt and sugar, blend well, then add the chicken with the soy sauce, rice wine and stock. Stir thoroughly and stir-fry for 1 minute. Sprinkle with the sesame oil to serve.

Roast meat stall in Kunming.

Steaming the duck and then frying it keeps the meat very moist and allows the marinade flavors to penetrate. For serving, poultry is traditionally chopped into bite-size pieces, rather than jointed, so that the pieces can be picked up with chopsticks.

CRISPY SKIN DUCK

NORTHERN CHEFS HAVE THEIR FAMOUS PEKING DUCK, BUT IN SICHUAN, CRISPY SKIN DUCK IS EQUALLY POPULAR. THIS DISH CAN ALSO BE MADE WITH BONELESS DUCK BREASTS, JUST ADJUST THE COOKING TIMES. SERVE THE DUCK WITH MANDARIN PANCAKES OR STEAMED FLOWER ROLLS.

4 1/2 lb duck
8 scallions, ends trimmed, smashed with the flat side of a cleaver
8 slices ginger, smashed with the flat side of a cleaver
3 tablespoons Shaoxing rice wine
2 tablespoons salt
2 teaspoons Sichuan peppercorns
1 star anise, smashed with the flat side of a cleaver
2 tablespoons light soy sauce
1 cup cornstarch
oil for deep-frying
hoisin sauce
Mandarin pancakes (page 277) or steamed breads (page 46)

SERVES 6

RINSE the duck, drain, and remove any fat from the cavity opening and around the neck. Cut off and discard the tail. Combine the scallions, ginger, rice wine, salt, Sichuan peppercorns and star anise. Rub the marinade all over the inside and outside of the duck. Place, breast side down, in a bowl with the remaining marinade and keep in the fridge for at least 1 hour. Put the duck and the marinade, breast side up, on a flameproof plate in a steamer, or cut into halves or quarters and put in several steamers.

STEAM over simmering water in a covered wok for 1 1/2 hours, replenishing with boiling water during cooking. Remove the duck, discard the marinade, and let cool. Rub the soy sauce over the duck and then dredge in the cornstarch, pressing lightly to make it adhere to the skin. Let the duck dry in the fridge for several hours until very dry.

FILL a wok one quarter full of oil. Heat the oil to 375°F, or until a piece of bread fries golden brown in 10 seconds when dropped in the oil. Lower the duck into the oil and fry, ladling the oil over the top, until the skin is crisp and golden.

DRAIN the duck and, using a cleaver, cut the duck through the bones into pieces. Serve plain or with hoisin sauce and pancakes or bread.

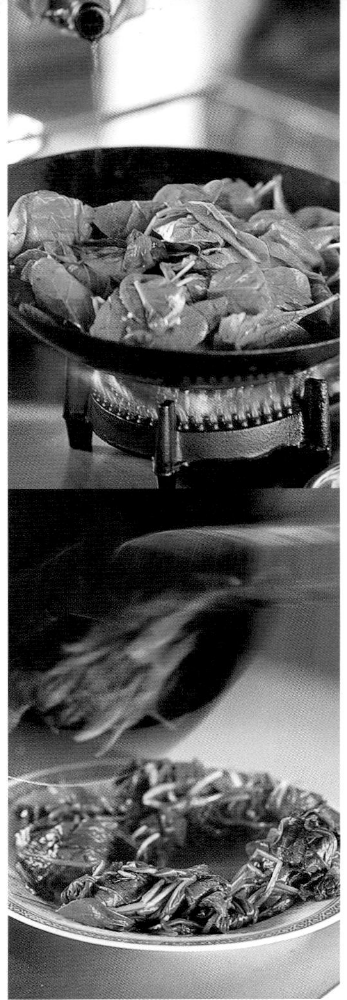

Cook the spinach for just a short amount of time so that it keeps its rich color.

Roasting seeds for the sesame oil outside a shop where it is sold in Chengdu.

宫保鸡丁

KUNG PAO CHICKEN

KUNG PAO IS ONE OF THE MOST CLASSIC HOT-AND-SOUR SICHUANESE SAUCES, AND CAN BE STIR-FRIED WITH SEAFOOD, PORK OR VEGETABLES AS WELL AS CHICKEN. THE SEASONINGS ARE FRIED IN OIL OVER HIGH HEAT, INTENSIFYING THE SPICINESS AND FLAVORING THE OIL.

11 oz skinned, boneless chicken breasts
3 tablespoons light soy sauce
3 tablespoons Shaoxing rice wine
2 teaspoons roasted sesame oil
1 tablespoon cornstarch
3/4 cup peeled water chestnuts
3 tablespoons oil
10 cups baby spinach leaves
1/2 teaspoon salt
3 garlic cloves, finely chopped
3/4 cup unsalted peanuts
1 scallion, finely chopped
1 tablespoon finely chopped ginger
1 teaspoon chili sauce
1 tablespoon sugar
1 teaspoon Chinese black rice vinegar
1/4 cup chicken stock (page 281)

SERVES 6

CUT the chicken into 1 inch cubes. Place the cubes in a bowl, add 2 tablespoons of the soy sauce, 2 tablespoons of the rice wine, 1 teaspoon of the sesame oil and 2 teaspoons of the cornstarch, and toss lightly. Marinate in the fridge for at least 20 minutes.

BLANCH the water chestnuts in a saucepan of boiling water, then refresh in cold water. Drain, pat dry and cut into thin slices.

HEAT a wok over high heat, add 1 teaspoon of the oil and heat until very hot. Stir-fry the spinach, salt, 2 teaspoons of the garlic and 2 teaspoons of the rice wine, turning constantly, until the spinach is just becoming limp. Remove the spinach from the wok, arrange around the edge of a platter, cover and keep warm.

REHEAT the wok over high heat, add 1 tablespoon of the oil and heat until very hot. Stir-fry half the chicken pieces, turning constantly, until the meat is cooked. Remove with a wire strainer or slotted spoon and drain. Repeat with 1 tablespoon of oil and the remaining chicken. Wipe out the pan.

DRY-FRY the peanuts in the wok or a saucepan until browned.

REHEAT the wok over high heat, add the remaining oil and heat until very hot. Stir-fry the scallion, ginger, remaining garlic and the chili sauce for 10 seconds, or until fragrant. Add the sliced water chestnuts and stir-fry for 15 seconds, or until heated through. Combine the sugar, black vinegar, chicken stock and remaining soy sauce, rice wine, sesame oil and cornstarch, add to the sauce and simmer until thickened. Add the cooked chicken and the peanuts. Toss lightly to coat with the sauce. Transfer to the center of the platter and serve.

HAINAN CHICKEN

HAINAN CHICKEN IS A MEAL OF CHICKEN, RICE AND SOUP, EATEN WITH A SCALLION OR CHILI SAUCE. ORIGINALLY FROM HAINAN ISLAND IN THE SOUTH OF CHINA, THIS DISH WAS BROUGHT TO SINGAPORE BY IMMIGRANTS AND IS NOW A SINGAPOREAN CLASSIC.

2 1/4 lb chicken
2 scallions, cut into 2 inch pieces
5 cilantro sprigs
3/4 teaspoon salt
4 slices ginger, smashed with the flat side of a cleaver
1/4 teaspoon black peppercorns
finely chopped scallion

DIPPING SAUCES
2 scallions, sliced
1 tablespoon finely grated ginger
1 teaspoon salt
3 tablespoons oil
3 tablespoons light soy sauce
1–2 red chiles, sliced

SERVES 4

RINSE the chicken, drain, and remove any fat from the cavity opening and around the neck. Cut off and discard the tail. Place the chicken in a large clay pot or braising pan. Add the scallion, cilantro, salt, ginger, peppercorns and enough water to cover the chicken. Cover and bring to a boil, then reduce the heat and simmer very gently for 30 minutes. Turn off the heat and allow the chicken to sit for 10 minutes. Remove the chicken from the pot and drain well. Skim off any impurities from the liquid and strain the liquid.

TO MAKE the dipping sauces, combine the scallions, ginger and salt in one small heatproof or metal bowl.

HEAT a wok over high heat, add the oil and heat until smoking. Allow it to cool slightly, then pour over the scallion mixture. The mixture will splatter. Stir well. Combine the soy sauce and chiles in another small bowl.

USING a cleaver, cut the chicken through the bones into bite-size pieces. Pour the stock into soup bowls, sprinkle with the finely chopped scallion, and serve with the chicken along with bowls of rice and the dipping sauces.

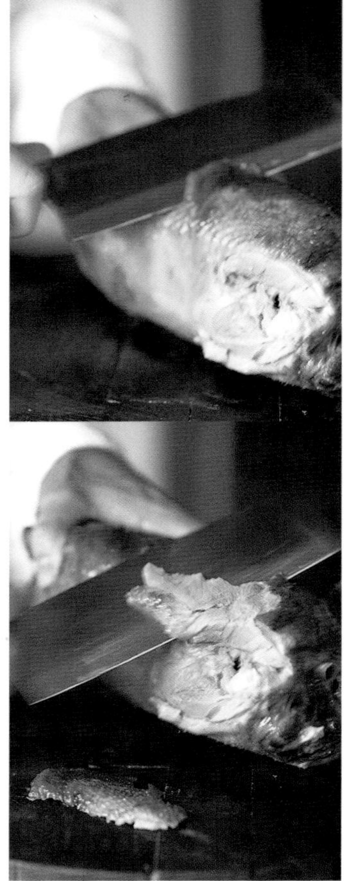

Carve the duck so that each slice has some crispy skin and tender meat. The skin can also be eaten separately, wrapped in the pancakes, while the meat is used in a stir-fry.

Commercially made pancakes are available in Asian markets, fresh or frozen, or from restaurants that sell carry-out ducks and barbecued meat.

北京烤鸭

PEKING DUCK

THIS DISH OWES ITS REPUTATION NOT SO MUCH TO THE WAY IT IS COOKED, BUT TO THE WAY IT IS THEATRICALLY CARVED AND EATEN ROLLED INTO PANCAKES. IN RESTAURANTS, THE DUCK IS COOKED IN A SPECIAL OVEN, BUT THIS RECIPE HAS BEEN MODIFIED FOR THE HOME KITCHEN.

5 lb duck
2 tablespoons maltose or honey, dissolved in 2 tablespoons water
1/2 cup hoisin sauce or plum sauce
24 Mandarin pancakes (page 277)
6–8 scallions, shredded
1/2 cucumber, shredded

SERVES 6

CUT the wing tips off the duck with a pair of poultry shears. Rinse the duck, drain, and remove any fat from the cavity opening and around the neck. Cut off and discard the tail. Plunge the duck into a pot of boiling water for 2–3 minutes to tighten the skin. Remove and drain, then dry thoroughly.

WHILE the skin is still warm, brush the duck all over with the maltose or honey and water solution, then hang it up to dry in a cool and airy place for at least 6 hours, or overnight, or keep it, uncovered, in the fridge.

PREHEAT the oven to 400°F. Place the duck, breast side up, on a rack in a roasting pan, and roast without basting or turning for 1 1/2 hours. Check to make sure the duck is not getting too dark and, if it is, cover it loosely with aluminum foil.

TO SERVE, remove the crispy duck skin in small slices by using a sharp carving knife, then carve the meat, or carve both together. Arrange on a serving plate.

TO EAT, spread about 1 teaspoon of the hoisin sauce or plum sauce in the center of a pancake, add a few strips of scallions, cucumber, duck skin and meat, roll up the pancake and turn up the bottom edge to prevent the contents from falling out.

THE QUANJUDE ROAST DUCK RESTAURANTS are perhaps the most famous Peking duck restaurants in Beijing. Established as early as 1864, the name Quanjude means 'everything is included'. More than just Peking duck restaurants, these restaurants specialize in all-duck dinners. Originally the menu included just four items: roast duck, stuffed duck neck, duck soup and stir-fried duck, but at the Quanjude

PEKING DUCK

DUCK DISHES HAVE ALWAYS BEEN CLASSICS OF THE CHINESE KITCHEN: ROASTED IN GUANGZHOU, CAMPHOR AND TEA-SMOKED IN SICHUAN, AND PRESSED IN NANJING, BUT IT IS IN THE CAPITAL THAT PEKING DUCK, PERHAPS CHINA'S MOST FAMOUS DISH, ORIGINATED.

True Peking duck must be made with a white-feathered mallard called a Peking duck. These ducks are bred on farms around Beijing and fattened up with grain for a few months to produce tender meat.

MAKING PEKING DUCK

The dish is prepared in different ways by different restaurants, though there are some principles that remain the same. After the duck is plucked, air is pumped in between the skin and body to inflate the bird, then the duck is blanched in boiling water. The crispy skin is formed by washing the duck with a maltose solution and leaving it to dry in a cool, dry place. The maltose, made from fermented barley, turns a dark reddish brown when cooked to give the bird a lacquered effect.

The duck is filled with boiling water to steam it from the inside and roasted in a specially made kiln-like oven. Inside the oven, the ducks are hung vertically or spit-roasted over fruit wood at very high temperatures for a relatively short time—this produces a truly crisp skin, but prevents the meat from drying out.

today you can order from more than 200 duck dishes, using every conceivable part of the duck, from deep-fried hearts to webs with mustard sauce and stewed tongues. The branch in Wangfujing has two duck kitchens, two pancake kitchens and two general kitchens for a restaurant that seats 800. The chefs are trained at the Beijing Culinary Institute for 3 years before working their way up through the kitchens.

PERFECT PEKING DUCK

The quality of the ingredients is paramount to the flavour of Peking duck. The Peking duck is specially bred to be plump and tender and is reared on a grain diet. Some restaurants add flavourings to the duck by varying the ingredients of the maltose solution or adding flavourings to the boiling water inside the cavity. However, Peking duck should not have a spicy or sweet aroma, instead the natural flavour of the duck juices and crispy skin should dominate.

Crispy skin is the true test of perfect Peking duck. This is achieved by separating the skin from the flesh, then drying the skin thoroughly before the duck is cooked. The wood-fired oven uses its high heat to cook the skin quickly, which also causes most of the fat to melt and run out, while the liquid that has been put inside the duck heats up and steams the flesh from the inside, keeping the meat moist.

THE WEATHER can be an important factor with Peking and roast ducks, and ducks can be seen hanging up outside all over China when it is cold and dry. To form a really crisp skin, the ducks must be thoroughly dried in air with a low humidity until the skin is like paper.

盐锅鸡

SALT-BAKED CHICKEN

THIS IS ANOTHER CANTONESE SPECIALTY THAT EMPLOYS A RATHER UNUSUAL COOKING METHOD. THE WHOLE CHICKEN IS WRAPPED IN CLOTH AND BAKED IN SALT, WHICH ACTS LIKE AN OVEN, KEEPING IN THE HEAT TO PRODUCE VERY SUCCULENT CHICKEN MEAT.

3 lb chicken
2 tablespoons light soy sauce
4 lb sea salt or coarse salt

FILLING
1 scallion, chopped
1 teaspoon grated ginger
2 star anise, crushed
1/2 teaspoon salt
4 tablespoons Mei Kuei Lu Chiew or brandy

DIPPING SAUCE
1 tablespoon oil
1 scallion, chopped
1 teaspoon chopped ginger
1/2 teaspoon salt
1/4 cup chicken and meat stock (page 281)

SERVES 4

RINSE the chicken, drain, and remove any fat from the cavity opening and around the neck. Cut off and discard the tail. Blanch the chicken in a saucepan of boiling water for 2–3 minutes, then refresh under cold water and dry well. Brush the chicken with the soy sauce and hang it up to dry in a cool and airy place for a couple of hours, or keep it, uncovered, in the fridge.

MEANWHILE, TO make the filling, combine the scallion, ginger, star anise, salt and Mei Kuei Lu Chiew. Pour the filling into the cavity of the chicken. Wrap the chicken tightly with a large sheet of cheesecloth.

HEAT the salt in a large clay pot or braising pan very slowly until very hot, then turn off the heat and remove and reserve about half the salt. Make a hole in the center of the salt and place the chicken in it, breast side up, then cover with the salt removed earlier so that the chicken is completely buried. Cover the clay pot or braising pan and cook over medium heat for 15–20 minutes, then reduce the heat to low and cook for 45–50 minutes. Allow to sit for at least 15–20 minutes before taking the chicken out. (The salt can be reused.)

TO MAKE the dipping sauce, heat the oil in a small wok or saucepan. Fry the scallion and ginger for 1 minute, then add the salt and stock. Bring to a boil, then reduce the heat and simmer for a couple of minutes.

REMOVE the chicken from the casserole and unwrap it. Using a cleaver, cut the chicken through the bones into bite-size pieces. Arrange on a serving dish and serve hot or cold with the dipping sauce.

Make sure every part of the chicken is covered in salt to seal in the flavor completely. The salt does not affect the flavor of the chicken as the wrapping and skin keep it from coming into contact with the flesh.

Table tennis played at an outside recreation area in Beijing.

RED-COOKED CHICKEN

RED-COOKED CHICKEN

RED-COOKING LIQUID
- 2 cinnamon or cassia sticks
- 1 1/2 star anise
- 2 pieces dried tangerine or orange peel, about 2 inches long
- 1/2 teaspoon fennel seeds
- 1 1/2 cups dark soy sauce
- 1/2 cup sugar
- 1/2 cup Shaoxing rice wine

- 3 lb chicken
- 1 tablespoon roasted sesame oil

SERVES 6

TO MAKE the red-cooking liquid, place all the ingredients in a clay pot or braising pan with 6 cups water, bring to a boil, then simmer for 30 minutes.

RINSE the chicken, drain, and remove any fat from the cavity opening and around the neck. Cut off and discard the tail. Place the chicken, breast side down, in the cooking liquid and cook for 1 1/2 hours, turning 2 or 3 times. Turn off the heat and leave in the liquid for 30 minutes, then remove. Brush the chicken with the sesame oil then, using a cleaver, cut the chicken through the bones into bite-size pieces. Spoon over a little liquid and serve hot or cold.

THE SAUCE can be reused as a "Master Sauce" (see page 290).

SOY CHICKEN

The soy sauce and sugar in the marinade turn the chicken skin a rich dark brown when cooked.

- 3 lb chicken
- 1 tablespoon ground Sichuan peppercorns
- 2 tablespoons grated ginger
- 2 tablespoons sugar
- 3 tablespoons Shaoxing rice wine
- 1 1/4 cups dark soy sauce
- 3/4 cup light soy sauce
- 2 1/2 cups oil
- 1 3/4 cups chicken and meat stock (page 281)
- 2 teaspoons roasted sesame oil

SERVES 4

RINSE the chicken, drain, and remove any fat from the cavity opening and around the neck. Cut off and discard the tail. Rub the Sichuan peppercorns and ginger all over the inside and outside of the chicken. Combine the sugar, rice wine and soy sauces, add the chicken and marinate in the fridge for at least 3 hours, turning occasionally.

HEAT a wok over high heat, add the oil and heat until very hot. Drain the chicken, reserving the marinade, and fry for 8 minutes until browned. Put in a clay pot or braising pan with the marinade and stock. Bring to a boil, then simmer, covered, for 35–40 minutes. Take off the heat for 2–3 hours, transferring to the fridge when cool. Drain the chicken, brush with oil and refrigerate for 1 hour.

USING a cleaver, chop the chicken through the bones into bite-size pieces, pour over a couple of tablespoons of sauce and serve.

THE SAUCE can be reused as a "Master Sauce" (see page 290).

椒盐炸鹌鹑

DEEP-FRIED QUAILS WITH SPICY SALT

FRESH QUAILS ARE BEST FOR THIS RECIPE BECAUSE ONCE FROZEN, QUAIL CAN BECOME QUITE DRY AND BLAND, AND TENDERNESS AND SUCCULENCE ARE THE MAIN CHARACTERISTICS OF THIS DISH.

4 quails
1 teaspoon spicy salt and pepper (page 285)
1 teaspoon sugar
1 tablespoon light soy sauce
1 tablespoon Shaoxing rice wine
2–3 tablespoons all-purpose flour
oil for deep-frying
1 scallion, finely chopped
1 red chile, finely chopped

SERVES 4

SPLIT EACH quail in half down the middle and clean well. Marinate with the spicy salt and pepper, the sugar, soy sauce and rice wine for 2–3 hours in the fridge, turning frequently. Coat each quail piece in the flour.

FILL a wok one quarter full of oil. Heat the oil to 375°F, or until a piece of bread fries golden brown in 10 seconds when dropped in the oil. Reduce the heat and fry the quail for 2–3 minutes on each side. Remove from the wok and drain on paper towels.

SOAK the scallion and chile in the hot oil (with the heat turned off) for 2 minutes. Remove with a wire strainer or slotted spoon and drain, then sprinkle over the quail pieces. Serve hot.

Erhai Lake in Yunnan.

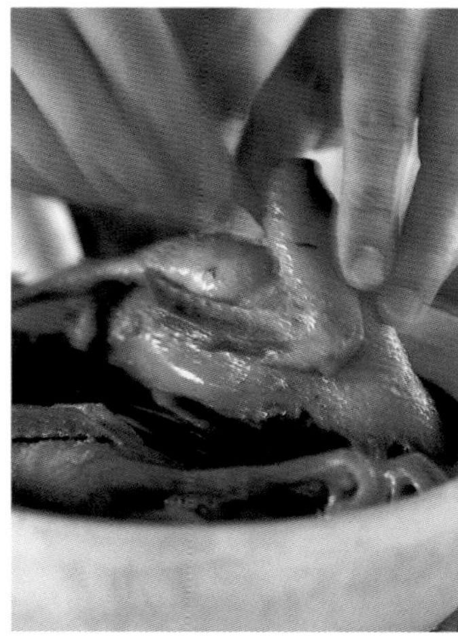

Marinate the quail long enough for the flavors to penetrate the meat.

油烧乳鸽

LACQUERED SQUAB

THIS COOKING METHOD GIVES THE SKIN OF THE SQUAB A SHINY, DEEP REDDISH-BROWN GLAZE. THE SIMMERING GIVES THE FLAVOR AND THE FINAL DEEP-FRYING CRISPS THE SKIN.

2 x 1 lb squab
4 slices ginger
4 scallions, cut into short pieces
4 tablespoons light soy sauce
3 tablespoons dark soy sauce
3 tablespoons Shaoxing rice wine
4 tablespoons rock sugar or dark brown sugar
1 teaspoon salt
2 cinnamon sticks
2 star anise
4 cups chicken stock (page 281)
oil for deep-frying

SERVES 4

BLANCH the squab in a saucepan of boiling water for 2 minutes, then remove and drain.

COMBINE the remaining ingredients except the oil in a clay pot or braising pan and bring to a simmer. Add the squab, cover and simmer for 20 minutes. Remove from the heat, take out the squab and allow to dry for at least 1 hour.

FILL a wok one quarter full of oil. Heat the oil to 375°F, or until a piece of bread fries golden brown in 10 seconds when dropped in the oil. Fry the squab until they are very crisp and brown. Drain well and sprinkle with salt. Using a cleaver, cut the squabs through the bones into bite-size pieces.

LACQUERED SQUAB

A chicken seller in Chengdu.

In China, rice wine can be bought directly out of the earthenware pots it is matured in.

柠檬鸡

LEMON CHICKEN

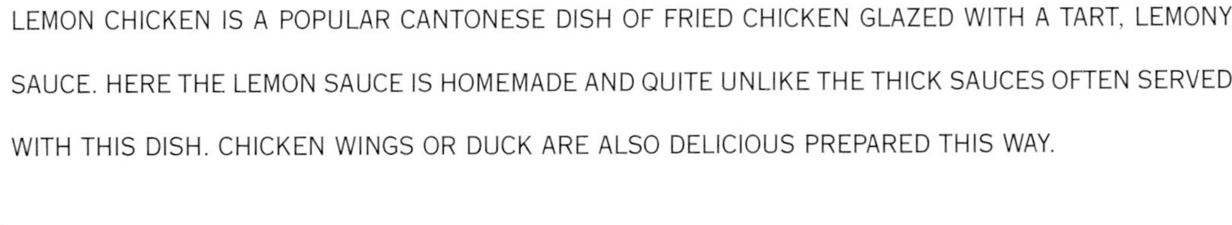

LEMON CHICKEN IS A POPULAR CANTONESE DISH OF FRIED CHICKEN GLAZED WITH A TART, LEMONY SAUCE. HERE THE LEMON SAUCE IS HOMEMADE AND QUITE UNLIKE THE THICK SAUCES OFTEN SERVED WITH THIS DISH. CHICKEN WINGS OR DUCK ARE ALSO DELICIOUS PREPARED THIS WAY.

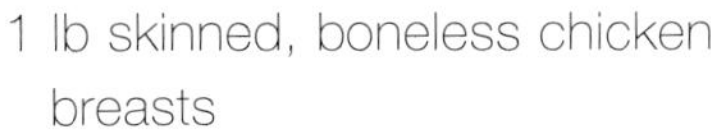

1 lb skinned, boneless chicken breasts
1 tablespoon light soy sauce
1 tablespoon Shaoxing rice wine
1 scallion, finely chopped
1 tablespoon finely chopped ginger
1 garlic clove, finely chopped
1 egg, lightly beaten
3/4 cup cornstarch
oil for deep-frying

LEMON SAUCE
2 tablespoons lemon juice
2 teaspoons sugar
1/2 teaspoon salt
1/2 teaspoon toasted sesame oil
3 tablespoons chicken stock (page 281) or water
1/2 teaspoon cornstarch

SERVES 6

CUT the chicken into slices. Place in a bowl, add the soy sauce, rice wine, scallion, ginger and garlic, and toss lightly. Marinate in the fridge for at least 1 hour, or overnight.

ADD the egg to the chicken mixture and toss lightly to coat. Drain any excess egg and coat the chicken pieces with the cornstarch. The easiest way to do this is to put the chicken and cornstarch in a plastic bag and shake it.

FILL a wok one quarter full of oil. Heat the oil to 375°F, or until a piece of bread fries golden brown in 10 seconds when dropped in the oil. Add half the chicken, a piece at a time, and fry, stirring constantly, for 3 1/2–4 minutes, or until golden brown. Remove with a wire strainer or slotted spoon and drain. Repeat with the remaining chicken. Reheat the oil and return all the chicken to the wok. Cook until crisp and golden brown. Drain the chicken. Pour off the oil and wipe out the wok.

TO MAKE the lemon sauce, combine the lemon juice, sugar, salt, sesame oil, stock and cornstarch.

REHEAT the wok over medium heat until hot, add the lemon sauce and stir constantly until thickened. Add the chicken and toss lightly in the sauce.

醉鸡

DRUNKEN CHICKEN

THERE ARE SEVERAL VERSIONS OF THIS POPULAR DISH, BUT IN THIS SIMPLE RECIPE, THE CHICKEN IS STEAMED IN THE "DRUNKEN" SAUCE, WHICH IS THEN POURED OVER TO SERVE.

3 lb chicken
1/2 cup Shaoxing rice wine
3 tablespoons Chinese spirit (Mou Tai) or brandy
3 slices ginger
3 scallions, cut into short pieces
2 teaspoons salt
1/4 teaspoon freshly ground black pepper
cilantro leaves

SERVES 4

RINSE the chicken, drain, and remove any fat from the cavity opening and around the neck. Cut off and discard the tail. Blanch the chicken in a saucepan of boiling water for 2–3 minutes, then refresh in cold water.

PLACE the chicken, breast side down, in a bowl. Add the rice wine, Chinese spirit, ginger, scallion and half the salt. Place the bowl in a steamer. Cover and steam over simmering water in a wok for 1 1/2 hours, replenishing with boiling water during cooking. Transfer the chicken to a dish, breast side up, reserving the cooking liquid.

POUR half the liquid into a wok or saucepan and add the remaining salt and the pepper. Bring to a boil, then pour the sauce over the chicken. Using a cleaver, cut the chicken through the bones into bite-size pieces. Garnish with the cilantro.

DRUNKEN CHICKEN

三杯鸡

THREE-CUP CHICKEN

THREE-CUP CHICKEN IS SO CALLED BECAUSE THE ORIGINAL RECIPE USES ONE CUP EACH OF RICE WINE, SOY SAUCE AND LARD. CHRISTINE YAN OF YMING RESTAURANT IN LONDON MODIFIED IT WITH THIS RECIPE THAT REPLACES THE LARD WITH STOCK, AND THE RESULT IS A MUCH HEALTHIER DISH.

1 lb skinned, boneless chicken thighs
1 tablespoon cornstarch
1 tablespoon oil
2 scallions, cut to short pieces
4 small pieces ginger
3 tablespoons Shaoxing rice wine
3 tablespoons light soy sauce
1/2 cup chicken and meat stock (page 281)
1/2 teaspoon toasted sesame oil

SERVES 4

CUT the chicken into 3/4 inch cubes. Combine the cornstarch with enough water to make a paste and toss the chicken cubes in the paste to coat.

HEAT the oil in a small clay pot or braising pan, lightly brown the chicken with the scallion and ginger, then add the rice wine, soy sauce and stock. Bring to a boil, then reduce the heat and simmer, covered, for 20–25 minutes. There should be a little liquid left—if there is too much, boil it off. Add the sesame oil and serve the chicken hot from the pot.

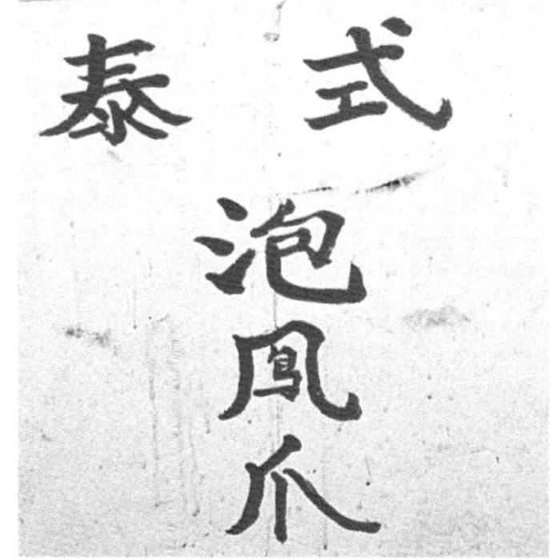

A sign proclaims "Thai-style chicken feet" for sale at an outside stall in Chengdu.

THREE-CUP CHICKEN

A shopping street in central Shanghai.

Ducks hanging up to dry after they have been plucked.

SHANGHAI SOY DUCK

THIS DUCK, SIMILAR TO CANTONESE SOY CHICKEN, IS TRADITIONALLY SERVED AT ROOM TEMPERATURE AS A FIRST COURSE, THOUGH THERE IS NO REASON WHY IT CAN'T BE SERVED AS A MAIN COURSE, HOT OR COLD. YOU CAN ALSO USE JOINTED PIECES OR DUCK BREASTS, JUST REDUCE THE COOKING TIME.

4 1/2 lb duck
2 teaspoons salt
4 scallions, each tied in a knot
4 x 1/2 inch slices ginger, smashed with the flat side of a cleaver
6 star anise
3 cinnamon or cassia sticks
1 tablespoon Sichuan peppercorns
1/2 cup Shaoxing rice wine
3/4 cup light soy sauce
1/2 cup dark soy sauce
3 oz rock sugar

SERVES 4

RINSE the duck, drain, and remove any fat from the cavity opening and around the neck. Cut off and discard the tail. Blanch the duck in a saucepan of boiling water for 2–3 minutes, then refresh in cold water, pat dry and rub the salt inside the cavity.

PLACE the duck, breast side up, in a clay pot or braising pan, and add the scallions, ginger, star anise, cinnamon, peppercorns, rice wine, soy sauces, rock sugar and enough water to cover. Bring to a boil, then reduce the heat and simmer, covered, for 40–45 minutes. Turn off the heat and allow the duck to cool in the liquid for 2–3 hours, transferring the clay pot to the fridge once it is cool enough. Keep in the fridge until completely cold (you can keep the duck in the liquid overnight and serve it the next day).

TO SERVE, remove the duck from the liquid and drain well. Using a cleaver, cut the duck through the bones into bite-size pieces.

TRADITIONALLY this dish is served at room temperature, but if you would like to serve it hot, put the clay pot with the duck and the liquid back on the stove and bring it to a boil. Simmer for 10 minutes, or until the duck is completely heated through.

THE SAUCE can be reused as a "Master Sauce" (see page 290).

棒棒鸡

BANG BANG CHICKEN

THIS CLASSIC SICHUAN-STYLE COLD PLATTER IS MADE FROM CHICKEN, CUCUMBER AND BEAN THREAD NOODLES, MIXED IN A SESAME OR PEANUT SAUCE. THE SESAME DRESSING IS THE AUTHENTIC ONE BUT THE PEANUT VERSION IS ALSO VERY GOOD.

1 1/2 cucumbers
1 teaspoon salt
1 oz bean thread noodles
1 teaspoon toasted sesame oil
8 oz cooked chicken, cut into shreds
2 scallions, green part only, finely sliced

SESAME DRESSING
1/4 teaspoon Sichuan peppercorns
3 garlic cloves
3/4 inch piece ginger
1/2 teaspoon chili sauce
3 tablespoons toasted sesame paste
2 tablespoons toasted sesame oil
2 1/2 tablespoons light soy sauce
1 tablespoon Shaoxing rice wine
1 tablespoon Chinese black rice vinegar
1 tablespoon sugar
3 tablespoons chicken stock (page 281)

OR

PEANUT DRESSING
1/2 cup smooth peanut butter
1 teaspoon light soy sauce
1 1/2 tablespoons sugar
2 teaspoons Chinese black rice vinegar
1 tablespoon Shaoxing rice wine
1 tablespoon toasted sesame oil
1 scallion, finely chopped
1 tablespoon finely chopped ginger
1 teaspoon chili sauce
2 1/2 tablespoons chicken stock (page 281)

SERVES 6

SLICE the cucumbers lengthwise and remove most of the seeds. Cut each half crosswise into thirds, then cut each piece lengthwise into thin slices that are 2 inches long and 3/4 inch wide. Place the slices in a bowl, add the salt, toss lightly, and set aside for 20 minutes. Pour off the water that has accumulated.

TO MAKE the sesame dressing, put the Sichuan peppercorns in a frying pan and cook over medium heat, stirring occasionally, for 7–8 minutes, or until golden brown and very fragrant. Cool slightly, then crush into a powder. Combine the garlic, ginger, chili sauce, sesame paste, sesame oil, soy sauce, rice wine, vinegar, sugar and stock in a blender, food processor or mortar and pestle. Blend to a smooth sauce the consistency of heavy cream. Stir in the Sichuan peppercorn powder. Pour into a bowl and set aside.

TO MAKE the peanut dressing, combine the peanut butter, soy sauce, sugar, vinegar, rice wine, sesame oil, scallion, ginger, chili sauce and stock in a blender, food processor or mortar and pestle. Blend until the mixture is the consistency of heavy cream, adding a little water if necessary. Pour into a bowl and set aside.

SOAK the bean thread noodles in hot water for 10 minutes, then drain and cut into 3 inch pieces. Blanch the noodles in a saucepan of boiling water for 3 minutes, then refresh in cold water and drain again. Toss the noodles in the sesame oil and arrange them on a large platter. Arrange the cucumber slices on top. Place the chicken shreds on top of the cucumber. Just before serving, pour the sesame or peanut dressing over the chicken. Sprinkle with the chopped scallions and serve.

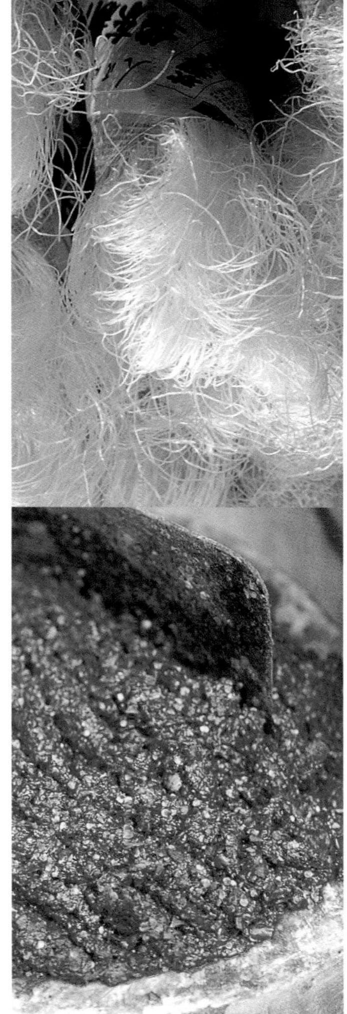

Peeling garlic in Sichuan.

白斩鸡

WHITE CUT CHICKEN

"WHITE CUT" IS A POACHING METHOD USED ALL OVER CHINA, WHERE A WHOLE CHICKEN IS COOKED IN A RELATIVELY SHORT TIME IN A WATER-BASED BROTH, THEN THE HEAT IS TURNED OFF AND THE RETAINED HEAT CARRIES OUT THE REMAINDER OF THE COOKING.

- $2\frac{1}{2}$ lb chicken
- 2 scallions, each tied in a knot
- 3 slices ginger, smashed with the flat side of a cleaver
- 3 tablespoons Shaoxing rice wine
- 1 tablespoon salt

DIPPING SAUCE

- 4 tablespoons dark soy sauce
- 1 tablespoon sugar
- 1 scallion, finely chopped
- 1 garlic clove, finely chopped
- 1 teaspoon finely chopped ginger
- 1 teaspoon roasted sesame oil

SERVES 4

RINSE the chicken, drain, and remove any fat from the cavity opening and around the neck. Cut off and discard the tail. Bring 6 cups water to a rolling boil in a clay pot or braising pan, and gently lower the chicken into the water with the breast side up. Add the scallions, ginger and rice wine, return to a boil, then add the salt and simmer, covered, for 15 minutes.

TURN OFF the heat and allow the chicken to cool in the liquid for 5–6 hours, without lifting the lid.

ABOUT 30 minutes before serving time, remove and drain the chicken. Using a cleaver, cut the chicken through the bones into bite-size pieces.

TO MAKE the dipping sauce, combine the soy sauce, sugar, scallion, garlic, ginger and sesame oil with a little of the cooking liquid. Divide the sauce among small saucers, one for each person. Each piece of the chicken is dipped before eating.

ALTERNATIVELY, pour the sauce over the chicken before serving, but use light soy sauce instead of dark soy sauce so as not to spoil the "whiteness" of the chicken.

Old men take their song birds out with them to the park when they meet their friends. The cages are hung up so the birds can sing together while their owners chat.

MEAT

木薯炒肉

MU SHU PORK

SINCE WHEAT IS THE STAPLE CROP IN NORTHERN CHINA, MEAT AND VEGETABLE DISHES ARE COMMONLY SERVED THERE WITH STEAMED BREAD OR PANCAKES INSTEAD OF RICE. THIS BEIJING DISH IS SERVED ROLLED IN MANDARIN PANCAKES, WHICH ARE FIRST SPREAD WITH HOISIN SAUCE.

You may find it easier to cut the meat into thin slices if you freeze it for 15 minutes first to firm it up.

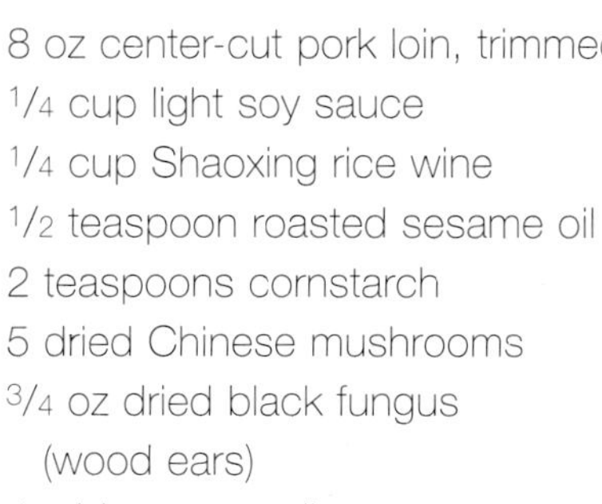

8 oz center-cut pork loin, trimmed
1/4 cup light soy sauce
1/4 cup Shaoxing rice wine
1/2 teaspoon roasted sesame oil
2 teaspoons cornstarch
5 dried Chinese mushrooms
3/4 oz dried black fungus (wood ears)
4 tablespoons oil
2 eggs, lightly beaten
4 garlic cloves, finely chopped
2 tablespoons finely chopped ginger
1 leek, white part only, finely shredded
1/4 small Chinese cabbage, shredded, stem sections and leafy sections separated
1/2 teaspoon sugar
1/4 teaspoon freshly ground black pepper
1/3 cup hoisin sauce
12 Mandarin pancakes (page 277)

SERVES 4

CUT the pork against the grain into slices about 1/4 inch thick, then cut into thin, matchstick-size shreds about 3/4 inch long. Put the shreds in a bowl, add 1 tablespoon of the soy sauce, 1 tablespoon of the rice wine, the sesame oil and 1 teaspoon of the cornstarch, and toss lightly to coat. Cover with plastic wrap and marinate in the fridge for 30 minutes.

SOAK the dried mushrooms in boiling water for 30 minutes, then drain and squeeze out any excess water. Remove and discard the stems and shred the caps. Soak the dried black fungus in cold water for 20 minutes, then drain and squeeze out any excess water. Shred the black fungus.

HEAT a wok over high heat, add 2 tablespoons of the oil and heat until very hot. Stir-fry the pork mixture for 2–3 minutes, until the meat is brown and cooked. Remove with a wire strainer or slotted spoon and drain. Rinse and dry the wok.

REHEAT the wok over high heat, add 1 tablespoon of the oil and heat until hot. Stir-fry the egg to scramble, then move to the side of the wok. Add 1 tablespoon of oil, heat until very hot, and stir-fry the garlic, ginger, mushrooms and black fungus for 10 seconds, or until fragrant. Add the leek and toss lightly for 1 1/2 minutes, then add the cabbage stems and stir-fry for 30 seconds. Add the leafy cabbage sections, and cook for 1 minute, or until the vegetables are just tender. Combine 1 1/2 tablespoons of the soy sauce, the remaining rice wine and cornstarch, the sugar, black pepper and the meat, add to the sauce and simmer until thickened.

COMBINE the hoisin sauce, remaining soy sauce and 1 1/2 tablespoons water in a small bowl. Serve the pork with the pancakes and sauce.

Harvesting bok choy in Liugan.

Roll the mixture into balls using the palms of your hands, then dust with cornstarch to prevent them from sticking when you cook them.

狮子头肉丸

LION'S HEAD MEATBALLS

THIS DISH IS SO NAMED BECAUSE THE LARGE MEATBALLS ARE SAID TO LOOK LIKE LION'S HEADS SURROUNDED BY A MANE OF BOK CHOY. ORIGINALLY THE MEATBALLS TENDED TO BE MADE FROM PORK AND PORK FAT AND WERE COARSER IN TEXTURE.

1 lb ground pork
1 egg white
4 scallions, finely chopped
1 tablespoon Shaoxing rice wine
1 teaspoon grated ginger
1 tablespoon light soy sauce
2 teaspoons sugar
1 teaspoon roasted sesame oil
1/2–3/4 lb bok choy
1 tablespoon cornstarch
oil for frying
2 cups chicken and meat stock (page 281)

SERVES 4

PUT the pork and egg white in a food processor and process briefly until you have a fluffy mixture, or mash the ground pork in a large bowl and gradually stir in the egg white, beating the mixture well until it is fluffy. Add the scallion, rice wine, ginger, soy sauce, sugar and sesame oil, season with salt and white pepper, and process or beat again briefly. Fry a small portion of the mixture and taste it, reseasoning if necessary. Divide the mixture into walnut-size balls.

SEPARATE the boy choy leaves and place in the bottom of a clay pot or braising pan.

DUST the meatballs with cornstarch. Heat a wok over high heat, add 1/2 inch oil and heat until very hot. Cook the meatballs in batches until they are browned all over. Drain well and add to the clay pot in an even layer. Pour off the oil and wipe out the wok.

REHEAT the wok over high heat until very hot, add the chicken stock and heat until it is boiling. Pour over the meatballs. Cover and bring very slowly to a boil. Simmer gently with the lid slightly open for 1 1/2 hours, or until the meatballs are very tender. Serve the meatballs in the dish they were cooked in.

A pickle stall in Sichuan.

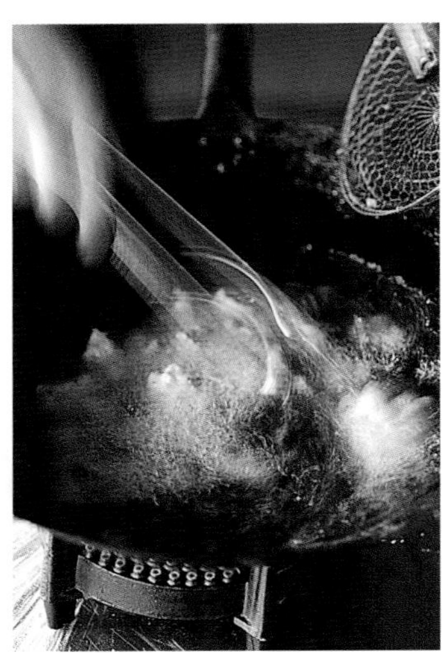

Deep-frying the pork gives it a crispy, well-browned outside while keeping the meat inside very tender.

酸甜肉

SWEET-AND-SOUR PORK

ALTHOUGH SWEET-AND-SOUR PORK IS OFTEN THOUGHT OF AS A WESTERN INVENTION, IT IS IN FACT CHINESE. IN THE ORIGINAL VERSION, THE PORK IS LIGHT AND CRISPY AND SERVED IN A PIQUANT SWEET-AND-SOUR SAUCE. IF YOU LIKE IT WITH PINEAPPLE, ADD 2 CUPS CUBED PINEAPPLE.

1 1/4 lb center-cut pork loin, trimmed
1 egg
3/4 cup cornstarch
1 tablespoon oil
1 onion, cubed
1 red pepper, cubed or cut into small triangles
2 scallions, cut into 3/4 inch pieces
2/3 cup Chinese pickles
1 cup clear rice vinegar
1/3 cup tomato ketchup
1 1/4 cups sugar
oil for deep-frying

SERVES 4

CUT the pork into 3/4 inch cubes and put it in a bowl with the egg, 1/2 cup of the cornstarch and 2 teaspoons water. Stir to coat all of the pieces of pork.

HEAT a wok over high heat, add the oil and heat until very hot. Stir-fry the onion for 1 minute. Add the pepper and scallions and cook for 1 minute. Add the pickles and toss together to combine. Add the rice vinegar, tomato ketchup and sugar and stir over low heat until the sugar dissolves. Bring to a boil, then simmer for 3 minutes.

COMBINE the remaining cornstarch with 1/4 cup water, add to the sweet-and-sour mixture and simmer until thickened. Set aside.

FILL a wok one quarter full of oil. Heat the oil to 350°F, or until a piece of bread fries golden brown in 15 seconds when dropped in the oil. Cook the pork in batches until golden brown and crispy. Return all of the pork to the wok, cook until crisp again, then remove with a wire strainer or slotted spoon and drain well. Add the pork pieces to the sauce, stir to coat, and reheat until bubbling.

红烧排骨

RED-COOKED PORK

RED-COOKING, OR BRAISING IN A SOY-SAUCE BASED LIQUID, IS A TECHNIQUE USED ALL OVER CHINA TO MAKE CHICKEN, MEAT OR FISH VERY TENDER WITH LITTLE EFFORT.

- 3 lb pork leg or fresh ham, with bone in and rind on
- 4 scallions, each tied in a knot
- 4 slices ginger, smashed with the flat side of a cleaver
- 3/4 cup dark soy sauce
- 4 tablespoons Shaoxing rice wine
- 1 teaspoon five-spice powder
- 2 oz rock sugar

SERVES 8

SCRAPE the pork rind to make sure it is free of any bristles. Blanch the pork in a saucepan of boiling water for 4–5 minutes. Rinse the pork and place in a clay pot or braising pan with 2 1/2 cups water, the scallions, ginger, soy sauce, rice wine, five-spice powder and sugar. Bring to a boil, then reduce the heat and simmer, covered, for 2 1/2–3 hours, turning several times, until the meat is very tender and falling from the bone.

IF THERE is too much liquid, remove the pork and reduce the sauce by boiling it for 10–15 minutes. Slice the pork and serve with the sauce poured over it.

RED-COOKED PORK

东坡肉

DONG PO PORK

NAMED AFTER A GOURMET STATESMAN OF THE SONG DYNASTY, THE PORK IS FRIED TO GIVE THE SKIN A GOOD COLOR AND TEXTURE, THEN SLOW COOKED TO MELTINGLY TENDER.

- 2 lb belly pork, rind on
- 2 tablespoons oil
- 6 scallions, sliced
- 8 slices ginger
- 3 oz rock sugar
- 1/4 cup dark soy sauce
- 1/4 cup light soy sauce
- 1/2 cup Shaoxing rice wine

SERVES 6

SCRAPE the pork rind to make sure it is free of any bristles. Blanch the pork in a saucepan of boiling water for 10 minutes, then drain well and dry thoroughly with paper towels.

HEAT a wok over high heat, add the oil and heat until very hot. Cook the pork until well browned and the skin is crisp and brown. Drain the pork.

PUT the scallions, ginger, sugar, soy sauces, rice wine and 1/2 cup water in a clay pot or braising pan. Bring to a boil, stirring until the sugar has dissolved. Add the pork, cover and simmer for 2 1/2–3 hours, or until very tender. Remove the pork and drain, straining the liquid. Cut the pork into very thin slices and serve with the sauce.

Make sure that the pork is very well browned and that the skin is crisp, otherwise it will be soggy after the second stage of cooking.

DONG PO PORK

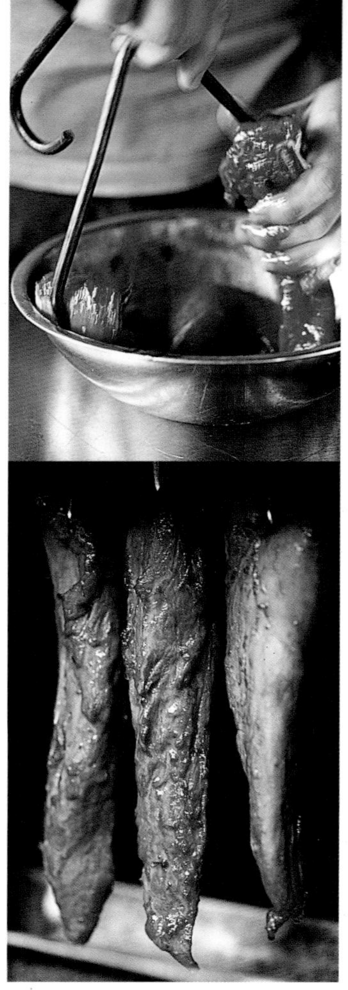

Hanging the char siu to roast above a tray of water creates a steamy atmosphere which helps keep the meat moist. Generally in China, char siu is bought from carry-out restaurants as most homes do not have an oven.

CHAR SIU

CHAR SIU, OR BARBECUED PORK, IS A CANTONESE SPECIALTY THAT CAN BE SEEN HANGING IN CHINESE RESTAURANTS. CHAR SIU MEANS "SUSPENDED OVER FIRE" AND IS TRADITIONALLY DYED A RED COLOR.

MARINADE
1 tablespoon rock sugar
1 tablespoon yellow bean sauce
1 tablespoon hoisin sauce
1 tablespoon oyster sauce
1 tablespoon fermented red bean curd
1 tablespoon Chinese spirit (Mou Tai) or brandy
1/2 teaspoon roasted sesame oil

1 1/2 lb center-cut pork loin, trimmed
2 tablespoons maltose or honey, dissolved with a little water

SERVES 4

TO MAKE the marinade, combine the ingredients. Cut the pork into 4 x 8 inch strips, add to the marinade and keep in the fridge for at least 6 hours.

PREHEAT the oven to 425°F. Put a baking dish filled with 2 1/2 cups boiling water in the bottom of the oven. Drain the pork, reserving the marinade. Put an S-shaped meat hook through one end of each strip and hang from the top rack.

ROAST FOR 10–15 minutes, then baste with the marinade. Reduce the heat to 350°F and roast for 8–10 minutes. Cool for 2–3 minutes, then brush with the maltose and lightly brown under a broiler for 4–5 minutes, turning to give a charred look around the edges.

CUT the meat into slices. Pour 3/4 cup liquid from the dish into the marinade. Bring to a boil and cook for 2 minutes. Strain and pour over the pork.

SPICY CRISPY PORK

香辣脆皮肉

SPICY CRISPY PORK

1 1/2 lb pork belly, rind on
1 teaspoon salt
1 teaspoon five-spice powder

DIPPING SAUCE
2 tablespoons light soy sauce
1 tablespoon dark soy sauce
1 tablespoon chili sauce (optional)

SERVES 6

SCRAPE the pork rind to make sure it is free of any bristles. Dry, then rub with the salt and five-spice powder. Keep uncovered in the fridge for at least 2 hours.

TO MAKE the dipping sauce, combine all of the ingredients.

PREHEAT the oven to 475°F. Place the pork, skin side up, on a rack in a roasting pan. Roast for 20 minutes, reduce the heat to 400°F and roast for 40–45 minutes until crispy. Cut into pieces and serve with the sauce.

芥菜焖三尘肉

BRAISED PORK BELLY WITH MUSTARD CABBAGE

MEAT FROM THE BELLY IS A CUT OF MEAT THAT NEEDS LONG, SLOW COOKING TO MAKE IT TENDER. THE RED BEAN CURD AND PRESERVED MUSTARD CABBAGE TEMPER THE RICHNESS OF THE MEAT BECAUSE THEY ARE BOTH STRONGLY FLAVORED.

8 oz preserved mustard cabbage
2 lb pork belly, rind on
2 tablespoons dark soy sauce
oil for frying

SAUCE
1 1/2 pieces fermented red bean curd
1 tablespoon yellow bean sauce
1 1/2 tablespoons oyster sauce
2 tablespoons dark soy sauce
2 teaspoons sugar
4 star anise
2 tablespoons oil
2 garlic cloves, bruised
4 slices ginger, smashed with the flat side of a cleaver

SERVES 6

SOAK the preserved mustard cabbage in cold water for 4 hours. Drain and wash well in a sink full of water until the water is clear of grit. Drain again, then cut the cabbage into 3/4 inch pieces.

SCRAPE the pork rind to make sure it is free of any bristles. Bring a large clay pot or braising pan full of water to a boil and add the pork belly. Simmer, covered, for 40 minutes, or until tender. Drain the pork and, when cool enough to handle, prick holes over the skin with a fork. Rub the soy sauce over the skin.

HEAT a wok with a lid over medium heat, add 3/4 inch of the oil and heat until hot. Add the pork belly, skin side down, and cook for 5–8 minutes, or until the skin is crispy, then turn over to brown the meat. Cover the wok slightly with the lid to protect you from the fat—the pork will sizzle violently as it cooks. Place the pork in a bowl of hot water for 30 minutes to make the skin bubble up and soften. Remove the pork from the bowl and cut it into 3/4 inch wide strips. Set aside.

TO MAKE the sauce, put the fermented bean curd, yellow bean sauce, oyster sauce, soy sauce, sugar and star anise in a bowl. Heat a wok over medium heat, add the oil and heat until hot. Cook the garlic for 30 seconds, then add the sauce mixture and the ginger. Cook for 1–2 minutes, or until aromatic.

ADD the pork and coat with the sauce, then add 3 cups water and mix well. Cover and bring to a boil, then reduce the heat and simmer for 40 minutes. Add the mustard cabbage and cook for 15 minutes. If the sauce is too thin, boil it, uncovered, for a few minutes, until it thickens.

A cured meat shop in Guangzhou.

Pig's feet need to be cooked for several hours in order to break down all the connective tissue and make them tender.

焖猪蹄

PICKLED PIG'S FEET

THIS RECIPE IS TRADITIONALLY SERVED TO NEW MOTHERS—THE GINGER IS SAID TO BE RESTORATIVE AND THE DISH SUPPOSEDLY HELPS MOTHERS PRODUCE PLENTY OF MILK FOR THEIR BABIES. THE HARD-BOILED EGGS ARE A SYMBOL OF LIFE AND CAN BE EATEN WITH THE MEAT.

1 lb young ginger, peeled and cut into 1 inch pieces
3 lb pig's feet or hocks, front and back legs
4 cups Chinese black rice vinegar
4 oz rock sugar
6 hard-boiled eggs (optional)

SERVES 6

PUT the ginger in a bowl of water. Bring a wok or saucepan of water to a boil, add the feet, return to a boil, then drain. Scrape the rind to make sure it is free of any bristles. Using a cleaver, cut each foot through the bone into 3 or 4 pieces.

DRAIN the ginger and lightly smash each piece with the side of a cleaver. Blanch the ginger in a saucepan of boiling water for 2 minutes, refresh in cold water and allow to cool.

PUT the vinegar and sugar in a wok or saucepan and bring to a boil, stirring to dissolve the sugar. Add the feet and ginger and simmer, covered, for 2 hours, then simmer, uncovered, for 1–2 hours until tender. Add the unpeeled eggs and cook for 5 minutes. Allow to cool, then refrigerate overnight. Remove any fat and bring to a boil. Serve hot or cold.

CRYSTAL-BOILED PORK

水晶猪肉

CRYSTAL-BOILED PORK

2 lb pork leg, bone removed and rind on
2 garlic cloves, finely chopped
1 scallion, finely chopped
1 teaspoon sugar
4 tablespoons light soy sauce
1 teaspoon roasted sesame oil
1 teaspoon chile oil (optional)

SERVES 8

SCRAPE the pork rind to make sure it is free of any bristles. Tie up like a package to hold its shape, then place in a clay pot or braising pan of boiling water, return to a boil and skim off any impurities. Simmer, covered, for 45–50 minutes.

TURN OFF the heat and cool the pork in the water, without taking off the lid, for at least 4 hours, transferring the pot or braising pan to the fridge once it is cool enough. Remove the pork from the liquid and drain, rind side up, for 2–3 hours.

CUT OFF the rind, leaving a thin layer of fat. Cut the pork against the grain into thin slices. Combine the remaining ingredients and pour over the pork.

A meat stand in an outdoor market in Sichuan.

Chinese spirits are sold in fancy packaging. The Wuliangye shown here is made from five grains: sorghum, corn, wheat and two kinds of rice.

酸甜红烧排骨

SPARERIBS WITH SWEET-AND-SOUR SAUCE

THIS DELICIOUS DISH IS CANTONESE IN ORIGIN. THE SAUCE SHOULD BE BRIGHT AND TRANSLUCENT, THE MEAT TENDER AND SUCCULENT, AND THE FLAVOR NEITHER TOO SWEET NOR TOO SOUR. IF YOU PREFER YOU CAN USE A BONELESS CUT OF PORK SUCH AS LOIN.

1 lb Chinese-style pork spareribs
1/4 teaspoon salt
1/4 teaspoon freshly ground black pepper
1 teaspoon sugar
1 tablespoon Chinese spirit (Mou Tai) or brandy
1 egg yolk, beaten
1 tablespoon cornstarch
oil for deep-frying

SAUCE
1 tablespoon oil
1 small green pepper, shredded
3 tablespoons sugar
2 tablespoons clear rice vinegar
1 tablespoon light soy sauce
1 tablespoon tomato paste
1/4 teaspoon roasted sesame oil
1/4 cup chicken and meat stock (page 281)
2 teaspoons cornstarch

SERVES 4

ASK the butcher to cut the slab of spareribs crosswise into thirds that measure 1 1/2–2 inches in length, or use a cleaver to do so yourself. Cut the ribs between the bones to separate them. Put the pieces in a bowl with the salt, pepper, sugar and Chinese spirit. Marinate in the fridge for at least 35 minutes, turning occasionally.

MEANWHILE, blend the egg yolk with the cornstarch and enough water to make a thin batter. Remove the spareribs from the marinade and coat them with the batter.

FILL a wok one quarter full of oil. Heat the oil to 350°F, or until a piece of bread fries golden brown in 15 seconds when dropped in the oil. Fry the spareribs in batches for 5 minutes until they are crisp and golden, stirring to separate them, then remove and drain. Reheat the oil and fry the spareribs again for 1 minute to darken their color. Remove and drain well on crumpled paper towels. Keep warm in a low oven.

TO MAKE the sauce, heat a wok over high heat, add the oil and heat until very hot. Stir-fry the green pepper for a few seconds, then add the sugar, rice vinegar, soy sauce, tomato paste, sesame oil and stock, and bring to a boil. Combine the cornstarch with enough water to make a paste, add to the sauce and simmer until thickened. Add the spareribs and toss to coat them with the sauce. Serve hot.

A tea seller in Guangzhou.

豆瓣炒牛肉

BEEF WITH PEPPERS AND BLACK BEAN SAUCE

LEAN STEAK IS A PARTICULARLY GOOD CUT OF BEEF FOR STIR-FRYING. THE TRADITIONAL VERSION OF THIS CANTONESE DISH CALLS FOR JUST GREEN PEPPERS, BUT THIS RECIPE USES ALL DIFFERENT COLORS TO MAKE A MORE ATTRACTIVE DISH.

1 1/2 lb beef top round steak, trimmed
1 tablespoon light soy sauce
2 teaspoons Shaoxing rice wine
1/2 teaspoon roasted sesame oil
1 teaspoon cornstarch
1 cup oil

BLACK BEAN SAUCE
1 tablespoon oil
1/4 cup finely chopped scallions
1 tablespoon finely chopped garlic
1 tablespoon salted, fermented black beans, rinsed and coarsely chopped
1 tablespoon finely chopped ginger
1 green pepper, shredded
1 red pepper, shredded
1 orange or yellow pepper, shredded
2 teaspoons light soy sauce
1 tablespoon Shaoxing rice wine
1 teaspoon sugar
2 1/2 tablespoons chicken stock (page 281)
1/2 teaspoon roasted sesame oil
2 teaspoons cornstarch

SERVES 6

CUT the beef against the grain into very thin slices. Cut each slice of beef into thin strips and place in a bowl. Add the soy sauce, rice wine, sesame oil, cornstarch and 1 tablespoon water, toss lightly to combine, then marinate in the fridge for 30 minutes. Drain the beef.

HEAT a wok over high heat, add the oil and heat until almost smoking. Add a third of the beef and cook, stirring constantly, for 1 minute, or until the pieces brown. Remove with a wire strainer or slotted spoon, then drain. Repeat with the remaining beef.

TO MAKE the black bean sauce, heat a wok over high heat, add the oil and heat until very hot. Stir-fry the scallions, garlic, black beans and ginger for 10 seconds, or until fragrant. Add the peppers and stir-fry for 1 minute, or until cooked.

COMBINE the soy sauce, rice wine, sugar, stock, sesame oil and cornstarch, add to the sauce and simmer until thickened. Add the beef and toss lightly to coat with the sauce.

红烧牛肉

RED-COOKED BEEF

THIS IS BASICALLY A STEW, SLOW-COOKED IN AN EQUAL MIXTURE OF SOY SAUCE, RICE WINE AND GINGER. THIS DISH IS A VERY HOME-STYLE ONE, MORE LIKELY FOUND IN SOMEONE'S KITCHEN THAN ON A RESTAURANT MENU.

- 1 lb boneless stewing beef, such as chuck or bottom round, trimmed
- 3 tablespoons Shaoxing rice wine
- 3 slices ginger
- 3 tablespoons dark soy sauce
- 2 oz rock sugar
- 3/4 lb carrots
- 1 teaspoon salt

SERVES 4

CUT the beef into 5/8 inch cubes and put in a clay pot or braising pan with enough water to cover. Add the rice wine and ginger, bring to a boil, skim off any impurities, then simmer, covered, for 35–40 minutes. Add the soy sauce and sugar and simmer for 10–15 minutes.

CUT the carrots into pieces roughly the same size as the beef, add to the saucepan with the salt and cook for 20–25 minutes.

RED-COOKED BEEF

五香牛肉

FIVE-SPICE BEEF

THIS IS A DELICIOUS BEEF RECIPE THAT IS VERY SIMPLE TO PREPARE. THE LIQUID IN WHICH THE BEEF HAS BEEN COOKED CAN BE REUSED FOR COOKING OTHER TYPES OF MEAT OR POULTRY, AND IS KNOWN AS LUSHUI ZHI—A "MASTER SAUCE."

- 1 1/2 lb boneless stewing beef, such as chuck or bottom round, trimmed
- 2 scallions, each tied in a knot
- 3 slices ginger, smashed with the flat side of a cleaver
- 4 tablespoons Chinese spirit (Mou Tai) or brandy
- 6 cups chicken and meat stock (page 281)
- 1 teaspoon salt
- 4 tablespoons light soy sauce
- 3 tablespoons dark soy sauce
- 1 tablespoon five-spice powder
- 5 oz rock sugar
- 1 scallion, finely sliced
- 1 teaspoon roasted sesame oil

SERVES 8

CUT the beef into 2–3 long strips and place in a clay pot or braising pan with the scallions, ginger, Chinese spirit and stock. Bring to a boil and skim off any impurities. Simmer, covered, for 15–20 minutes.

ADD the salt, soy sauces, five-spice powder and sugar to the beef, return to a boil, then simmer, covered, for 25–30 minutes.

ALLOW the beef to cool in the liquid for 1 hour, then remove, drain, and continue to cool for 3–4 hours. Just before serving, slice thinly against the grain and sprinkle with the chopped scallion and sesame oil.

THE SAUCE can be reused as a "Master Sauce" (see page 290).

Tying the scallions into knots bruises the flesh and allows more flavor to come out.

FIVE-SPICE BEEF

蒙古火锅

MONGOLIAN HOTPOT

THE HOTPOT WAS INTRODUCED TO NORTHERN CHINA BY THE MONGOLIANS, BUT IT SOON BECAME SO POPULAR THAT REGIONAL VARIATIONS EVOLVED. TRADITIONALLY LAMB OR BEEF IS USED, AS IN THIS SLIGHTLY ADAPTED VERSION OF THE NORTHERN CLASSIC.

The Great Wall of China.

A hotpot restaurant in Yunnan.

11 oz beef top round steak, trimmed
1 tablespoon light soy sauce
1/3 cup Shaoxing rice wine
1/2 teaspoon roasted sesame oil
1/2 lb Chinese (Napa) cabbage, stems removed and leaves cut into 2 inch squares
1 tablespoon oil
2 garlic cloves, smashed with the flat side of a cleaver
3 cups chicken stock (page 281)
1/2 teaspoon salt
1 oz bean thread noodles
1/2 lb Chinese mushrooms (shiitake) or button mushrooms
4 cups baby spinach

DIPPING SAUCE
2 tablespoons light soy sauce
1 tablespoon Shaoxing rice wine
1 teaspoon Chinese black rice vinegar
1 teaspoon sugar
1/2 teaspoon chili sauce or dried chili flakes (optional)
1/2 scallion, finely chopped
1 teaspoon finely chopped ginger
1 garlic clove, finely chopped

SERVES 6

CUT the beef against the grain into paper-thin slices. Place in a bowl and add the soy sauce, 1 tablespoon of the rice wine and the sesame oil, toss lightly, and arrange the slices on a platter.

SEPARATE the hard cabbage pieces from the leafy ones. Heat a wok over high heat, add the oil and heat until very hot. Stir-fry the hard cabbage pieces and garlic for several minutes, adding 1 tablespoon of water. Add the leafy cabbage pieces and stir-fry for several minutes. Add the remaining rice wine, chicken stock and salt, and bring to a boil. Reduce the heat and simmer for 20 minutes.

SOAK the bean thread noodles in hot water for 10 minutes, then drain and cut into 6 inch pieces. Arrange the mushrooms, spinach and noodles on several platters and place on a table where a heated Mongolian hotpot has been set up. (If you do not have a Mongolian hotpot, use an electric frying pan or an electric wok.)

COMBINE the dipping sauce ingredients and divide among 6 bowls. Put a bowl of dipping sauce at each diner's place.

POUR the cabbage soup mixture into the hotpot and bring to a boil. To eat, each diner takes a slice of meat, dips it into the hot stock until the meat is cooked, then dips the meat into the dipping sauce, and eats. The mushrooms, noodles and spinach are cooked in the same way and dipped in the sauce before eating. Supply small wire strainers to cook the noodles so they stay together. The mushrooms and noodles should cook for 5 to 6 minutes, but the spinach should only take about 1 minute. Once all the ingredients have been eaten, the soup is eaten.

香脆牛肉片

CRISPY SHREDDED BEEF

THE ORIGINS OF THIS DISH ARE A BIT OBSCURE, THOUGH SOME CLAIM THAT IT IS FROM SICHUAN OR HUNAN, PROBABLY BECAUSE IT IS SPICY. MAKE SURE THE BEEF IS REALLY CRISPY WHEN YOU FRY IT.

13 oz beef top round steak, trimmed
2 eggs, beaten
1/2 teaspoon salt
4 tablespoons cornstarch
oil for deep-frying
2 carrots, finely shredded
2 scallions, shredded
1 garlic clove, finely chopped
2 red chiles, shredded
4 tablespoons superfine sugar
3 tablespoons Chinese black rice vinegar
2 tablespoons light soy sauce

SERVES 4

CUT the beef into thin shreds. Combine the eggs, salt and cornstarch, then coat the shredded beef with the batter. Mix well.

FILL a wok one quarter full of oil. Heat the oil to 350°F, or until a piece of bread fries golden brown in 15 seconds when dropped in the oil. Cook the beef for 3–4 minutes, stirring to separate, then remove and drain. Cook the carrots for 1 1/2 minutes, then remove and drain. Pour out the oil, reserving 1 tablespoon.

REHEAT the reserved oil over high heat until very hot and stir-fry the scallion, garlic and chiles for a few seconds. Add the beef, carrots, sugar, vinegar and soy sauce and stir to combine.

CRISPY SHREDDED BEEF

青葱炒牛肉

STIR-FRIED BEEF WITH SCALLIONS

THIS NORTHERN DISH COMBINES DELICIOUSLY TENDER BEEF WITH A LIGHT GLAZE OF SOY SAUCE AND SUGAR AND FRIED SCALLIONS. YOU CAN SERVE IT WITH MANDARIN PANCAKES OR RICE.

1 lb beef top round steak, trimmed
2 garlic cloves, finely chopped
2 tablespoons light soy sauce
1 tablespoon Shaoxing rice wine
2 teaspoons sugar
1 tablespoon cornstarch
3 tablespoons oil
5 scallions, green part only, cut into thin strips

SAUCE
3 tablespoons light soy sauce
2 teaspoons sugar
1/2 teaspoon roasted sesame oil

SERVES 6

CUT the beef against the grain into slices 3/4 inch thick, then cut into bite-size pieces. Combine in a bowl with the garlic, soy sauce, rice wine, sugar and cornstarch. Marinate in the fridge for at least 1 hour. Drain.

TO MAKE the sauce, combine all the ingredients.

HEAT a wok over high heat, add the oil and heat until very hot. Cook the beef in 2 batches for 1 1/2 minutes, or until brown. Remove and drain. Pour out the oil, reserving 1 tablespoon.

REHEAT the reserved oil over high heat until very hot and stir-fry the scallion for 1 minute. Add the beef and the sauce. Toss well.

STIR-FRIED BEEF WITH SCALLIONS

BEEF WITH OYSTER SAUCE

- 10 oz beef top round steak, trimmed
- 1 teaspoon sugar
- 1 tablespoon dark soy sauce
- 2 teaspoons Shaoxing rice wine
- 2 teaspoons cornstarch
- 4 dried Chinese mushrooms
- oil for deep-frying
- 4 slices ginger
- 1 scallion, cut into short pieces
- 3/4 cup snow peas, ends trimmed
- 1 small carrot, thinly sliced
- 1/2 teaspoon salt
- 2–3 tablespoons chicken and meat stock (page 281)
- 2 tablespoons oyster sauce

SERVES 4

CUT the beef against the grain into thin bite-size slices. Combine with half the sugar, the soy sauce, rice wine, cornstarch and 2 tablespoons water. Marinate in the fridge for several hours, or overnight.

SOAK the dried mushrooms in boiling water for 30 minutes, then drain and squeeze out any excess water. Remove and discard the stems and cut the caps in half, or quarters if large.

FILL a wok one quarter full of oil. Heat the oil to 180°C (350°F), or until a piece of bread fries golden brown in 15 seconds when dropped in the oil. Cook the beef for 45–50 seconds, stirring to separate the pieces, and remove as soon as the color changes. Drain well in a colander. Pour out the oil, reserving 2 tablespoons.

REHEAT the reserved oil over high heat until very hot and stir-fry the ginger and scallion for 1 minute. Add the snow peas, mushrooms and carrot and stir-fry for 1 minute, then add the salt, stock and remaining sugar and stir-fry for 1 minute. Toss with the beef and oyster sauce.

STEAMED BEEF WITH RICE FLOUR

蒸面粉牛肉

STEAMED BEEF WITH RICE FLOUR

- 1 lb beef top round steak, trimmed
- 2 tablespoons soy sauce
- 1 tablespoon chile bean paste (toban jiang)
- 1 tablespoon Shaoxing rice wine
- 1 tablespoon finely chopped ginger
- 1/4 teaspoon freshly ground white pepper
- 1 tablespoon oil
- 3/4 cup glutinous rice flour
- 1/2 teaspoon ground cinnamon
- 1 teaspoon roasted sesame oil
- 1 scallion, shredded

SERVES 4

CUT the beef into 3/4 inch slices and cut the slices into bite-size pieces. Combine with the soy sauce, chile bean paste, rice wine, ginger, pepper and oil. Marinate in the fridge for 30 minutes.

DRY-FRY the rice flour in a wok until it is brown and smells roasted. Add the cinnamon. Drain the beef and toss in the rice flour to coat the slices.

PLACE the beef slices in a steamer lined with waxed paper punched with holes. Cover and steam over simmering water in a wok for 20 minutes. Sprinkle with the sesame oil and garnish with the shredded scallion.

蒙古羊肉

MONGOLIAN LAMB

- 10 oz lamb steak
- 2 teaspoons finely chopped ginger
- 1 scallion, chopped
- 2 teaspoons ground Sichuan peppercorns
- 1 teaspoon salt
- 2 tablespoons light soy sauce
- 1 tablespoon yellow bean sauce
- 1 tablespoon hoisin sauce
- 1 teaspoon five-spice powder
- 2 tablespoons Shaoxing rice wine
- oil for deep-frying
- crisp lettuce leaves
- 1/3 cup hoisin sauce, extra
- 1/2 cucumber, shredded
- 6 scallions, shredded

SERVES 4

CUT the lamb along the grain into 6 long strips. Combine with the ginger, scallion, pepper, salt, soy sauce, yellow bean and hoisin sauces, five-spice powder and rice wine. Marinate in the fridge for at least 2 hours. Put the lamb and marinade in a flameproof dish in a steamer. Cover and steam for 2 1/2–3 hours over simmering water in a wok, replenishing with boiling water during cooking. Remove the lamb from the liquid and drain well.

FILL a wok one quarter full of oil. Heat the oil to 350°F, or until a piece of bread fries golden brown in 15 seconds when dropped in the oil. Cook the lamb for 3–4 minutes, then remove and drain. Cut the lamb into bite-size shreds.

TO SERVE, place some lamb in the lettuce leaves with some hoisin sauce, cucumber and scallions and roll up into a package.

Making bread and pancakes at a street stall in Beijing.

韭菜炒羊肉

STIR-FRIED LAMB AND LEEKS

- 10 oz lamb steak
- 1/4 teaspoon ground Sichuan peppercorns
- 1/2 teaspoon sugar
- 1 tablespoon light soy sauce
- 2 teaspoons Shaoxing rice wine
- 2 teaspoons cornstarch
- 1/2 teaspoon roasted sesame oil
- 3 tablespoons dried black fungus (wood ears)
- 2 1/2 cups oil
- 4 small pieces ginger
- 1 1/2 cups young leeks, white part only, cut into short lengths
- 2 tablespoons yellow bean sauce

SERVES 4

CUT the lamb into thin slices and combine with the Sichuan peppercorns, sugar, soy sauce, rice wine, cornstarch and sesame oil. Marinate in the fridge for at least 2 hours.

SOAK the dried black fungus in cold water for 20 minutes, then drain and squeeze out any excess water.

HEAT a wok over high heat, add the oil and heat until very hot. Stir-fry the lamb for 1 minute, or until the color changes. Remove and drain. Pour out the oil, reserving 2 tablespoons.

REHEAT the reserved oil over high heat until very hot and stir-fry the ginger, leeks and black fungus for 1 minute, then add the yellow bean sauce, blend well, and add the lamb. Continue stirring for 1 minute.

STIR-FRIED LAMB AND LEEKS

BEAN CURD

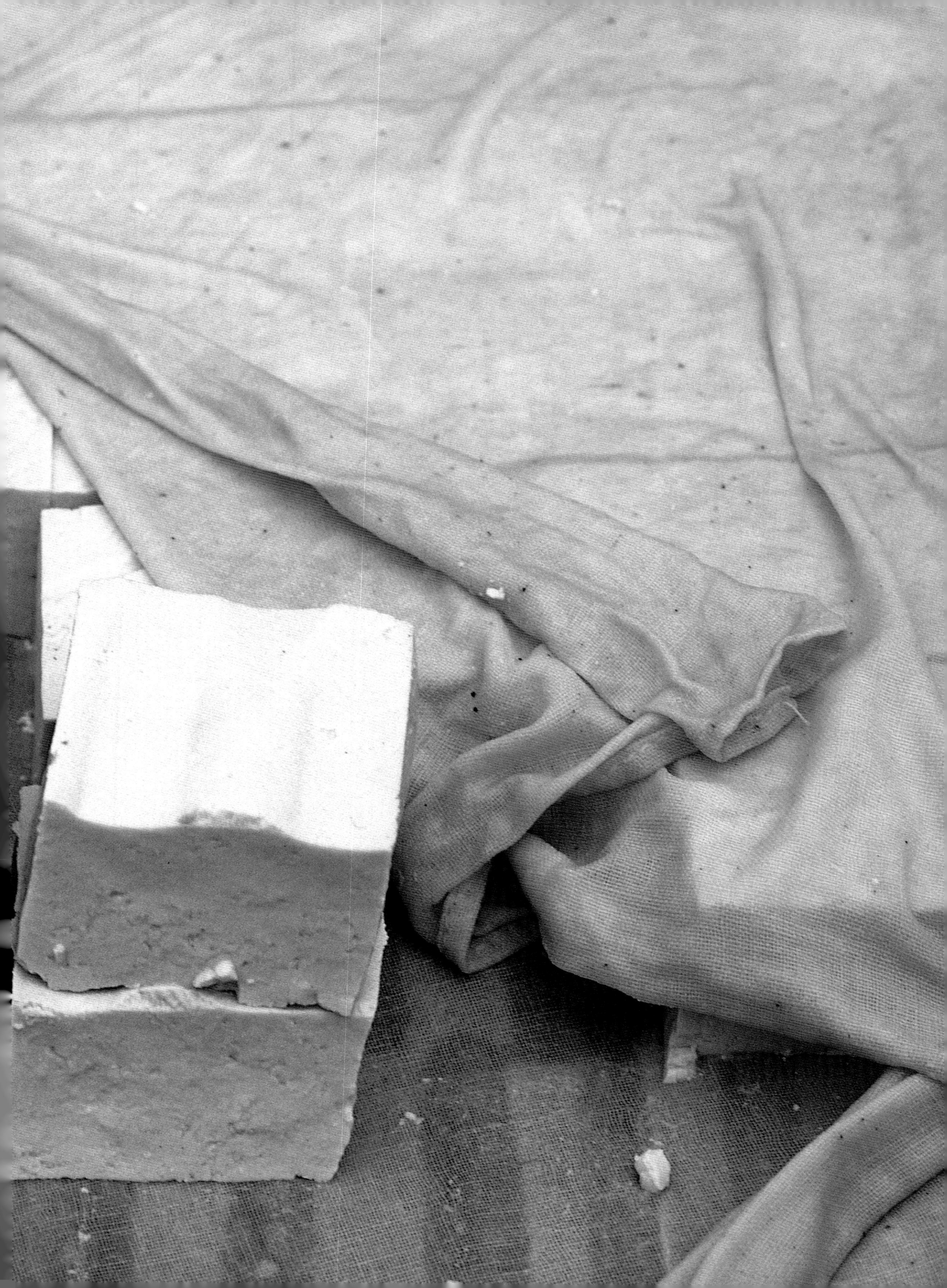

香菇焖豆腐

BRAISED BEAN CURD WITH CHINESE MUSHROOMS

SOME PEOPLE FIND BEAN CURD BLAND, BUT BY COOKING IT WITH STRONGLY FLAVORED MUSHROOMS, YOU HAVE A WELL-BALANCED DISH WITH A CONTRAST IN COLOR, AROMA, FLAVOR AND TEXTURE.

10 oz firm bean curd, drained
1 3/4 oz dried Chinese mushrooms
4 tablespoons oil
1 teaspoon salt
1 teaspoon sugar
1 tablespoon Shaoxing rice wine
1/2 teaspoon roasted sesame oil
1 teaspoon cornstarch
1 tablespoon light soy sauce

SERVES 4

CUT the bean curd into strips. Soak the dried mushrooms in boiling water for 30 minutes, then drain, reserving the soaking liquid, and squeeze out any excess water. Remove and discard the stems. Cut the caps in half.

HEAT a wok over high heat, add the oil and heat until very hot. Stir-fry the mushrooms for 35 seconds, then add 1/2 cup of the reserved liquid and bring to a boil. Add the bean curd, salt, sugar and rice wine, and stir very gently to blend well. Braise for 2 minutes, making sure there is enough liquid to prevent the bean curd from sticking to the wok, then sprinkle with the sesame oil.

COMBINE the cornstarch and soy sauce with enough of the reserved liquid to make a paste. Add to the sauce and simmer to form a clear, light glaze.

FERMENTED BEAN CURD WITH ASIAN GREENS

青菜炒腐酱

FERMENTED BEAN CURD WITH ASIAN GREENS

USE ANY SELECTION OF ASIAN GREENS THAT YOU WISH—CHOY SUM, BOK CHOY, CHINESE CABBAGE, CHINESE BROCCOLI AND WATER SPINACH ARE ALL SUITABLE. FERMENTED WHITE BEAN CURD IS STRONG, ESPECIALLY IF IT CONTAINS CHILES, SO DON'T BE TEMPTED TO ADD ANY MORE TO THE RECIPE.

1 1/4 lb choy sum
1/2 lb bok choy
1 tablespoon oil
3 garlic cloves, crushed
3 tablespoons fermented white bean curd
1 teaspoon light soy sauce
3 tablespoons oyster sauce
2 teaspoons sugar
1 teaspoon roasted sesame oil

SERVES 4

CUT the choy sum horizontally into thirds and the bok choy into thirds and then quarters. Trim off any roots that may hold the pieces together, then wash well and dry thoroughly.

HEAT a wok over high heat, add the oil and heat until very hot. Stir-fry the garlic and bean curd for 1 minute. Add the choy sum stems and stir-fry for 1 minute, then add the leaves and bok choy and stir-fry for 1–2 minutes, or until the vegetables just start to wilt. Add the soy and oyster sauces, sugar and sesame oil and toss everything together.

Selling snacks in Yunnan.

麻婆豆腐

MA PO DOUFU

A QUINTESSENTIAL SICHUAN-STYLE DISH, SUPPOSEDLY NAMED AFTER AN OLD WOMAN WHO SERVED THIS IN HER RESTAURANT AND WHOSE POCKMARKED COMPLEXION LED TO THE DISH BEING CALLED MA PO DOUFU, "POCKMARKED GRANDMOTHER'S DOUFU." SOFT BEAN CURD IS TRADITIONALLY USED.

- 1 1/2 lb soft or firm bean curd, drained
- 1/2 lb ground beef or pork
- 2 tablespoons dark soy sauce
- 1 1/2 tablespoons Shaoxing rice wine
- 1/2 teaspoon roasted sesame oil
- 2 teaspoons Sichuan peppercorns
- 1 tablespoon oil
- 2 scallions, finely chopped
- 2 garlic cloves, finely chopped
- 2 teaspoons finely chopped ginger
- 1 tablespoon chile bean paste (toban jiang), or to taste
- 1 cup chicken and meat stock (page 281)
- 1 1/2 teaspoons cornstarch
- 1 scallion, finely shredded

SERVES 6

CUT the bean curd into cubes. Place the meat in a bowl with 2 teaspoons of the soy sauce, 2 teaspoons of the rice wine and the sesame oil, and toss lightly. Dry-fry the Sichuan peppercorns in a wok or frying pan until brown and aromatic, then crush lightly.

HEAT a wok over high heat, add the oil and heat until very hot. Stir-fry the meat until browned, mashing and chopping to separate the pieces. Remove the meat with a wire strainer or slotted spoon and heat the oil until any liquid from the meat has evaporated. Add the scallions, garlic and ginger and stir-fry for 10 seconds, or until fragrant. Add the chile bean paste and stir-fry for 5 seconds.

COMBINE the stock with the remaining soy sauce and rice wine. Add to the wok, bring to a boil, then add the bean curd and meat. Return to a boil, reduce the heat to medium and cook for 5 minutes, or until the sauce has reduced by a quarter. If you are using soft bean curd, do not stir or it will break up.

COMBINE the cornstarch with enough water to make a paste, add to the sauce and simmer until thickened. Season if necessary. Serve sprinkled with the scallion and Sichuan peppercorns.

Fresh bean curd and chile pastes are readily available at the markets in China.

BRAISED BEAN CURD

焖豆腐

BRAISED BEAN CURD

BEAN CURD PICKS UP ITS FLAVOR FROM THE INGREDIENTS IT IS COOKED WITH. THE VEGETABLES SHOULD BE COOKED THROUGH, BUT NOT SO MUCH THAT THEY ARE SOFT AND MUSHY.

8 dried Chinese mushrooms
3 1/3 cups Chinese cabbage or choy sum
7 oz firm bean curd, drained
1/4 lb carrots
1/4 lb baby corn
3–4 tablespoons oil
2 tablespoons light soy sauce or oyster sauce
1 teaspoon salt
1/2 teaspoon sugar
1 tablespoon Shaoxing rice wine
2 scallions, cut into short pieces
1 teaspoon roasted sesame oil

SERVES 4

SOAK the dried mushrooms in boiling water for 30 minutes, then drain, reserving the liquid, and squeeze out any excess water. Remove and discard the stems and cut the caps in half.

CUT the cabbage into large pieces and the bean curd into 12 cubes. Diagonally cut the carrots. Leave the corn whole if small, or cut into pieces.

LINE a clay pot, braising pan or saucepan with the Chinese cabbage and pour in 1/4 cup of the reserved liquid. Heat a wok over high heat, add half the oil and heat until very hot. Lightly brown the bean curd for 2–3 minutes, transfer to the pot and add the soy or oyster sauce.

REHEAT the wok over high heat, add the remaining oil and heat until very hot. Stir-fry the carrots, corn and mushrooms for 1 minute. Add the salt, sugar and rice wine, blend well, then transfer to the pot. Bring to a boil, place the scallions on top, then simmer, covered, for 15–20 minutes. Sprinkle with the sesame oil.

Soft bean curd is sold by shops and traveling carts and is eaten as a snack. Here it is dressed with honey.

小葱辣椒拌豆腐

SOFT BEAN CURD WITH CHILE AND SCALLIONS

THIS RECIPE PERFECTLY SETS OFF THE SOFT, COOL SMOOTHNESS OF THE BEAN CURD BY ADDING A HOT, HIGHLY SPICED DRESSING. SERVE WITH RICE AND STIR-FRIED GREENS FOR A HEALTHY MEAL.

1/2 lb soft bean curd, drained
2 scallions, thinly sliced
1 red chile, thinly sliced
2 tablespoons chopped cilantro
2 tablespoons soy sauce
1/3 cup oil
1 teaspoon roasted sesame oil

SERVES 4

CUT the bean curd into cubes and put it on a flameproof plate.

SCATTER the scallions, chile, cilantro and soy sauce over the bean curd. Put the oils in a small saucepan and heat until they are smoking, then immediately pour the oils over the bean curd.

SOFT BEAN CURD WITH CHILE AND SCALLIONS

THE LEE KUM KEE factory at Xinhui, China, makes soy sauce according to traditional methods. It uses premium soya beans, wheat flour and its own unique starter culture *(left)* rather than chemicals. The resulting soy sauce is analyzed for quality by a soy sauce master before bottling. To make the sauce, the beans are first cleaned, soaked, defatted and cooked by steaming *(middle and right)*.

SOY

SOYA BEANS ARE RARELY EATEN WHOLE, BUT WHEN TRANSFORMED INTO SOY SAUCE, BEAN CURD, SOY MILK, VEGETABLE OIL, FERMENTED BEANS, BEAN PASTES OR SHAPED INTO NOODLES, THEY BECOME ONE OF THE ESSENTIAL INGREDIENTS OF CHINESE COOKING.

Soya beans have grown in China for perhaps 5,000 years, and it is from here that they spread to the rest of Asia. Importantly, they provide a valuable source of protein in a country where the diet sometimes includes little meat. Soya beans are sprouted as bean sprouts, which benefit from being cooked as they have a strong flavour, and sometimes eaten from the pod as a snack or thrown into stir-fries, but the protein in them can generally only be unlocked through processing the relatively undigestable beans in various ways.

SOY SAUCE

Invented in China over 2,000 years ago, soy sauce *(jiang you)* is one of the traditional seven necessities of a Chinese household, along with tea, salt, oil, vinegar, rice and firewood. First brought to Europe in the seventeenth century, soya beans are actually called after the sauce rather than the other way around, though the name is really a misnomer, as it is not so much a sauce as a flavouring extracted from fermented beans. Properly prepared soy sauce is made from mixing the beans with wheat flour to form a paste. This mixture is then fermented using two different *Aspergillus* moulds. Once the maturing process is complete, the sauce is strained and bottled. The fermentation produces a mix of flavours—salt, amino acids, sugars, acids, esters and alcohols—and the final flavour of each batch is controlled by the soy sauce master.

AT THE KUNG WO BEAN CURD FACTORY in Sham Shui Po, Hong Kong, 100 kg of beans a day are soaked for 5 hours, then ground up with water to make soy milk. This milk is boiled, left to settle, and the milk separated from the sediment. Finally the milk is coagulated *(far left)*. Curds are put into a mould and drained to form blocks *(middle)*, or poured into vats to set as soft bean curd and scooped into bowls *(right)*

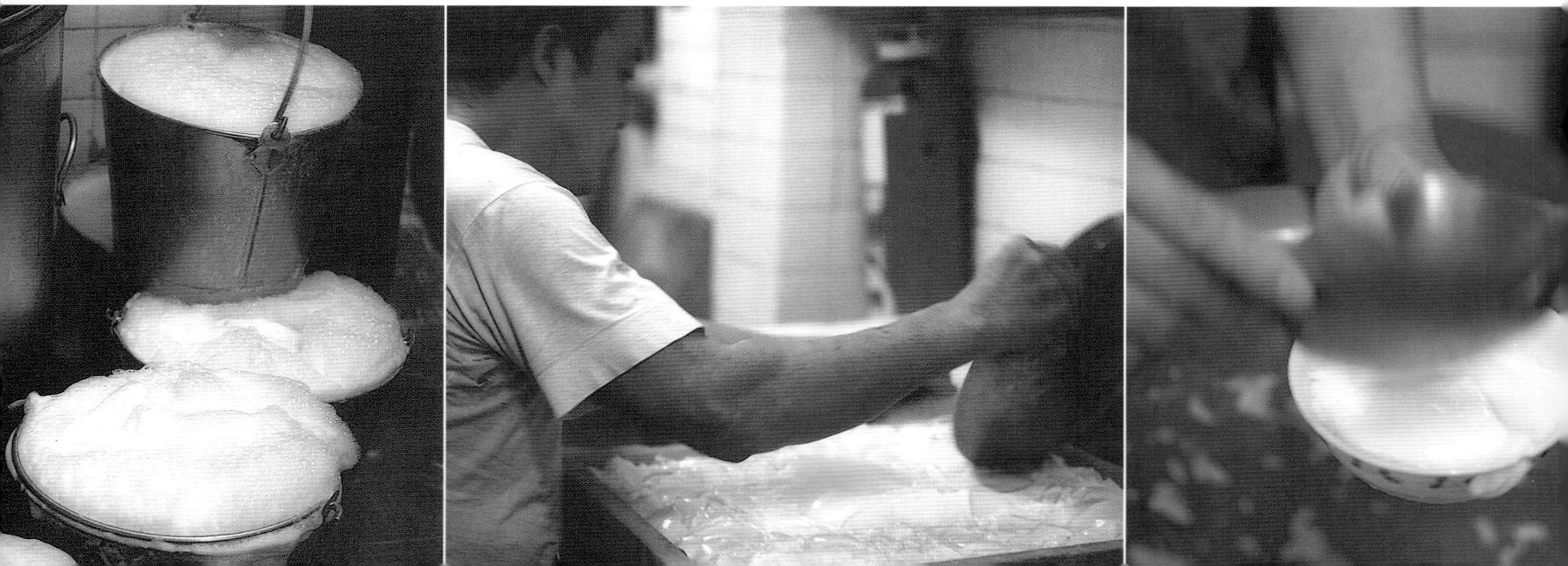

After spraying with the starter culture and wheat flour *(left)*, they are left to ferment for a few days. The mixture is then put in a fermentation tank with brine *(middle)* and fermented for 3 months, circulating it by drawing liquid from the bottom and spraying it back in at the top *(right)*. The raw soy is drawn off, and the sediment is allowed to settle. The soy sauce is then analyzed, filtered, sterilized and bottled.

Chinese cooking uses both light and dark soy sauces. Light soy *(shengchou)* comes from the first pressing and has a light colour and a delicate, salty flavour. It is often just labelled as soy sauce and is used with white meat, fish and vegetables. Dark soy *(laochou)* is aged for longer than light, giving it a brownish-black colour and thicker texture. It sometimes has caramel added as well and is used with red meats and for red-cooking and braising. Chinese food is seasoned in the kitchen, so both types are often mixed within recipes. In Guangzhou, soy is always provided at the table as a condiment, unlike in the rest of China.

BEAN CURD

Bean curd or dofu (tofu in Japanese) is eaten all over China Fresh bean curd does not have much flavour of its own and is very versatile—it absorbs the flavourings and seasonings of the ingredients it is mixed with and can be cooked by any method. The Chinese also prize its unique texture. Bean curd is made in a similar way to cheese. Dried beans are soaked, then crushed with water to make soy 'milk', boiled and coagulated. The curd is left to set and drain like fresh cheese. Soft tofu is allowed to retain a lot of moisture, while firm tofu is better drained, and pressed tofu has had almost all of its moisture removed.

BEAN CURD PRODUCTS

Bean curd can also be processed into other forms:

FERMENTED BEAN CURD a seasoning ingredient made from fermented, dried cubes of curd, marinated with chillies, spices and alcohol (white tofu) and served as a spicy side dish, or coloured red with red fermented rice (red tofu) and used as a potent condiment or to flavour congee.

MOULDY BEAN CURD rancid bean curd with a strong taste that has been left to develop blue veins or a furry white rind. It is used as a pungent ingredient in cooking.

BEAN CURD SKIN made by lifting off the skin that forms on top of boiling soy milk before coagulation and drying it. The brittle sheets and rolled sticks need to be soaked before use.

and served warm to the breakfast trade with syrup. Later in the day, bowls of refrigerated soft bean curd are served as a savoury or sweet snack *(left)*. Soy milk, which has been strained after the milk is boiled and not coagulated, is sold as a cold drink *(middle)* and the blocks *(right)* are sold by weight and also turned into fermented bean curd, deep-fried puffs and a snack of fried, stuffed bean curd in the shop.

Transporting bean curd in Hangzhou.

The Temple of Heaven in Beijing.

北方豆腐

NORTHERN-STYLE BEAN CURD

THIS DISH WAS APPARENTLY A FAVORITE OF DOWAGER EMPRESS TZU-HSI IN THE NINETEENTH CENTURY, AND IT'S STILL A POPULAR CLASSIC IN CHINA TODAY. THE BEAN CURD IS FIRST FRIED, THEN SIMMERED SO THAT IT MELTS IN YOUR MOUTH.

2 lb firm bean curd, drained
oil for deep-frying
1 cup cornstarch
2 eggs, lightly beaten
1 tablespoon finely chopped ginger
1 1/3 cups chicken stock (page 281)
2 tablespoons Shaoxing rice wine
1 teaspoon salt, or to taste
1/2 teaspoon sugar
1 1/2 teaspoons roasted sesame oil
2 scallions, green part only, finely chopped

SERVES 6

HOLDING a cleaver parallel to the cutting surface, slice each bean curd cake in half horizontally. Cut each piece into 1 1/4 inch squares.

FILL a wok one quarter full of oil. Heat the oil to 375°F, or until a piece of bread fries golden brown in 10 seconds when dropped in the oil. Coat each piece of bean curd in the cornstarch, then dip in the beaten egg to coat. Cook the bean curd in batches for 3–4 minutes on each side, or until golden brown. Remove with a wire strainer or slotted spoon and drain in a colander. Pour out the oil, reserving 1 teaspoon.

REHEAT the reserved oil over high heat until very hot and stir-fry the ginger for 5 seconds, or until fragrant. Add the stock, rice wine, salt and sugar, and bring to a boil. Add the fried bean curd and pierce the pieces with a fork so that they will absorb the cooking liquid. Cook over medium heat for 20 minutes, or until all the liquid is absorbed. Drizzle the sesame oil over the bean curd, toss carefully to coat, sprinkle with the scallions and serve.

An outdoor haircut in Beijing.

豆干包

STUFFED BEAN CURD

SEVERAL VERSIONS EXIST OF THIS HIGHLY POPULAR DISH, WHICH IS THOUGHT TO BE A HAKKA RECIPE FROM THE SOUTHEAST OF CHINA. THE STUFFING HERE IS A MIXTURE OF SHRIMP AND PORK AND THOUGH THE RECIPE MAY APPEAR RATHER COMPLICATED, IT IS WORTH THE EFFORT.

Push the stuffing fairly firmly into the slit in the bean curd—the pocket should be open at one end and the stuffing showing.

- 6 x 2 inch square cakes firm bean curd, drained
- 2 dried Chinese mushrooms
- 2 oz shrimp
- 2 oz ground pork
- a pinch of salt
- 1/2 egg white, beaten
- 1 teaspoon Shaoxing rice wine
- 1 teaspoon light soy sauce
- 1–2 teaspoons cornstarch
- 3–4 tablespoons oil
- 1/4 cup chicken and meat stock (page 281)
- 2 tablespoons oyster sauce
- 1 scallion, sliced

SERVES 4

PARBOIL the bean curd in a saucepan of lightly salted boiling water for 2–3 minutes to harden, then drain. Cut each cake into 2 triangular pieces and make a slit at the bottom of each triangle.

SOAK the dried mushrooms in boiling water for 30 minutes, then drain and squeeze out any excess water. Remove and discard the stems and finely chop the caps. Peel and devein the shrimp and chop them finely until they are almost a paste. Put the mushrooms and shrimp in a bowl with the pork, salt, egg white, rice wine, soy sauce and enough cornstarch to hold the mixture together. Fill the slit of each bean curd piece with stuffing (the pieces will gape open and show the stuffing).

HEAT a wok over high heat, add the oil and heat until very hot. Cook the stuffed bean curd for 2 minutes on each side, or until golden. Pour off any excess oil. Add the stock and oyster sauce, bring to a boil and braise for 5–6 minutes. Sprinkle with the scallion.

STIR-FRIED BEAN CURD IN YELLOW BEAN SAUCE

豆瓣酱炒豆腐

STIR-FRIED BEAN CURD IN YELLOW BEAN SAUCE

- 3/4 lb firm bean curd, drained
- 2 tablespoons oil
- 1 garlic clove, crushed
- 1 1/2 tablespoons yellow bean sauce
- 2 teaspoons oyster sauce
- 2 teaspoons sugar
- 2 teaspoons cornstarch
- 1 scallion, cut into 3/4 inch lengths
- 5 cilantro sprigs

SERVES 4

CUT the bean curd into bite-size pieces. Heat the wok over medium heat, add the oil and heat until hot. Cook the bean curd until it is golden brown on both sides.

ADD the garlic, yellow bean sauce, oyster sauce and sugar and toss until well combined. Combine the cornstarch with 2/3 cup water, add to the sauce with the scallion and simmer until the sauce has thickened and the scallion has softened slightly. If the sauce is still a little thick, add a little water. Garnish with cilantro sprigs.

焖面筋

BRAISED GLUTEN

GLUTEN IS A WHEAT FLOUR DOUGH THAT HAS HAD THE STARCH WASHED AWAY SO IT IS SPONGY AND POROUS, SIMILAR TO BEAN CURD, BUT MUCH FIRMER. IN CHINA, GLUTEN IS USED AS A MOCK MEAT AS IT CAN BE COOKED IN THE SAME WAY. YOU CAN USE 10 OZ STORE-BOUGHT GLUTEN IN THIS RECIPE.

2 lb all-purpose flour
1 1/2 teaspoons salt
oil for deep-frying
1 teaspoon sugar
1 tablespoon light soy sauce
3–4 tablespoons vegetable stock (page 281)
1/4 teaspoon roasted sesame oil

SERVES 4

SIFT the flour into a bowl with 1 teaspoon of the salt and gradually add 2 1/2 cups warm water to make a dough. Knead until smooth, then cover with a damp cloth and allow to rest in a warm place for 55–60 minutes.

RINSE the dough under cold water and wash off all the starch by pulling, stretching and squeezing the dough with your hands. You should have about 10 oz gluten after 10–15 minutes of washing and squeezing. Extract as much water as you can by squeezing the dough hard, then cut the dough into bite-size pieces. Dry thoroughly.

FILL a wok one quarter full of oil. Heat the oil to 350°F, or until a piece of bread fries golden brown in 15 seconds when dropped in the oil. Cook the gluten pieces for 3 minutes, or until golden. Remove and drain. Pour the oil from the wok, leaving 1 teaspoon.

REHEAT the reserved oil over high heat until very hot and add the gluten, remaining salt, sugar, soy sauce and stock, bring to a boil and braise for 2–3 minutes, or until the liquid has evaporated. Sprinkle with the sesame oil. Serve hot or cold.

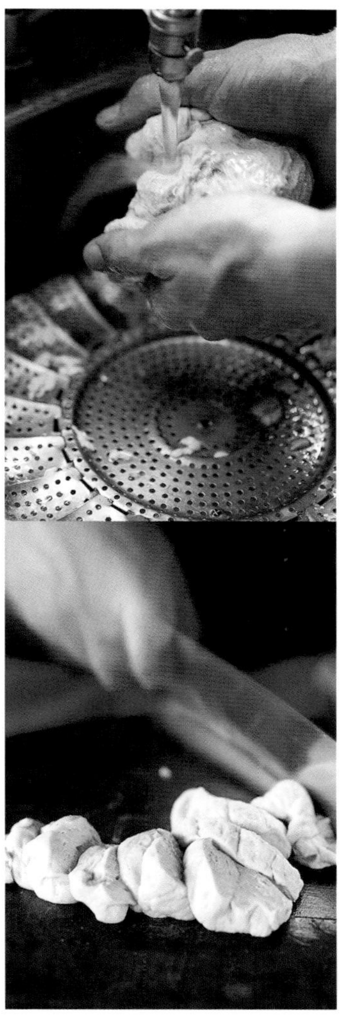

Wash the gluten thoroughly under running water to get rid of the starch. You should end up with a firm, sliceable piece of gluten.

A Buddhist temple in Sichuan.

Incense and temple offerings are on sale at stores in the streets around temples.

MOCK DUCK

GLUTEN IS USED IN VEGETARIAN CHINESE COOKING TO TAKE THE PLACE OF MEAT IN RECIPES. RATHER THAN RESEMBLING DUCK, THIS DISH IS COOKED AS DUCK WOULD BE COOKED. YOU CAN MAKE THE GLUTEN OR USE 10 OZ STORE-BOUGHT GLUTEN—PLAIN OR SHAPED LIKE PIECES OF DUCK.

2 lb all-purpose flour
1 teaspoon salt
$1\frac{1}{2}$ tablespoons cornstarch
2 tablespoons oil
1 green pepper, diced
$\frac{1}{3}$ cup vegetable stock (page 281)
2 tablespoons light soy sauce
2 teaspoons Shaoxing rice wine
1 teaspoon sugar
1 teaspoon roasted sesame oil

SERVES 4

SIFT the flour into a bowl with the salt and gradually add $2\frac{1}{2}$ cups warm water to make a dough. Knead until smooth, then cover with a damp cloth and allow to rest in a warm place for 55–60 minutes.

RINSE the dough under cold water and wash off all the starch by pulling, stretching and squeezing the dough with your hands. You should have about 10 oz gluten after 10–15 minutes of washing and squeezing. Extract as much water as you can by squeezing the dough hard, then cut the dough into bite-size pieces. Dry thoroughly.

TOSS the gluten in 1 tablespoon of the cornstarch. Heat a wok over high heat, add the oil and heat until very hot. Quickly stir-fry the gluten until it is browned all over, then remove from the wok. Stir-fry the pepper until it starts to brown around the edges, then remove. Pour off any excess oil.

ADD the stock, soy sauce, rice wine and sugar to the wok and bring to a boil. Return the gluten and pepper and simmer for 1 minute.

COMBINE the remaining cornstarch with enough water to make a paste, add to the sauce and simmer until thickened. Sprinkle with the sesame oil and serve.

VEGETABLES

Tiger lily buds, or golden needles, are dried unopened lilies. When reconstituted they resemble limp bean sprouts.

Bean curd puffs are cubes of deep-fried bean curd. They have a spongy interior that soaks up liquid and flavors well.

Lighting candles at a Buddhist temple.

佛跳墙

BUDDHA'S DELIGHT

THE ORIGINAL RECIPE FOR THIS WELL-KNOWN VEGETARIAN DISH USED NO LESS THAN EIGHTEEN DIFFERENT INGREDIENTS TO REPRESENT THE EIGHTEEN BUDDHAS. NOWADAYS, ANYTHING BETWEEN SIX TO EIGHT INGREDIENTS IS USUAL PRACTICE.

1/4 cup tiger lily buds
6–8 dried Chinese mushrooms
1/4 oz dried black fungus (wood ears)
5 oz braised gluten (page 198) or store-bought braised gluten, drained
2 oz bean curd puffs
1 cup bean sprouts
1 carrot
4 tablespoons oil
1/2 cup snow peas, ends trimmed
1 teaspoon salt
1/2 teaspoon sugar
4 tablespoons vegetable stock (page 281)
2 tablespoons light soy sauce
1/2 teaspoon roasted sesame oil

SERVES 4

SOAK the tiger lily buds in boiling water for 30 minutes. Rinse and drain the tiger lily buds, and trim off any roots if they are hard. Soak the dried mushrooms in boiling water for 30 minutes, then drain and squeeze out any excess water. Remove and discard the stems and cut the caps in half (or quarters if large). Soak the dried black fungus in cold water for 20 minutes, then drain and squeeze out any excess water. Cut any large pieces of fungus in half.

CUT the gluten and bean curd into small pieces. Wash the bean sprouts, discarding any husks and straggly end pieces, and dry thoroughly. Diagonally cut the carrot into thin slices.

HEAT a wok over high heat, add the oil and heat until very hot. Stir-fry the carrot for 30 seconds, then add the snow peas and bean sprouts. Stir-fry for 1 minute, then add the gluten, bean curd, tiger lily buds, mushrooms, black fungus, salt, sugar, stock and soy sauce. Toss everything together, then cover and braise for 2 minutes at a gentle simmer.

ADD the sesame oil, toss it through the mixture and serve hot or cold.

炒生菜

STIR-FRIED LETTUCE

LETTUCE IS GENERALLY EATEN COOKED IN CHINA AND LOTS OF DIFFERENT VARIETIES ARE AVAILABLE. LETTUCE IS ADDED TO SOUPS, STIR-FRIES AND CASSEROLES, AS WELL AS COOKED ON ITS OWN AS A VEGETABLE. YOU CAN USE ANY CRISP LETTUCE FOR THIS RECIPE.

- $1^1/_2$ lb iceberg or Romaine lettuce
- 1 tablespoon oil
- 4 tablespoons oyster sauce
- 1 teaspoon roasted sesame oil

SERVES 4

CUT the lettuce in half and then into wide strips, trimming off any roots that may hold the pieces together. Wash well and dry thoroughly (if too much water clings to the lettuce it will cause it to steam rather than fry).

HEAT a wok over high heat, add the oil and heat until very hot. Toss the lettuce pieces around the wok until they start to wilt, then add the oyster sauce and toss everything together. Sprinkle with the sesame oil, season and serve.

炒豆芽

BEAN SPROUTS STIR-FRY

BEAN SPROUTS CAN MEAN EITHER SOY BEAN SPROUTS OR MUNG BEAN SPROUTS AND BOTH ARE USED IN THIS RECIPE. SOY BEAN SPROUTS ARE SLIGHTLY BIGGER AND MORE ROBUST FOR COOKING, AS WELL AS BEING MORE COMMONLY FOUND IN CHINA.

- $2^1/_2$ cups mung bean sprouts
- 3 cups soy bean sprouts
- 1 tablespoon oil
- 1 red chile, finely chopped
- 1 scallion, finely chopped
- 2 tablespoons light soy sauce

SERVES 4

WASH the bean sprouts, discarding any husks and straggly end pieces, and drain thoroughly.

HEAT a wok over high heat, add the oil and heat until very hot. Stir-fry the chile and scallion for 30 seconds, add the bean sprouts and toss until they start to wilt. Add the soy sauce and toss for 1 minute, then season and serve.

BEAN SPROUTS STIR-FRY

STIR-FRIED LETTUCE

Fresh bamboo shoots.

炒双冬

STIR-FRIED TWIN WINTER

THIS SIMPLE DISH IS CALLED "TWIN WINTER" BECAUSE BOTH MUSHROOMS AND BAMBOO SHOOTS ARE AT THEIR BEST IN THE WINTER MONTHS. ANOTHER VERSION OF THIS DISH, TRIPLE WINTER, USES BAMBOO SHOOTS AND MUSHROOMS WITH CABBAGE.

- 12 dried Chinese mushrooms
- 1 1/4 cups fresh or canned bamboo shoots, rinsed and drained
- 3 tablespoons oil
- 2 tablespoons light soy sauce
- 2 teaspoons sugar
- 2 teaspoons cornstarch
- 1/2 teaspoon roasted sesame oil

SERVES 4

SOAK the dried mushrooms in boiling water for 30 minutes, then drain, reserving the liquid, and squeeze out any excess water. Remove and discard the stems and cut the caps in half (or quarters if large). Cut the bamboo shoots into small pieces the same size as the mushrooms.

HEAT a wok over high heat, add the oil and heat until very hot. Stir-fry the mushrooms and bamboo shoots for 1 minute. Add the soy sauce and sugar, stir a few times, then add 1/2 cup of the reserved liquid. Bring to a boil and braise for 2 minutes, stirring constantly.

COMBINE the cornstarch with enough water to make a paste, add to the sauce and simmer until thickened. Sprinkle with the sesame oil, blend well and serve.

STIR-FRIED CHINESE CABBAGE

炒包菜

STIR-FRIED CHINESE CABBAGE

CHINESE CABBAGE IS A COOL-WEATHER CROP, BUT IT CAN NOW BE BOUGHT ALL YEAR ROUND. THERE ARE TWO KINDS; ONE HAS A GREEN, FINE LEAF, THE OTHER IS YELLOW AND TIGHTLY CURLED.

- 1 oz dried shrimp
- 1 tablespoon oil
- 3/4 lb Chinese (Napa) cabbage, cut into 1/2 inch strips
- 1 tablespoon light soy sauce
- 2 teaspoons sugar
- 1 tablespoon clear rice vinegar
- 2 teaspoons roasted sesame oil

SERVES 4

SOAK the dried shrimp in boiling water for 1 hour, then drain.

HEAT a wok over high heat, add the oil and heat until very hot. Toss the Chinese cabbage for 2 minutes, or until wilted. Add the shrimp, soy sauce, sugar and rice vinegar and cook for 1 minute. Sprinkle with the sesame oil and serve.

Preserved mustard cabbage *(bottom, second from left)* for sale in Beijing.

回锅长豆

DOUBLE-COOKED YARD-LONG BEANS

THIS SICHUAN-STYLE RECIPE IS SO NAMED BECAUSE THE BEANS, AFTER BEING FRIED UNTIL TENDER, ARE THEN COOKED AGAIN WITH SEASONINGS AND A SAUCE. TRADITIONALLY YARD-LONG, OR SNAKE, BEANS ARE USED. THESE ARE AVAILABLE IN CHINESE MARKETS, BUT HARICOT VERTS ARE ALSO DELICIOUS.

2 lb yard-long (snake) beans or haricot verts, trimmed
6 oz ground pork or beef
2 tablespoons light soy sauce
$1\frac{1}{2}$ tablespoons Shaoxing rice wine
$\frac{1}{2}$ teaspoon roasted sesame oil
oil for deep-frying
5 tablespoons finely chopped preserved mustard cabbage
3 scallions, finely chopped
$1\frac{1}{2}$ teaspoons sugar

SERVES 6

DIAGONALLY cut the beans into 2 inch pieces. Lightly chop the ground meat with a cleaver until it becomes slightly fluffy. Put the meat in a bowl, add 1 teaspoon of the soy sauce, 1 teaspoon of the rice wine and the sesame oil and stir vigorously to combine.

FILL a wok one quarter full of oil. Heat the oil to 350°F, or until a piece of bread fries golden brown in 15 seconds when dropped in the oil. Add $\frac{1}{3}$ of the beans, covering the wok with the lid as they are placed in the oil to prevent the oil from splashing. Cook for $3\frac{1}{2}$–4 minutes, stirring constantly, until they are tender and golden brown at the edges. Remove with a wire strainer or slotted spoon and drain. Reheat the oil and repeat with the remaining beans. Pour the oil from the wok, leaving 1 tablespoon.

REHEAT the reserved oil over high heat until very hot, add the ground meat and stir-fry until the color changes, mashing and chopping to separate the pieces of meat. Push the meat to the side and add the preserved mustard cabbage and scallions. Stir-fry over high heat for 15 seconds, or until fragrant. Add the beans with the remaining soy sauce and rice wine, sugar and 1 tablespoon water, and return the meat to the center of the pan. Toss lightly to coat the beans with the sauce.

Meat, such as this pork, is ground by hand using two cleavers at a market.

CHINESE BROCCOLI IN OYSTER SAUCE

CHINESE BROCCOLI DIFFERS FROM ITS WESTERN RELATIVE IN THAT THE STEMS ARE LONG, THE FLORETS ARE TINY, AND THE FLAVOR IS SLIGHTLY BITTER. SOME VERSIONS ARE PURPLE IN COLOR. CHINESE BROCCOLI IS AVAILABLE IN CHINESE MARKETS.

2 lb Chinese broccoli (gai lan)
1 1/2 tablespoons oil
2 scallions, finely chopped
1 1/2 tablespoons grated ginger
3 garlic cloves, finely chopped
3 tablespoons oyster sauce
1 1/2 tablespoons light soy sauce
1 tablespoon Shaoxing rice wine
1 teaspoon sugar
1 teaspoon roasted sesame oil
1/2 cup chicken stock (page 281)
2 teaspoons cornstarch

SERVES 6

WASH the broccoli well. Discard any tough-looking stems and diagonally cut into 3/4 inch pieces through the stem and the leaf. Blanch the broccoli in a saucepan of boiling water for 2 minutes, or until the stems and leaves are just tender, then refresh in cold water and dry thoroughly.

HEAT a wok over high heat, add the oil and heat until very hot. Stir-fry the scallions, ginger and garlic for 10 seconds, or until fragrant. Add the broccoli and cook until the broccoli is heated through. Combine the remaining ingredients, add to the wok, stirring until the sauce has thickened, and toss to coat the broccoli.

SICHUAN-STYLE SPICY EGGPLANT

THE TENDER FLESH OF THE EGGPLANT ABSORBS FLAVORS AND IT IS THE PERFECT CARRIER FOR BOTH SPICY AND DELICATE SAUCES. THIS RECIPE USES THIN EGGPLANTS (USUALLY REFERRED TO AS JAPANESE EGGPLANT), BUT IF THEY ARE UNAVAILABLE, USE SMALL, TENDER WESTERN ONES.

1 lb thin eggplants
1/2 teaspoon salt
3 tablespoons light soy sauce
1 tablespoons Shaoxing rice wine
1 tablespoon roasted sesame oil
2 teaspoons clear rice vinegar
1 teaspoon sugar
1 scallion, finely chopped
2 garlic cloves, finely chopped
1 teaspoon chile bean paste (toban jiang)

SERVES 6

PEEL the eggplants and trim off the ends. Cut the eggplants in half lengthwise and cut each half into strips 3/4 inch thick. Cut the strips into 2 inch pieces. Place the epplants in a bowl, add the salt and toss lightly, then set aside for 1 hour. Pour off any water that has accumulated.

ARRANGE the eggplant on a flameproof plate and place in a steamer. Cover and steam over simmering water in a wok for 20 minutes, or until tender. Combine the remaining ingredients in a bowl, then pour the sauce over the eggplant, tossing lightly to coat.

SICHUAN-STYLE SPICY EGGPLANT

蒜爆炒豆苗

STIR-FRIED PEA SHOOTS WITH GARLIC

PEA SHOOTS ARE THE DELICATE LEAVES AT THE TOP OF PEA PLANTS. THEY ARE PARTICULARLY GOOD WHEN STIR-FRIED SIMPLY WITH A LITTLE OIL AND GARLIC. IF UNAVAILABLE, SPINACH OR ANY OTHER LEAFY GREEN MAY BE SUBSTITUTED.

- 3/4 lb pea shoots
- 1 teaspoon oil
- 2 garlic cloves, finely chopped
- 1 1/2 tablespoons Shaoxing rice wine
- 1/4 teaspoon salt

SERVES 6

TRIM the tough stems and wilted leaves from the pea shoots. Wash well and dry thoroughly.

HEAT a wok over high heat, add the oil and heat until very hot. Add the pea shoots and garlic and toss lightly for 20 seconds, then add the rice wine and salt, and stir-fry for 1 minute, or until the shoots are slightly wilted, but still bright green. Transfer to a platter, leaving behind most of the liquid. Serve hot, at room temperature, or cold.

Selling pea shoots in Dali.

炒莲藕

STIR-FRIED LOTUS ROOT

THE LOTUS IS A SYMBOL OF PURITY IN BUDDHIST CULTURE AS THE ROOTS, WHICH GROW IN MUD, ARE CLEAN AND PURE DESPITE THEIR MUDDY ORIGINS. LOTUS ROOT CAN BE EATEN RAW OR COOKED AND HAS A CRISP, CRUNCHY TEXTURE.

- 1 lb fresh lotus root or 3/4 lb pre-packaged lotus root
- 1 tablespoon oil
- 1 garlic clove, thinly sliced
- 10 very thin slices ginger
- 2 scallions, finely chopped
- 2 oz Chinese ham, rind removed, diced
- 1 tablespoon Shaoxing rice wine
- 1 tablespoon light soy sauce
- 1 teaspoon sugar

SERVES 4

IF USING fresh lotus root, peel, cut into slices, wash well and drain thoroughly. Pre-packaged lotus root just needs to be washed, sliced and drained thoroughly.

HEAT a wok over high heat, add the oil and heat until very hot. Stir-fry the garlic and ginger for 30 seconds. Add the scallion, ham and lotus root and stir-fry for 1 minute, then add the rice wine, soy sauce and sugar and cook for 2–3 minutes, or until the lotus root is tender but still crisp.

STIR-FRIED LOTUS ROOT

STIR-FRIED PEA SHOOTS WITH GARLIC

Market crops near Guilin.

STIR-FRIED EGGS AND TOMATOES

番茄炒蛋

STIR-FRIED EGGS AND TOMATOES

THIS IS A SIMPLE DISH OF SCRAMBLED EGGS FLAVORED WITH TOMATOES, SCALLIONS AND SESAME OIL, WHICH CAN BE EATEN ON ITS OWN OR AS A SIDE DISH. YOU CAN MAKE THIS IN A WOK OR IN A NONSTICK FRYING PAN.

4 eggs
2 teaspoons roasted sesame oil
1 tablespoon oil
2 scallions, finely chopped
2 very ripe large tomatoes, roughly chopped

SERVES 4

BEAT the eggs with the sesame oil and season with salt. Heat a wok or nonstick frying pan over high heat, add the oil and heat until very hot. Stir-fry the scallions for 30 seconds, then add the tomatoes and stir-fry for 30 seconds. Add the eggs and stir until the eggs are set.

Chinese celery is similar to celery but has darker stems and a more pronounced flavor.

芹菜沙律

CELERY SALAD

YOU CAN OMIT THE DRIED SHRIMP USED AS A GARNISH FROM THIS DELICIOUS SALAD IF YOU ARE A VEGETARIAN. USE YOUNG CELERY THAT DOES NOT HAVE STRINGS RUNNING THROUGH IT IF YOU CAN, OTHERWISE PULL OUT THE STRINGS BEFORE SLICING.

2 tablespoons dried shrimp
2 tablespoons Shaoxing rice wine
8 Chinese celery or celery stalks
1 tablespoon light soy sauce
1 tablespoon sugar
1 tablespoon clear rice vinegar
1 teaspoon roasted sesame oil
1 tablespoon finely chopped ginger

SERVES 4

SOAK the dried shrimp in the rice wine for 1 hour.

CUT the celery into thin slices and blanch in a saucepan of boiling water for 1–2 minutes, then refresh in cold water and dry thoroughly. Arrange the celery on a serving dish.

COMBINE the soaked shrimp and rice wine with the soy sauce, sugar, rice vinegar, sesame oil and ginger. Blend well and pour over the celery just before serving.

酿苦瓜炒豆瓣酱

STUFFED BITTER MELON IN BLACK BEAN SAUCE

BITTER MELON LIVES UP TO ITS NAME—IT REALLY IS BITTER, AND SOMETHING OF AN ACQUIRED TASTE. BUY RIPER MELONS, WHICH ARE MORE YELLOW IN COLOR, AS THESE ARE A LITTLE SWEETER. BLANCHING THE MELON IN BOILING WATER ALSO GETS RID OF A LITTLE BITTERNESS.

BLACK BEAN SAUCE
- 2 tablespoons salted, fermented black beans, rinsed and coarsely chopped
- 2 garlic cloves, finely chopped
- 2 teaspoons finely chopped ginger
- 2–3 small red chiles, seeded and thinly sliced
- 2 teaspoons oyster sauce
- 2 teaspoons soy sauce
- 3 teaspoons sugar

- 3 bitter melons
- 1 lb firm white fish fillets, such as cod, halibut or monkfish, skin removed
- 3 teaspoons finely chopped ginger
- 3 teaspoons light soy sauce
- 1 teaspoon roasted sesame oil
- 3/4 oz finely chopped cilantro
- 2 scallions, thinly sliced
- 1/4 teaspoon freshly ground white pepper
- 2 1/2 tablespoons cornstarch
- 2 tablespoons oil

SERVES 4

TO MAKE the black bean sauce, combine the black beans, garlic, ginger, chiles, oyster sauce, soy sauce and sugar in a small bowl. Set aside.

SLICE the bitter melons into rings about 1 inch wide. Remove the seeds and membranes and blanch the pieces in a saucepan of boiling water for 2–3 minutes, then refresh in cold water and dry thoroughly.

FINELY CHOP the fish fillets with a cleaver or in a food processor and place in a bowl with the ginger, soy sauce, sesame oil, cilantro, scallions, pepper and 1 tablespoon of the cornstarch, stirring to combine. Set aside in the fridge for up to 1 hour to allow the flavors to develop.

LIGHTLY COAT the bitter melon in 1 tablespoon of the cornstarch to help the stuffing stick to it. Fill the center of each piece with the fish mixture. Heat a wok over high heat, add the oil and heat until very hot. Cook the bitter melon in batches, without turning, until golden brown. Remove from the wok and keep warm.

ADD the black bean sauce to the wok and stir-fry over medium heat for 1 minute. Add the stuffed melon pieces and coat with the sauce.

COMBINE the remaining cornstarch with about 1/2 cup water, add to the sauce and simmer until thickened.

Press the filling firmly into the hollow in each piece of melon so that it stays intact when the melon is fried.

CHINESE BROCCOLI WITH SOY SAUCE

CHINESE BROCCOLI (GAI LAN) IS A QUICK AND EASY VEGETABLE TO PREPARE. ALTHOUGH IT CAN BE USED IN STIR-FRIES OR WITH MORE COMPLICATED SAUCES, IT GOES EQUALLY WELL WITH A SIMPLE DRIZZLE OF OYSTER SAUCE AND SOY SAUCE.

Chinese broccoli (gai lan) comes in both the more common green and a dark reddish-purple variety.

3/4–1 lb Chinese broccoli (gai lan)
2 tablespoons oil
1 tablespoon oyster sauce
2 tablespoons light soy sauce

SERVES 4

WASH the broccoli well. Discard any tough-looking stems and cut the rest of the stems in half. Blanch the broccoli in a saucepan of boiling water for 2 minutes, or until the stems and leaves are just tender, then refresh in cold water and dry thoroughly. Arrange in a serving dish.

HEAT a wok over high heat, add the oil and heat until very hot. Carefully pour the hot oil over the Chinese broccoli (it will splatter). Gently toss the oil with the Chinese broccoli and drizzle with the oyster sauce and soy sauce. Serve hot.

STIR-FRIED BOK CHOY

BOK CHOY COMES IN SEVERAL VARIETIES AND SIZES. SOME TYPES HAVE LONG WHITE STEMS AND VERY GREEN LEAVES, OTHERS, SUCH AS BABY BOK CHOY, HAVE SHORTER PALE-GREEN STEMS AND LEAVES. ALL TYPES ARE INTERCHANGEABLE IN RECIPES.

3/4 lb bok choy
2 tablespoons oil
2 garlic cloves, smashed with the flat side of a cleaver
3 thin slices ginger, smashed with the flat side of a cleaver
3 tablespoons chicken stock (page 281)
1 teaspoon sugar
salt or light soy sauce, to taste
1 teaspoon roasted sesame oil

SERVES 4

CUT the bok choy into 2–3 inch pieces. Trim off any roots that may hold the pieces together, then wash well and dry thoroughly.

HEAT a wok over high heat, add the oil and heat until very hot. Stir-fry the garlic and ginger for 30 seconds. Add the bok choy and stir-fry until it begins to wilt, then add the stock and sugar and season with the salt or soy sauce. Simmer, covered, for 2 minutes, or until the stems and leaves are tender but still green. Add the sesame oil and serve hot.

CHINESE BROCCOLI WITH SOY SAUCE

酸辣包心菜

HOT-AND-SOUR CABBAGE

THIS SPICY PICKLE OR SIDE DISH IS WELL LOVED IN MANY PARTS OF CHINA, ALTHOUGH IT IS ESPECIALLY POPULAR IN HANGZHOU, A CITY IN EAST CHINA THAT BOASTS GREAT FOOD. IT MAY BE MADE WITH OTHER VEGETABLES BESIDES CABBAGE AND CAN BE EATEN HOT, WARM OR COLD.

1 small Chinese (Napa) cabbage
3 tablespoons light soy sauce
1/2 teaspoon salt
2 tablespoons sugar
4 tablespoons Chinese black rice vinegar
1 tablespoon oil
1 red chile, finely chopped
2 1/2 tablespoons finely chopped ginger
1 1/2 red peppers, cut into 1/4 inch dice
1 1/2 tablespoons Shaoxing rice wine
1 teaspoon roasted sesame oil

SERVES 6

SEPARATE the cabbage leaves and trim off the stems. Cut the leaves lengthwise into 1/2 inch wide strips, separating the stem sections from the leafy sections.

COMBINE the soy sauce, salt, sugar and Chinese black vinegar and set aside.

HEAT a wok over high heat, add the oil and heat until very hot. Stir-fry the red chile and ginger for 15 seconds. Add the red peppers and stir-fry for 30 seconds, then add the rice wine and stir-fry for 30 seconds. Add the stem sections of the cabbage, toss lightly and cook for 1 minute. Add the leafy sections and toss lightly, then pour in the soy sauce mixture, tossing lightly to coat. Cook for 30 seconds, then add the sesame oil. Serve hot, at room temperature, or cold.

Chinese cabbages for sale in a Beijing market. The cabbages are often covered in blankets to protect them from frost.

黑椒炒白菜

FLAT CABBAGE WITH BLACK PEPPER

FLAT CABBAGE (TAT SOI) HAS SMALL, DARK-GREEN, SHINY LEAVES WITH A WHITE STEM. IT IS SOMETIMES CALLED ROSETTE CABBAGE. THE LEAVES NEED TO BE WASHED THOROUGHLY BEFORE THEY ARE USED AS THEY HARBOR A LOT OF DIRT.

1 flat cabbage (tat soi)
1 tablespoon oil
2 garlic cloves, sliced
1/4 teaspoon freshly ground black pepper
2 teaspoons Shaoxing rice wine
light soy sauce, to taste
2 teaspoons roasted sesame oil

SERVES 4

SEPARATE the cabbage leaves, wash well and dry thoroughly.

HEAT a wok over high heat, add the oil and heat until very hot. Stir-fry the garlic for a few seconds. Add the cabbage leaves and stir-fry until they have just wilted. Add the pepper and rice wine and toss together. Season with the soy sauce and add the sesame oil.

FLAT CABBAGE WITH BLACK PEPPER

芥末白菜卷

CABBAGE ROLLS WITH MUSTARD

Blanching the leaves first makes them easier to roll. Make sure you only spread a thin layer of mustard on each.

MUSTARD SEEDS COME FROM PLANTS BELONGING TO THE CABBAGE FAMILY, WHICH HAVE GROWN IN CHINA FOR CENTURIES. ALTHOUGH IT WAS TRADITIONALLY GROWN FOR ITS LEAVES, MUSTARD IS ALSO SOMETIMES USED AS A SPICE IN ITS GROUND FORM, OR MADE UP INTO A PASTE AS A CONDIMENT.

1 Chinese (Napa) cabbage
3 tablespoons English mustard powder
1 tablespoon light soy sauce
1 tablespoon clear rice vinegar
1 teaspoon roasted sesame oil

SERVES 4

SEPARATE the cabbage leaves and blanch them in a saucepan of boiling water for 1 minute, then refresh in cold water and dry thoroughly.

COMBINE the mustard powder, soy sauce, rice vinegar and sesame oil, then add enough cold water to make a stiff but spreadable paste.

TRIM the cabbage leaves into long strips about 2 inch wide. For each roll, use 3 strips. Lay a bottom strip on the work surface and cover with a thin layer of mustard, lay another strip on top covered with a layer of mustard, finish with a final strip and some mustard, then roll up. Repeat with the remaining cabbage to make four rolls. Put the rolls, standing upright, on a flameproof plate in a steamer. Cover and steam over simmering water in a wok for 20 minutes.

虾酱炒菠菜

STIR-FRIED WATER SPINACH WITH SHRIMP SAUCE

STIR-FRIED WATER SPINACH WITH SHRIMP SAUCE

2 lb water spinach (ong choy)
$2\frac{1}{2}$ tablespoons oil
2 teaspoons Chinese shrimp paste
3 garlic cloves, crushed
1–2 red chiles, seeded and chopped
2 teaspoons oyster sauce
2 teaspoons sugar

SERVES 4

WASH the water spinach well and dry thoroughly. Remove any tough lower stalks and only use the young stems and leaves.

HEAT a wok over high heat, add $1\frac{1}{2}$ tablespoons of the oil and heat until very hot. Stir-fry the water spinach for 1 minute, or until it begins to wilt. Drain in a colander.

ADD the remaining oil to the wok with the shrimp paste, garlic and chiles, and toss over medium heat to release the flavors for 30 seconds to 1 minute. Add the water spinach, oyster sauce and sugar and toss for 1 minute.

RICE & NOODLES

金丝鸡蛋挂面
飞麟粮制品厂
选
质
出品
（0875） 2849220

蛋炒饭

EGG FRIED RICE

EGG FRIED RICE

IN CHINA, PLAIN COOKED RICE IS SERVED WITH EVERYDAY MEALS, WHILE FRIED RICE IS ONLY EATEN AS A SNACK ON ITS OWN OR AT BANQUETS, WHEN IT IS SERVED AT THE END OF THE MEAL. THIS VERSION IS HOWEVER QUITE SIMPLE, SO IT WOULD GO WELL AS A SIDE DISH.

4 eggs
1 scallion, chopped
2 oz fresh or frozen peas (optional)
3 tablespoons oil
1 quantity cooked rice (page 274)

SERVES 4

BEAT the eggs with a pinch of salt and 1 teaspoon of the scallion. Cook the peas in a saucepan of simmering water for 3–4 minutes for fresh or 1 minute for frozen.

HEAT a wok over high heat, add the oil and heat until very hot. Reduce the heat, add the eggs and lightly scramble. Add the rice before the eggs are set too hard, increase the heat and stir to separate the rice grains and break the eggs into small bits. Add the peas and the remaining scallion and season with salt. Stir constantly for 1 minute.

YANGZHOU FRIED RICE WITH SHRIMP

YANGZHOU FRIED RICE WITH SHRIMP

THIS WELL-KNOWN FRIED RICE DISH HAILS FROM YANGZHOU, A CITY IN THE EAST. IT CAN BE SERVED BY ITSELF AS A LIGHT MEAL OR WITH SOUP. THE SECRET TO NON-LUMPY FRIED RICE IS USING COOKED RICE THAT HAS BEEN CHILLED, THEN LEFT OUT TO REACH ROOM TEMPERATURE.

4 oz cooked shrimp
1 cup fresh or frozen peas
1 tablespoon oil
3 scallions, finely chopped
1 tablespoon finely chopped ginger
2 eggs, lightly beaten
1 quantity cooked rice (page 274)
1 1/2 tablespoons chicken stock (page 281)
1 tablespoon Shaoxing rice wine
2 teaspoons light soy sauce
1/2 teaspoon salt, or to taste
1/2 teaspoon roasted sesame oil
1/4 teaspoon freshly ground black pepper

SERVES 4

PEEL the shrimp and cut then in half through the back, removing the vein. Cook the peas in a saucepan of simmering water for 3–4 minutes for fresh or 1 minute for frozen.

HEAT a wok over high heat, add the oil and heat until hot. Stir-fry the scallions and ginger for 1 minute. Reduce the heat, add the eggs and lightly scramble. Add the shrimp and peas and toss lightly to heat through, then add the rice before the eggs are set too hard, increase the heat and stir to separate the rice grains and break the eggs into small bits.

ADD the stock, rice wine, soy sauce, salt, sesame oil and pepper, and toss lightly.

PEARL BALLS

THIS FAMOUS DISH ORIGINATED IN HUNAN PROVINCE, ONE OF CHINA'S MAJOR RICE BASINS. ONCE STEAMED, THE STICKY RICE THAT FORMS THE COATING FOR THESE MEATBALLS TURNS INTO PEARL-LIKE GRAINS. TRADITIONALLY, GLUTINOUS OR SWEET RICE IS USED, BUT YOU COULD USE RISOTTO RICE.

Roll the meatballs so they are completely coated in the glutinous rice, then press the rice on firmly so it sticks.

1 3/4 cups glutinous or sweet rice
8 dried Chinese mushrooms
1 cup peeled water chestnuts
1 lb ground pork
1 small carrot, grated
2 scallions, finely chopped
1 1/2 tablespoons finely chopped ginger
2 tablespoons light soy sauce
1 tablespoon Shaoxing rice wine
1 1/2 teaspoons roasted sesame oil
2 1/2 tablespoons cornstarch
soy sauce

SERVES 6

PUT the rice in a bowl and, using your fingers as a rake, rinse under cold running water to remove any dust. Drain the rice in a colander, then place it in a bowl with enough cold water to cover. Set aside for 1 hour. Drain the rice and transfer it to a baking sheet in an even layer.

SOAK the dried mushrooms in boiling water for 30 minutes, then drain and squeeze out any excess water. Remove and discard the stems and chop the caps.

BLANCH the water chestnuts in a saucepan of boiling water for 1 minute, then refresh in cold water. Drain, pat dry and finely chop them.

PLACE the pork in a bowl, add the mushrooms, water chestnuts, carrot, scallions, ginger, soy sauce, rice wine, sesame oil and cornstarch. Stir the mixture vigorously to combine.

ROLL the mixture into 3/4 inch balls, then roll each meatball in the glutinous rice so that it is completely coated. Lightly press the rice to make it stick to the meatball. Arrange the pearl balls well spaced in 3 steamers lined with waxed paper punched with holes or some damp cheesecloth. Cover and steam over simmering water in a wok, reversing the steamers halfway through, for 25 minutes. If the rice is still *al dente*, continue to cook for a little longer until it softens. Serve with the soy sauce.

A haircut in Lijiang.

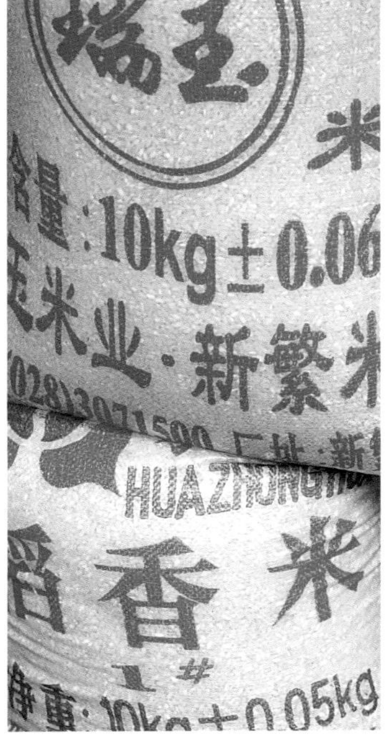

蒸鸡腊肠饭

STEAMED CHICKEN AND SAUSAGE RICE

THIS WARMING CANTONESE DISH IS TRADITIONALLY COOKED IN SMALL CLAY POTS SO THERE IS ONE POT FOR EACH INDIVIDUAL. CHINESE SAUSAGE (LAP CHEONG) TASTES A LITTLE LIKE A SWEET SALAMI, BUT IT MUST BE COOKED BEFORE EATING.

4 dried Chinese mushrooms
8 oz skinned boneless chicken thighs
1 teaspoon Shaoxing rice wine
2 teaspoons cornstarch
3 Chinese sausages (lap cheong)
1 cup long-grain rice
1 scallion, chopped

SAUCE
2 tablespoons light soy sauce
1 tablespoon Shaoxing rice wine
1/2 teaspoon superfine sugar
1/2 garlic clove, chopped (optional)
1/2 teaspoon chopped ginger
1/2 teaspoon roasted sesame oil

SERVES 4

SOAK the dried mushrooms in boiling water for 30 minutes, then drain and squeeze out any excess water. Remove and discard the stems and shred the caps.

CUT the chicken into bite-size pieces and combine with a pinch of salt, the rice wine and cornstarch.

PLACE the sausages on a plate in a steamer. Cover and steam over simmering water in a wok for 10 minutes, then thinly slice on the diagonal.

PUT the rice in a bowl and, using your fingers as a rake, rinse under cold running water to remove any dust. Drain the rice in a colander. Place in a large clay pot or braising pan and add enough water so that there is 3/4 inch of water above the surface of the rice. Bring the water slowly to a boil, stir, then place the chicken pieces and mushrooms on top of the rice, with the sausage slices on top of them. Cook, covered, over very low heat for 15–18 minutes, or until the rice is cooked.

TO MAKE the sauce, combine the soy sauce, rice wine, sugar, garlic, ginger and sesame oil in a small saucepan and heat until nearly boiling. Pour the sauce over the chicken and sausage and garnish with the chopped scallion.

白粥加各样小菜

PLAIN CONGEE WITH ACCOMPANIMENTS

CONGEE IS EATEN IN CHINA FOR BREAKFAST OR AS AN ALL-DAY SNACK. PLAIN CONGEE IS SERVED WITH LOTS OF DIFFERENT CONDIMENTS TO SPRINKLE OVER IT AND OFTEN A FRIED DOUGH STICK.

1 cup short-grain rice
9 cups litres chicken stock (page 281) or water
light soy sauce, to taste
sesame oil, to taste

TOPPINGS
3 scallions, chopped
4 tablespoons chopped cilantro
1 oz sliced pickled ginger
4 tablespoons finely chopped preserved turnip
4 tablespoons roasted peanuts
2 one-thousand-year-old eggs, cut into slivers
2 tablespoons toasted sesame seeds
2 fried dough sticks, diagonally sliced

SERVES 4

PUT the rice in a bowl and, using your fingers as a rake, rinse under cold running water to remove any dust. Drain the rice in a colander. Place in a clay pot, braising pan or saucepan and stir in the stock or water. Bring to a boil, then reduce the heat and simmer very gently, stirring occasionally, for 1¾–2 hours, or until it has a porridge-like texture and the rice is breaking up.

ADD a sprinkling of soy sauce, sesame oil and white pepper to season the congee. The congee can be served plain, or choose a selection from the toppings listed and serve in bowls alongside the congee for guests to help themselves.

Fried dough sticks are available in Chinese markets and are sold as long thin sticks, best eaten fresh on the day they are made, or broiled until crisp again.

鱼粥

FISH CONGEE

EVERYDAY CONGEE, OR RICE PORRIDGE, IS USUALLY SERVED WITH A FEW SIMPLE ACCOMPANIMENTS, BUT IT IS SOMETIMES COOKED INTO A MORE SUBSTANTIAL MEAL BY ADDING FISH OR MEAT.

1 cup short-grain rice
9 cups chicken stock (page 281) or water
½ lb firm white fish fillets, such as cod, halibut or monkfish, skin removed and cut into small cubes
1 tablespoon finely shredded ginger
light soy sauce, to taste
2 scallions, chopped

SERVES 4

PUT the rice in a bowl and, using your fingers as a rake, rinse under cold running water to remove any dust. Drain the rice in a colander. Place in a clay pot, braising pan or saucepan and stir in the stock or water. Bring to a boil, then reduce the heat and simmer very gently, stirring occasionally, for 1¾–2 hours, or until it has a porridge-like texture and the rice is breaking up.

ADD the fish, ginger and a little soy sauce and bring to a boil for 1 minute. Garnish with the chopped scallions.

FISH CONGEE

Rice terraces at Longsheng.

什锦粥

RAINBOW CONGEE

TO THE CHINESE, CONGEE IS A VERSATILE DISH. IT IS A FAVORITE COMFORT FOOD, A DISH PREPARED FOR CONVALESCENTS BECAUSE IT IS SO SOOTHING TO EAT, AND A FILLING AND FLAVORFUL SNACK.

A game of mahjong in Chengdu.

1 cup short-grain rice
2 dried Chinese mushrooms
3/4 cup snow peas, ends trimmed
2 Chinese sausages (lap cheong)
2 tablespoons oil
1/4 red onion, finely diced
1 carrot, cut into 1/2 inch dice
8–9 cups chicken stock (page 281) or water
1/4 teaspoon salt
3 teaspoons light soy sauce

SERVES 6

PUT the rice in a bowl and, using your fingers as a rake, rinse under cold running water to remove any dust. Drain the rice in a colander.

SOAK the dried mushrooms in boiling water for 30 minutes, then drain and squeeze out any excess water. Remove and discard the stems and chop the caps into 1/4 inch dice. Cut the snow peas into 1/2 inch pieces.

PLACE the sausages on a plate in a steamer. Cover and steam over simmering water in a wok for 10 minutes, then cut them into 1/4 inch pieces.

HEAT a wok over medium heat, add the oil and heat until hot. Stir-fry the sausage until it is brown and the fat has melted out of it. Remove with a wire strainer or slotted spoon and drain. Pour out the oil, reserving 1 tablespoon.

REHEAT the reserved oil over high heat until very hot. Stir-fry the red onion until soft and transparent. Add the mushrooms and carrot and stir-fry for 1 minute, or until fragrant.

PUT the mushroom mixture in a clay pot, braising pan or saucepan and stir in 8 cups of stock or water, the salt, soy sauce and the rice. Bring to a boil, then reduce the heat and simmer very gently, stirring occasionally, for 1 3/4–2 hours, or until it has a porridge-like texture and the rice is breaking up. If it is too thick, add the remaining stock and return to a boil. Toss in the snow peas and sausage, cover and let stand for 5 minutes before serving.

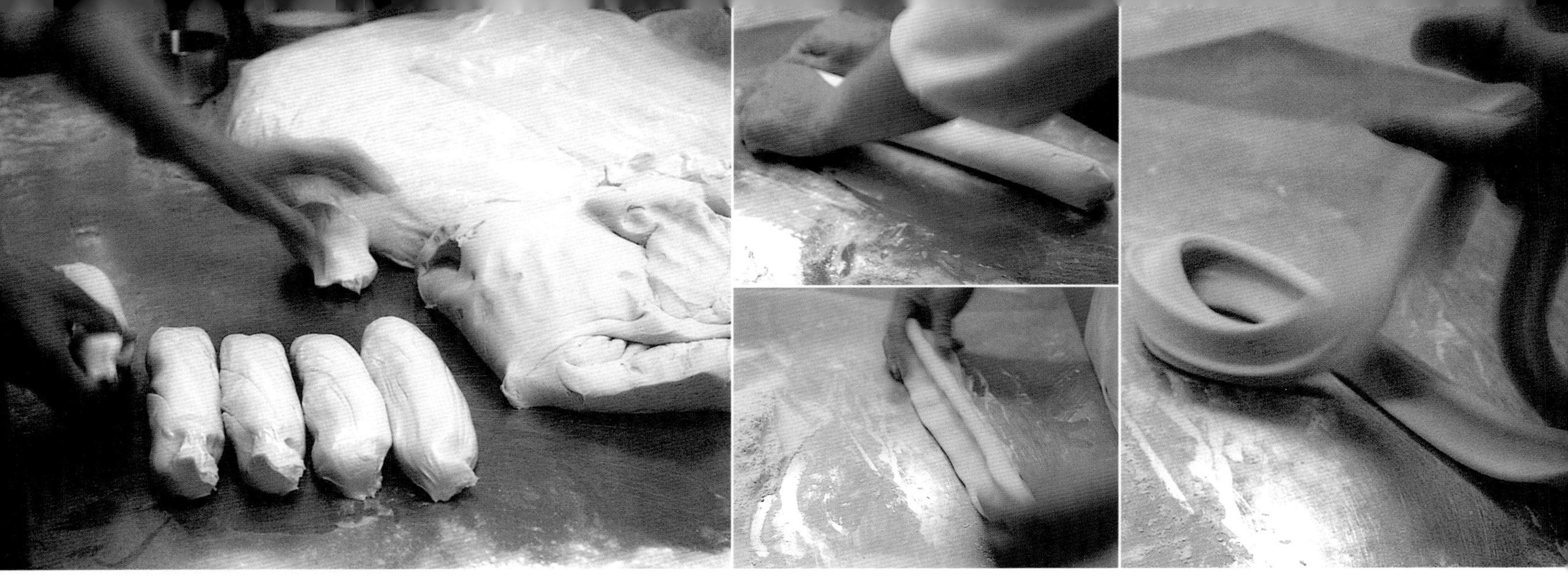

WHEAT NOODLES are still made by hand in China, and these 'pulled' or 'hand-drawn' noodles are an ancient art. At the Malan restaurants in Beijing, they follow a century-old recipe from Lanzhou in northwestern China. First, a large batch of dough is made from strong wheat flour, water and a little vegetable oil (to make the dough soft), left to rest, then worked to stretch the gluten. Portions are rolled into tubes and pulled

NOODLES

NOODLES GEOGRAPHICALLY DIVIDE CHINA, FROM THE COOL NORTH, WHERE HARDY WHEAT IS A STAPLE MADE INTO *MIAN*—WHEAT-FLOUR NOODLES—DOWN TO THE WARM, HUMID SOUTH, WHERE GROUND RICE IS TURNED INTO RICE NOODLES—*FEN*.

Though both kinds of noodles are now eaten all over China, noodles remain more of a staple in the North than the South, where a bowl of rice is the usual accompaniment to a meal.

TYPES OF NOODLES

Mian is the name for noodles made from wheat and barley, though it is often used as the general name for all noodles across China. They can be dried or fresh, made by machine or hand, and eggs can be added to the flour and water paste to make egg noodles, a Cantonese speciality.

Fen is the Chinese word for the flour made from millet and rice, and also refers to noodles made from ground rice. Popular in the South, they are also known as Sha He noodles after a town near Guangzhou, renowned for the quality of its noodles. Fresh rice noodles are formed in sheets and cut up after steaming to make the soft white noodles often found in dim sum. Dried rice noodles come in various thicknesses, from flat rice sticks to strand-like vermicelli, and are usually machine-made.

Fen also refers to non-grain noodles that are not regarded as 'true' noodles made from a staple ingredient such as wheat or rice. *Fen si,* or bean thread noodles, are made of mung bean flour, and their translucent appearance is reflected in their English names of cellophane or glass noodles. *Gan si* are made from pressed bean curd.

amount of strands until the required thickness of noodle is reached (noodles for men are traditionally thicker than for women to provide more 'energy'). The thicker end of the noodles (the lump of dough that forms as the noodles are folded) is twisted off and the noodles gathered into a skein. The noodles must now be handled quickly and gently. They are dropped into a continually boiling pot of water and cooked for a couple of

horizontally to arm's length, folded back and stretched again until the dough is soft and elastic. The noodle-maker then starts to let the dough stretch to the floor in an arc, folding it just before it touches so the dough twists up like a coiled rope. Now strong enough to be split into strands, the dough is folded over and over, keeping each folded piece separate by dusting it in the flour on the work surface. Every fold doubles the

EATING NOODLES

Noodles are most often served up in bowls of soup or as roadside snacks in China, especially in the South, where they are rarely served in restaurants and are considered a home-cooking style dish. In the North, noodles are served with meals, and are also found in small restaurants or stalls dedicated to just a few noodle dishes, where the noodles are often hand-thrown to order, then boiled in large pots.

Noodles are a symbol of longevity in Chinese gastronomy and are sometimes eaten on special occasions. Very long, they are rarely cut as to do this may bring bad luck.

Most areas of China have a special noodle dish associated with the region. In Beijing, these are *la mian,* the pulled noodles *(shown above)* that are also known as Dragon's whiskers. In Sichuan, crossing-the-bridge noodles and ants climbing trees are favourite dishes, while fried Singapore noodles are actually from Fujian.

COOKING NOODLES

NOODLES IN SOUP the most common way to eat noodles, dropped into broth, sometimes topped with a little meat, vegetables or seafood, and always eaten as a snack, never as a soup or main course.

BRAISED NOODLES noodles in a thick sauce (which they may have been cooked in), with meat, vegetables or seafood.

FRIED NOODLES crisp- or soft-fried noodles, tossed with meat, vegetables or seafood and flavourings. Stir-fried noodles may be eaten as part of a meal—usually at home, as they are considered home-cooking style dishes. The Chinese name for fried noodles is *chao mian*, corrupted in English to *chow mein*.

TOSSED NOODLES plain boiled noodles, served with a meat sauce and fresh vegetables to mix through, and often eaten cold in the summer.

WON TONS made from an egg noodle dough, won ton wrappers are usually filled with meat and the dumplings poached in soup or fried.

minutes, then lifted out with chopsticks into a bowl. Malan's special recipe is based on five different colours. The broth (transparent) is made with beef and chicken stock, chinese herbs and a little MSG and is poured over the noodles. To this are added sliced turnip (white), chilli (red), coriander and spring onion (green) and noodles (yellow)—the colours are thought to influence the taste. A little cooked beef finishes the dish.

蒜苗炒牛肉面

FRESH NOODLES WITH BEEF AND GARLIC CHIVES

1/2 lb beef top round steak, trimmed
2 large garlic cloves, crushed
3 tablespoons oyster sauce
2 teaspoons sugar
1 tablespoon dark soy sauce
3 teaspoons cornstarch
1/4 teaspoon roasted sesame oil
3 tablespoons oil
1 red pepper, thinly sliced
1/4 lb Chinese garlic chives, cut into 2 inch pieces
2 lb fresh rice noodle rolls, cut into 3/4 inch thick slices and separated slightly
chili sauce

SERVES 6

CUT the beef against the grain into thin bite-size strips. Combine with the garlic, 1 tablespoon of the oyster sauce, 1 teaspoon of the sugar, 2 teaspoons of the soy sauce, the cornstarch and sesame oil. Marinate in the fridge for at least 30 minutes, or overnight.

HEAT a wok over high heat, add the oil and heat until very hot. Stir-fry the pepper for 1–2 minutes, or until it begins to soften. Add the beef and toss until it changes color. Add the garlic chives and noodles and toss for 1–2 minutes, or until they soften. Add the remaining oyster sauce, sugar and soy sauce and toss well until combined.

SERVE with some chili sauce on the side.

Slice the fresh noodle roll into thick slices, which will unroll and separate into noodles.

COLD TOSSED NOODLES

THIS IS A SUMMER DISH THAT PROVIDES A VERY REFRESHING SNACK FOR A HOT AFTERNOON OR EVENING. THE DRESSING CAN BE VARIED ACCORDING TO PERSONAL PREFERENCE BY ADDING MORE OR LESS CHILI SAUCE OR PRESERVED TURNIP. OMIT THE SHRIMP FOR A VEGETARIAN DISH.

DRESSING
3/4 oz dried shrimp
3 tablespoons Shaoxing rice wine
3 tablespoons light soy sauce
2 tablespoons clear rice vinegar
1 teaspoon chili sauce
1 tablespoon finely chopped ginger
2 tablespoons chopped preserved turnip
1 teaspoon roasted sesame oil

1 lb fresh or 3/4 lb dried egg noodles
1 tablespoon oil
2 scallions, finely shredded

SERVES 6

TO MAKE the dressing, soak the dried shrimp in boiling water for 1 hour, then drain, coarsely chop and soak in the rice wine for 15 minutes. Combine the shrimp, soy sauce, rice vinegar, chili sauce, ginger, preserved turnip and sesame oil.

COOK the noodles in a saucepan of salted boiling water for 2–3 minutes if fresh and 10 minutes if dried, then drain and rinse in cold water. Combine with the oil and spread the noodles out on a dish.

POUR the dressing over the top of the noodles and sprinkle with the shredded scallions. Toss at the table before serving.

COLD TOSSED NOODLES

荷兰豆炒牛肉烩炸面

CRISPY NOODLES WITH BEEF AND SNOW PEAS

THIS CANTONESE DISH IS A FAVORITE ACROSS THE GLOBE. THE CRISP NOODLES WITH THEIR BEEF AND SNOW PEA TOPPING ARE DRENCHED IN A VELVETY OYSTER SAUCE.

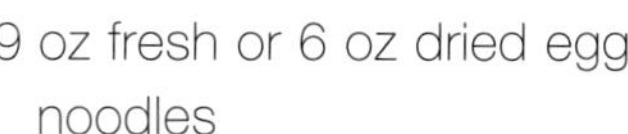

- 9 oz fresh or 6 oz dried egg noodles
- 1 1/2 teaspoons roasted sesame oil
- 3/4 lb beef top round steak, trimmed
- 1 tablespoon dark soy sauce
- 2 teaspoons Shaoxing rice wine
- 1/2 teaspoon sugar
- 1 garlic clove, finely chopped
- 1 teaspoon cornstarch
- 1 cup snow peas, ends trimmed
- 3 tablespoons oil

SAUCE

- 1 tablespoon finely chopped ginger
- 1 scallion, finely chopped
- 1 1/4 cups chicken stock (page 281)
- 3 tablespoons oyster sauce
- 1 tablespoon Shaoxing rice wine
- 1/2 teaspoon dark soy sauce
- 1 teaspoon sugar
- 1/2 teaspoon roasted sesame oil
- 1 1/2 tablespoons cornstarch

SERVES 4

COOK the noodles in a saucepan of salted boiling water for 2–3 minutes if fresh and 10 minutes if dried, then drain and combine with 1 teaspoon of the sesame oil. Place the noodles in 4 small cake pans or flat-bottomed bowls and allow to cool.

CUT the beef against the grain into slices about 1/8 inch thick, then cut into 1 1/2 inch squares. Combine the beef, soy sauce, rice wine, sugar, garlic, cornstarch and the remaining seame oil and toss lightly. Marinate in the fridge for at least 1 hour.

BLANCH the snowpeas in a saucepan of boiling water for 15 seconds. Drain and refresh immediately in cold water. Dry thoroughly.

HEAT a wok over high heat, add 2 tablespoons of the oil and heat until almost smoking. Invert the noodle cakes, one at a time, into the wok and fry on both sides until golden brown, swirling the pan from time to time to move the noodles so that they cook evenly. Put the noodles on a plate and keep warm and crisp in a low oven.

REHEAT the wok over high heat, add the remaining oil and heat until very hot. Drain the beef and stir-fry in batches for 1 minute, or until the beef changes color. Remove with a wire strainer or slotted spoon, and drain. Pour out the oil, reserving 2 tablespoons.

TO MAKE the sauce, reheat the reserved oil over high heat until very hot and stir-fry the ginger and scallion for 10 seconds, or until fragrant. Add the remaining sauce ingredients, except the cornstarch, and bring to a boil. Combine the cornstarch with enough water to make a paste, add to the sauce and simmer until thickened.

ADD the beef and snow peas, toss to coat with the sauce, and pour the mixture over the noodles.

A pot of boiling water for cooking noodles in Chengdu.

新加坡炒面

SINGAPORE NOODLES

10 oz rice vermicelli
2 tablespoons dried shrimp
4 oz barbecued pork (char siu)
1 cup bean sprouts
4 tablespoons oil
2 eggs, beaten
1 onion, thinly sliced
1 teaspoon salt
1 tablespoon Chinese curry powder
2 tablespoons light soy sauce
2 scallions, shredded
2 red chiles, shredded

SERVES 4

SOAK the noodles in hot water for 10 minutes, then drain. Soak the dried shrimp in boiling water for 1 hour, then drain. Thinly shred the pork. Wash the bean sprouts and drain thoroughly.

HEAT a wok over high heat, add 1 tablespoon of the oil and heat until very hot. Pour in the egg and make an omelet. Remove from the wok and cut into small pieces.

REHEAT the wok over high heat, add the remaining oil and heat until very hot. Stir-fry the onion and bean sprouts with the pork and shrimp for 1 minute, then add the noodles, salt, curry powder and soy sauce, blend well and stir for 1 minute. Add the omelet, scallions and chiles and toss to combine.

SINGAPORE NOODLES

担担面

DAN DAN MIAN

A COMMON STREET FOOD SNACK IN SICHUAN, THIS DISH IS NOW POPULAR ALL OVER THE NORTH OF CHINA AND THE RECIPE VARIES FROM STAND TO STAND.

1 tablespoon Sichuan peppercorns
7 oz ground pork
2 oz preserved turnip, rinsed and finely chopped
2 tablespoons light soy sauce
2 tablespoons oil
2 garlic cloves, crushed
2 tablespoons grated ginger
4 scallions, finely chopped
2 tablespoons sesame paste or smooth peanut butter
2 tablespoons light soy sauce
2 teaspoons chile oil
3/4 cup chicken stock (page 281)
3/4 lb thin wheat flour noodles

SERVES 4

DRY-FRY the Sichuan peppercorns in a wok or frying pan until brown and aromatic, then crush lightly. Combine the pork with the preserved turnip and soy sauce and allow to marinate for a few minutes. Heat a wok over high heat, add the oil and heat until very hot. Stir-fry the pork until crisp and browned. Remove and drain well.

ADD the garlic, ginger and scallions to the wok and stir-fry for 30 seconds, then add the sesame paste, soy sauce, chile oil and stock and simmer for 2 minutes.

COOK the noodles in a saucepan of salted boiling water for 4–8 minutes, then drain well. Divide among 4 bowls, ladle the sauce over the noodles, then top with the crispy pork and Sichuan peppercorns.

Making wheat noodles by pulling them by hand. The noodles are made fresh for each customer and cooked immediately.

DAN DAN MIAN

Make sure you separate all the ground meat as it cooks, or it will form large lumps and not resemble ants at all.

Lunch in Chengdu.

蚂蚁上树

ANTS CLIMBING TREES

THE UNUSUAL NAME OF THIS SPICY SICHUAN-STYLE DISH IS SUPPOSED TO COME FROM THE FACT THAT IT BEARS A RESEMBLANCE TO ANTS CLIMBING TREES, WITH LITTLE PIECES OF GROUND PORK COATING LUSTROUS BEAN THREAD NOODLES.

4 oz pork or beef
1/2 teaspoon light soy sauce
1/2 teaspoon Shaoxing rice wine
1/2 teaspoon roasted sesame oil
4 oz bean thread noodles
1 tablespoon oil
2 scallions, finely chopped
1 tablespoon finely chopped ginger
1 garlic clove, finely chopped
1 teaspoon chile bean paste (toban jiang), or to taste
2 scallions, green part only, finely chopped

SAUCE
1 tablespoon light soy sauce
1 tablespoon Shaoxing rice wine
1/2 teaspoon salt
1/2 teaspoon sugar
1/2 teaspoon roasted sesame oil
1 cup chicken stock (page 281)

SERVES 4

COMBINE the ground meat with the soy sauce, rice wine and sesame oil. Soak the bean thread noodles in hot water for 10 minutes, then drain.

HEAT a wok over high heat, add the oil and heat until very hot. Stir-fry the ground meat, mashing and separating it, until it changes color and starts to brown. Push the meat to the side of the wok, add the scallions, ginger, garlic and chile bean paste and stir-fry for 5 seconds, or until fragrant. Return the meat to the center of the pan.

TO MAKE the sauce, combine all the ingredients. Add the sauce to the meat mixture and toss lightly. Add the noodles and bring to a boil. Reduce the heat to low and cook for 8 minutes, or until almost all the liquid has evaporated. Sprinkle with the chopped scallions.

Making noodle dishes at a market in Yunnan.

什锦面

RAINBOW NOODLES

THIS DISH OF SHRIMP, BEAN SPROUTS AND THIN RICE NOODLES IS ENLIVENED WITH A TOUCH OF CHINESE CURRY POWDER. MUCH MILDER THAN ITS INDIAN COUNTERPART AND SIMILAR TO FIVE-SPICE POWDER, YOU COULD USE A MILD INDIAN CURRY POWDER INSTEAD.

7 oz shrimp
1 tablespoon Shaoxing rice wine
2 1/2 tablespoons finely chopped ginger
1 teaspoon roasted sesame oil
10 oz rice vermicelli
2 leeks, white part only
4 tablespoons oil
1 1/2 tablespoons Chinese curry powder
2 1/4 cups bean sprouts
1/4 cup chicken stock (page 281) or water
2 tablespoons light soy sauce
1 teaspoon salt
1/2 teaspoon sugar
1/2 teaspoon freshly ground black pepper

SERVES 4

PEEL the shrimp, leaving the tails intact. Using a sharp knife, score lengthwise along the back of each and remove the vein. Place in a bowl, add the rice wine, 2 teaspoons of the ginger and the sesame oil, and toss to coat.

SOAK the noodles in hot water for 10 minutes, then drain. Cut the leeks into roughly 2 inch pieces and shred finely. Wash well and dry thoroughly.

HEAT a wok over high heat, add 1 tablespoon of the oil and heat until very hot. Stir-fry the shrimp in batches for 1 1/2 minutes, or until they turn opaque. Remove with a wire strainer or slotted spoon and drain. Pour out the oil and wipe out the wok.

REHEAT the wok over high heat, add the remaining oil and heat until very hot. Stir-fry the curry powder for a few seconds, or until fragrant. Add the leeks and remaining ginger and stir-fry for 1 1/2 minutes. Add the bean sprouts and cook for 20 seconds, then add the shrimp, stock or water, soy sauce, salt, sugar and pepper, and stir to combine.

ADD the noodles and toss until they are cooked through and have absorbed all the sauce. Transfer to a serving dish and serve.

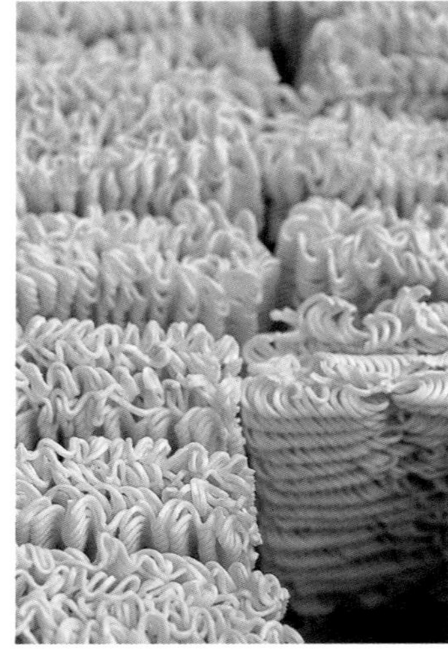

BLACK MUSHROOM NOODLES

THIS VEGETARIAN NOODLE DISH IS STRONGLY FLAVORED WITH CHINESE BLACK MUSHROOMS, CARROTS, LEEKS, GARLIC AND GINGER. TRADITIONALLY THE NOODLE CAKES ARE PAN-FRIED, BUT THEY CAN ALSO BE BROILED UNTIL CRISP, WHICH USES LESS OIL.

Chinese, or black, mushrooms are also known as shiitake mushrooms. They can be bought fresh when in season and dried all year round.

9 oz fresh or 6 oz dried egg noodles
1 1/2 teaspoons roasted sesame oil
5 dried Chinese mushrooms
2 leeks, white part only
2 carrots
1 tablespoon oil
2 garlic cloves, finely chopped
1 tablespoon finely chopped ginger
2 tablespoons Shaoxing rice wine
2 tablespoons light soy sauce
1 tablespoon oyster sauce
1/4 teaspoon freshly ground black pepper
1 1/2 tablespoons cornstarch

SERVES 4

COOK the noodles in a saucepan of salted boiling water for 2–3 minutes if fresh and 10 minutes if dried, then drain and combine with 1/2 teaspoon of the sesame oil.

PREHEAT the broiler, shape the noodles into 4 loose mounds on a lightly greased baking sheet and broil for 10 minutes on each side, turning once, until golden brown. Keep warm in a low oven.

SOAK the dried mushrooms in boiling water for 30 minutes, then drain, reserving the soaking liquid, and squeeze out any excess water. Remove and discard the stems and shred the caps. Cut the leeks into 2 inch pieces, then into 1/2 inch wide strips. Wash well and dry thoroughly. Cut the carrots to the same size as the leeks.

HEAT a wok over high heat, add the oil and heat until very hot. Stir-fry the garlic and ginger until fragrant. Add the leeks and carrots and stir-fry for 1 minute. Add the rice wine and mushrooms and cook for 1 minute.

ADD the soy and oyster sauces, pepper, remaining sesame oil and 1/3 cup of the reserved liquid. Combine the cornstarch with enough water to make a paste, add to the sauce and simmer until thickened. Put the noodles on a plate and spoon over with the sauce.

彩桥面

CROSSING-THE-BRIDGE NOODLES

LEGEND HAS IT THAT THIS DISH WAS INVENTED BY A WOMAN WHO HAD TO TAKE HER HUSBAND'S FOOD TO HIM EACH DAY. TO KEEP THE SOUP HOT FOR THE LONG JOURNEY, SHE FLOATED OIL ON TOP. THE SOUP MUST BE SERVED CLOSE TO BOILING AS YOU COOK THE FOOD IN IT.

1/4 lb shrimp
1/4 lb skinned boneless chicken breasts
1/4 lb squid bodies
1/4 lb Chinese ham, thinly sliced
8 dried Chinese mushrooms
1 1/3 cups bean sprouts
11 oz fresh rice noodles or 8 oz rice stick noodles
chili sauce
light soy sauce
4 cups chicken stock (page 281)
4 scallions, finely chopped

SERVES 4

PEEL the shrimp and cut them in half through the back, removing the vein. Slice the shrimp and the chicken breast thinly on the diagonal.

OPEN up the squid bodies by cutting down one side, scrub off any soft jelly-like substance and slice thinly on the diagonal. Arrange the shrimp, chicken, squid and ham on a plate, cover and refrigerate until needed.

SOAK the dried mushrooms in boiling water for 30 minutes, then drain and squeeze out any excess water. Remove and discard the stems. Add the mushrooms to the plate. Wash the bean sprouts and drain thoroughly. Add to the plate.

SEPARATE the rice noodles into 4 bundles. If you are using dried rice noodles, soak in hot water for 10 minutes, then drain.

GIVE EACH guest a small saucer of chili sauce and a saucer of soy sauce. Place the ingredients and dipping sauces on the table. Heat 4 soup bowls either in a low oven or by running them under very hot water for a few minutes. Put the chicken stock in a clay pot, braising pan or saucepan with the scallions and bring to a boil. When the stock has reached a rolling boil, fill the soup bowls.

GIVE EACH guest a hot bowl filled with stock and let them cook the meat, vegetables and noodles in the stock. You can be authentic and add a dash of oil to each bowl to seal in the heat, but it isn't really necessary.

A canal running through Lijiang.

In China, cassia bark *(middle)* is more often used than cinnamon to make this recipe.

桂皮牛肉面

CINNAMON BEEF NOODLES

- 1 teaspoon oil
- 10 scallions, cut into 1 1/2 inch pieces, lightly smashed with the flat side of a cleaver
- 10 garlic cloves, thinly sliced
- 6 slices ginger, smashed with the flat side of a cleaver
- 1 1/2 teaspoons chile bean paste (toban jiang)
- 2 cassia or cinnamon sticks
- 2 star anise
- 1/2 cup light soy sauce
- 2 lb chuck steak, trimmed and cut into 1 1/2 inch cubes
- 1/2 lb rice stick noodles
- 1/2 lb baby spinach
- 3 tablespoons finely chopped scallion

SERVES 6

HEAT a wok over medium heat, add the oil and heat until hot. Stir-fry the scallions, garlic, ginger, chile bean paste, cassia and star anise for 10 seconds, or until fragrant. Transfer to a clay pot, braising pan or saucepan. Add the soy sauce and 9 cups water. Bring to a boil, add the beef, then return to a boil. Reduce the heat and simmer, covered, for 1 1/2 hours, or until the beef is very tender. Skim the surface occasionally to remove impurities and fat. Remove and discard the ginger and cassia.

SOAK the noodles in hot water for 10 minutes, then drain and divide among 6 bowls. Add the spinach to the beef and bring to a boil. Spoon the beef mixture over the noodles and sprinkle with the chopped scallion.

LONGEVITY NOODLES

长寿面

LONGEVITY NOODLES

NOODLES SYMBOLIZE A LONG LIFE BECAUSE OF THEIR LENGTH AND ARE THEREFORE SERVED AT SPECIAL OCCASIONS SUCH AS BIRTHDAYS AND FEAST DAYS. THE NOODLES FOR THIS DISH ARE PARTICULARLY LONG AND CAN BE BOUGHT LABELED AS LONGEVITY NOODLES.

- 1/2 lb precooked longevity or dried egg noodles
- 1 cup bean sprouts
- 1/3 cup fresh or canned bamboo shoots, rinsed and drained
- 1 tablespoon oil
- 1 tablespoon finely chopped ginger
- 4 scallions, thinly sliced
- 1 tablespoon light soy sauce
- 1 teaspoon roasted sesame oil
- 1/4 cup chicken stock (page 281)

SERVES 4

IF USING dried egg noodles, cook in a saucepan of salted boiling water for 10 minutes, then drain. Wash the bean sprouts and drain thoroughly. Shred the bamboo shoots.

HEAT a wok over high heat, add the oil and heat until very hot. Stir-fry the ginger for a few seconds, then add the bean sprouts, bamboo shoots and scallions and stir-fry for 1 minute. Add the soy sauce, sesame oil and stock and bring to a boil. Add the longevity or dried egg noodles and toss together until the sauce is absorbed.

叉烧面/汤

CHAR SIU NOODLE SOUP

NOODLES IN SOUP ARE FAR MORE POPULAR THAN FRIED NOODLES (CHOW MEIN) IN CHINA. LIKE FRIED RICE, NOODLE DISHES ARE EATEN AS SNACKS RATHER THAN SERVED AS PART OF AN EVERYDAY MEAL. THIS IS A BASIC RECIPE—YOU CAN USE DIFFERENT INGREDIENTS FOR THE TOPPING.

4 dried Chinese mushrooms
7 oz barbecue pork (char siu)
1/3 cup fresh or canned bamboo shoots, rinsed and drained
2 cups green vegetable, such as spinach, bok choy or Chinese (Napa) cabbage
2 scallions
14 oz fresh or 11 oz dried egg noodles
4 cups chicken and meat stock (page 281)
2–3 tablespoons oil
1 teaspoon salt
1/2 teaspoon sugar
1 tablespoon light soy sauce
1 teaspoon Shaoxing rice wine
1/4 teaspoon roasted sesame oil

SERVES 4

SOAK the dried mushrooms in boiling water for 30 minutes, then drain and squeeze out any excess water. Remove and discard the stems and shred the caps. Thinly shred the pork, bamboo shoots, green vegetable and scallions.

COOK the noodles in a saucepan of salted boiling water for 2–3 minutes if fresh and 10 minutes if dried, then drain and place in 4 bowls. Bring the stock to a boil, then reduce the heat to simmering.

HEAT a wok over high heat, add the oil and heat until very hot. Stir-fry the pork and half the scallions for 1 minute, then add the mushrooms, bamboo shoots and green vegetable and stir-fry for 1 minute. Add the salt, sugar, soy sauce, rice wine and sesame oil and blend well.

POUR the stock over the noodles and top with the meat mixture and the remaining scallions.

烧鸭面/汤

ROAST DUCK NOODLE SOUP

THIS IS A QUICK AND EASY SNACK OR MEAL. CANTONESE-STYLE ROAST DUCK CAN BE BOUGHT AT CHINESE AND CARRY-OUT RESTAURANTS. ASK FOR IT TO BE CHOPPED INTO BITE-SIZE PIECES.

ROAST DUCK NOODLE SOUP

1 lb fresh or 11 oz dried egg noodles
4 cups chicken stock or chicken and meat stock (page 281)
3/4 lb roast duck, chopped
1/4 lb bok choy, shredded
2 tablespoons soy sauce
1/4 teaspoon roasted sesame oil

SERVES 4

COOK the noodles in a saucepan of salted boiling water for 2–3 minutes if fresh and 10 minutes if dried, then drain and place in 4 bowls. Bring the stock to a boil, then reduce the heat and keep at simmering point.

TOP EACH bowl with the duck, bok choy, soy sauce and sesame oil. Pour over the stock.

CHAR SIU NOODLE SOUP

Rice noodles being sold in a market in Yunnan.

Shred the steamed scallops into pieces. They have a strong flavor and are best eaten in small pieces.

干贝海鲜面

NOODLES WITH SEAFOOD AND DRIED SCALLOPS

THIS NOODLE DISH IS RATHER GRAND TO BE A SIMPLE SNACK. NOT ONLY DOES IT INCLUDE FRESH SEAFOOD, IT ALSO HAS DRIED SCALLOPS AS AN ADDED FLAVORING. DRIED SCALLOPS, ALSO KNOWN AS CONPOY, ARE REGARDED AS A DELICACY AND HAVE A RICH FLAVOR.

4 dried scallops (conpoy)
12 shrimp
7 oz squid bodies
13 oz thin rice stick noodles
1 tablespoon oil
2 tablespoons shredded ginger
2 scallions, thinly sliced
3 cups Chinese (Napa) cabbage, finely shredded
1 cup chicken stock (page 281)
2 tablespoons light soy sauce
2 tablespoons Shaoxing rice wine
1 teaspoon roasted sesame oil

SERVES 4

PUT the dried scallops in a flameproof bowl with 1 tablespoon water and put them in a steamer. Cover and steam over simmering water in a wok for 30 minutes, or until they are completely tender. Remove the scallops and shred the meat.

PEEL the shrimp and cut them in half through the back, removing the vein.

OPEN up the squid bodies by cutting down one side, scrub off any soft jelly-like substance, then score the inside of the flesh with a fine crisscross pattern, making sure you do not cut all the way through. Cut the squid into 3 x 2 inch pieces.

SOAK the noodles in hot water for 10 minutes, then drain.

HEAT a wok over high heat, add the oil and heat until very hot. Stir-fry the ginger and scallions for 1 minute, then add the shrimp and squid and stir-fry until just opaque. Add the scallops and Chinese cabbage and toss together. Pour in the stock, soy sauce and rice wine and boil for 1 minute. Add the noodles and sesame oil, toss together and serve.

云吞汤

WON TON SOUP

WON TON LITERALLY TRANSLATED MEANS "SWALLOWING A CLOUD". WON TONS, KNOWN AS HUN TUN OUTSIDE OF GUANGZHOU, ARE CATEGORIZED AS NOODLES AS THEY USE THE SAME DOUGH AS EGG NOODLES. WON TON SOUP CAN ALSO INCLUDE EGG NOODLES—ADD SOME IF YOU LIKE.

1/2 lb shrimp
1/2 cup peeled water chestnuts
1/2 lb lean ground pork
3 1/2 tablespoons light soy sauce
3 1/2 tablespoons Shaoxing rice wine
1 1/2 teaspoons salt
1 1/2 teaspoons roasted sesame oil
1/2 teaspoon freshly ground black pepper
1 teaspoon finely chopped ginger
1 1/2 tablespoons cornstarch
30 square or round won ton wrappers
6 cups chicken stock (page 281)
1 lb spinach, trimmed (optional)
2 scallions, green part only, finely chopped

SERVES 6

PEEL AND devein the shrimp. Place in a kitchen towel and squeeze out as much moisture as possible. Grind the shrimp to a coarse paste using a sharp knife or a food processor.

BLANCH the water chestnuts in boiling water for 1 minute, then refresh in cold water. Drain, pat dry and roughly chop them. Place the shrimp, water chestnuts, pork, 2 teaspoons of the soy sauce, 2 teaspoons of the rice wine, 1/2 teaspoon of the salt, 1/2 teaspoon of the sesame oil, the black pepper, ginger and cornstarch in a mixing bowl. Stir vigorously to combine.

PLACE a teaspoon of filling in the center of one won ton wrapper. Brush the edge of the wrapper with a little water, fold in half and then bring the two folded corners together and press firmly. Place the won tons on a cornstarch-dusted baking sheet.

BRING a saucepan of water to a boil. Cook the won tons, covered, for 5–6 minutes, or until they have risen to the surface. Using a wire strainer or slotted spoon, remove the won tons and divide them among 6 bowls.

PLACE the stock in a saucepan with the remaining soy sauce, rice wine, salt and sesame oil, and bring to a boil. Add the spinach and cook until just wilted. Pour the hot stock over the won tons and sprinkle with the chopped scallions.

The easiest way to make the won tons is to shape them in the same way as tortellini.

DESSERTS

Squeeze the juice out of the ginger by twisting it up in a piece of cheesecloth.

生姜布丁

GINGER PUDDING

THIS DESSERT CAN ALSO BE EATEN AS A SNACK. THE GINGER JUICE CAUSES THE HOT MILK TO COAGULATE AND FORMS A GINGER-FLAVORED PUDDING WITH A SLIPPERY SMOOTH TEXTURE. IT IS IMPORTANT TO USE YOUNG, SWEET FRESH GINGER OR THE FLAVOR WILL BE TOO HARSH.

7 oz young ginger
1 tablespoon sugar
2 cups milk

SERVES 4

GRATE the ginger as finely as you can, collecting any juice. Place it in a piece of cheesecloth, twist the top hard and squeeze out as much juice as possible. You will need 4 tablespoons. Alternatively, push the ginger through a juicer.

PUT 1 tablespoon of ginger juice and 1 teaspoon of sugar each into 4 bowls. Put the milk in a saucepan and bring to a boil, then divide among the bowls. Allow to set for 1 minute (the ginger juice will cause the milk to solidify). Serve warm.

杏仁豆腐（加水果）

ALMOND BEAN CURD WITH FRUIT

DURING HOT WEATHER IN CHINA, REFRESHING FRUIT SALADS MADE FROM PINEAPPLE, MANGO, PAPAYA, MELON, LYCHEE AND LOQUAT ARE POPULAR SNACKS. THE MILKY SQUARE OF ALMOND JELLY THAT GOES WITH THIS FRUIT SALAD IS SAID TO RESEMBLE BEAN CURD, HENCE THE NAME.

$2\frac{1}{2}$ tablespoons powdered gelatin or 6 gelatin sheets
$\frac{1}{3}$ cup superfine sugar
2 teaspoons almond extract
$\frac{1}{2}$ cup condensed milk
13 oz can lychees in syrup
13 oz can loquats in syrup
$\frac{1}{2}$ papaya, cut into cubes
$\frac{1}{2}$ melon, cut into cubes

SERVES 6

PUT $\frac{1}{2}$ cup water in a saucepan. If you are using powdered gelatin, sprinkle it on the water and let it dissolve for 1 minute. If you are using sheets, soak in the water until floppy. Heat the mixture slightly, stirring constantly to dissolve the gelatin.

PLACE the sugar, almond extract and condensed milk in a bowl and stir to combine. Slowly add $5\frac{1}{2}$ cups water, stirring to dissolve the sugar. Stir in the dissolved gelatin. Pour into a chilled 9 inch square pan. Chill for at least 4 hours, or until set.

DRAIN HALF the syrup from the lychees and the loquats. Place the lychees and loquats with their remaining syrup in a large bowl. Add the cubed papaya and melon. Cut the almond bean curd into diamond-shaped pieces and arrange on plates, then spoon the fruit around the bean curd.

ALMOND BEAN CURD WITH FRUIT

新年甜汤圆

NEW YEAR SWEET DUMPLINGS

THESE GLUTINOUS SWEET DUMPLINGS ARE MADE FOR THE CHINESE NEW YEAR AND ARE OFTEN EATEN IN A SWEET SOUP. THEY CAN BE FILLED WITH A NUT OR BEAN PASTE.

$^1/_4$ cup black sesame paste, red bean paste or smooth peanut butter
4 tablespoons superfine sugar
$1^1/_2$ cups glutinous rice flour
1 oz rock sugar

MAKES 24

COMBINE the sesame paste with the sugar.

SIFT the rice flour into a bowl and stir in $^3/_4$ cup boiling water. Knead carefully (the dough will be very hot) to form a soft, slightly sticky dough. Dust your hands with extra rice flour, roll the dough into a cylinder, then divide it into cherry-size pieces. Cover the dough with a kitchen towel and, using one piece at a time, form each piece of dough into a flat round, then gather it into a cup shape. The dough should be fairly thin.

FILL EACH cup shape with 1 teaspoon of paste and fold the top over, smoothing the dough so you have a round ball with no visible seams.

BRING 4 cups water to a boil, add the rock sugar and stir until dissolved. Return to a boil, add the dumplings in batches and simmer for 5 minutes, or until they rise to the surface. Serve warm with a little of the syrup.

New Year dumplings are widely available in the markets and night markets of China during the New Year celebrations.

炸香蕉

FRIED FRAGRANT BANANAS

$^1/_2$ cup self-rising flour
2 tablespoons milk
1 tablespoon butter, melted
1 tablespoon superfine sugar
4 apple or lady finger bananas, or 3 ordinary bananas
oil for deep-frying
honey (optional)

SERVES 4

COMBINE the flour, milk, butter and sugar, then add enough water to make a thick batter.

CUT the bananas into $1^1/_4$ inch chunks.

FILL a wok one quarter full of oil. Heat the oil to 350°F, or until a piece of bread fries golden brown in 15 seconds when dropped in the oil. Dip the banana pieces, a few at a time, into the batter and then fry them for 3 minutes, or until they are well browned on all sides. Drain on paper towels. Serve the bananas drizzled with honey for extra sweetness.

FRIED FRAGRANT BANANAS

Packaged eight-treasure rice.

Fresh longans.

八宝饭

EIGHT-TREASURE RICE

THIS CHINESE RICE PUDDING IS A FAVORITE AT BANQUETS AND CHINESE NEW YEAR. THE EIGHT TREASURES VARY, BUT CAN ALSO INCLUDE OTHER PRESERVED FRUITS.

12 whole blanched lotus seeds
12 jujubes (dried Chinese dates)
20 fresh or canned gingko nuts, shelled
1 cup glutinous rice
2 tablespoons sugar
2 teaspoons oil
1 oz slab sugar
8 candied cherries
6 dried longans, pitted
4 almonds or walnuts
1 cup red bean paste

SERVES 8

SOAK the lotus seeds and jujubes in bowls of cold water for 30 minutes, then drain. Remove the pits from the jujubes. If using fresh gingko nuts, blanch in a saucepan of boiling water for 5 minutes, then refresh in cold water and dry thoroughly.

PUT the glutinous rice and 1 1/4 cups water in a heavy-bottomed saucepan and bring to a boil. Reduce the heat to low and simmer for 10–15 minutes. Stir in the sugar and oil.

DISSOLVE the slab sugar in 3/4 cup water and bring to a boil. Add the lotus seeds, jujubes and gingko nuts and simmer for 1 hour, or until the lotus seeds are soft. Drain, reserving the liquid.

GREASE a 4-cup flameproof bowl and decorate the bottom with the lotus seeds, jujubes, gingko nuts, cherries, longans and almonds. Smooth 2/3 of the rice over this to form a shell on the surface of the bowl. Fill with the bean paste, cover with the remaining rice and smooth the surface.

COVER the rice with greased aluminum foil and put the bowl in a steamer. Cover and steam over simmering water in a wok for 1–1 1/2 hours, replenishing with boiling water during cooking.

TURN the pudding out onto a plate and pour the reserved sugar liquid over the top. Serve hot.

Eight-treasure rice can be made in any round dish. If you want it to sit higher on the plate, then choose a deep bowl. Remember that the pattern you make on the bottom will come out on top.

蜂蜜蒸梨

STEAMED PEARS IN HONEY

THIS RECIPE COMBINES SWEET PEARS WITH JUJUBES, SMALL RED DATES THAT ARE THOUGHT TO HAVE MEDICINAL BENEFITS. THEY ARE SOLD DRIED, BUT CAN BE LEFT OUT IF THEY ARE UNAVAILABLE.

3/4 cup jujubes (dried Chinese dates)
6 nearly ripe pears
6 tablespoons honey

SERVES 6

SOAK the jujubes in hot water for 1 hour, changing the water twice. Drain, remove pits and cut crosswise into strips.

CUT a slice off the bottom of each pear so that it will sit flat. Cut a 1 inch piece off the top and set it aside. Using a fruit corer or knife, remove the cores without cutting right through to the bottom.

ARRANGE the pears upright on a flameproof plate. Place 1 tablespoon of honey and some jujubes into the cavity of each pear. Replace the tops and, if necessary, fasten with cocktail sticks.

PUT the plate in a steamer. Cover and steam over simmering water in a wok for 30 minutes, or until tender when pierced with a knife. Serve hot or cold.

STEAMED PEARS IN HONEY

杏仁饼

ALMOND COOKIES

ALMONDS ARE USED FOR SWEET RATHER THAN SAVORY DISHES IN CHINA. THESE COOKIES MAKE GREAT SNACKS AND CAN ALSO BE SERVED ALONGSIDE DESSERTS SUCH AS ALMOND BEAN CURD.

1/2 cup unsalted butter, softened
3/4 cup sugar
1 egg, lightly beaten
1 1/2 cups all-purpose flour
1/2 teaspoon baking powder
1/2 teaspoon salt
1 cup finely chopped almonds
1 teaspoon almond extract
1 egg, lightly beaten, extra
25 whole blanched almonds

MAKES 25

PREHEAT the oven to 350°F. Lightly grease a baking sheet. Cream the butter and sugar for 5 minutes. Add the egg and beat until smooth. Sift together the flour, baking powder and salt and slowly add to the butter, stirring until smooth. Add the almonds and extract and stir until smooth.

DROP tablespoons of the mixture onto the baking sheet, spacing them about 1 1/4 inches apart. Dip your thumb into some flour and make an indentation in the center of each cookie. Brush each cookie with the beaten egg and place an almond in the center of each indentation. Bake for 10–12 minutes, or until the cookies are golden and puffed. Cool slightly, then transfer to a rack to cool completely.

Dip your thumb in some flour and make an indent in each cookie to hold the almonds.

BASICS

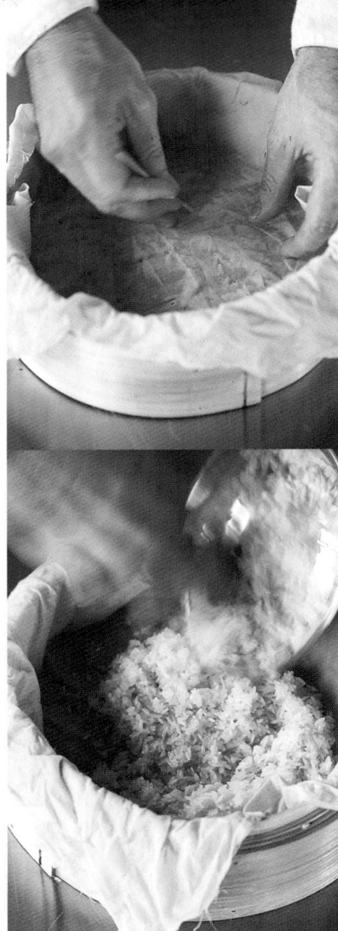

For steamed rice, line a steamer with waxed paper punched with holes or cheesecloth to let in the steam. Spread out the rice in an even layer.

白饭

BOILED OR STEAMED RICE

1 cup white long-grain rice

SERVES 4

PUT the rice in a bowl and, using your fingers as a rake, rinse under cold running water to remove any dust. Drain the rice in a colander.

TO BOIL the rice, put the rice and 1 2/3 cups water in a heavy-bottomed saucepan and bring to a boil. Reduce the heat to low and simmer, covered, for 15–18 minutes, or until the water has evaporated and craters appear on the surface.

TO STEAM the rice, spread the rice in a steamer lined with waxed paper punched with holes or damp cheesecloth. Cover and steam over simmering water in a wok for 35–40 minutes, or until tender.

FLUFF the rice with a fork to separate the grains. Serve or use as directed.

锅巴

CRISPY RICE

CRISPY RICE IS A GREAT WAY TO USE UP LEFTOVER RICE, ALTHOUGH YOU CAN MAKE IT FROM SCRATCH, AS HERE. THE DEEP-FRIED RICE IS PUT IN THE BOTTOM OF BOWLS AND A SOUP SUCH AS TOMATO AND EGG (PAGE 60) OR MIXED VEGETABLE (PAGE 63) IS POURED OVER IT TO MAKE THE RICE SIZZLE.

2/3 cup white long-grain rice

SERVES 4

PUT the rice in a bowl and, using your fingers as a rake, rinse under cold running water to remove any dust. Drain the rice in a colander.

PUT the rice and 3/4 cup water in a heavy-bottomed saucepan and bring to the boil. Reduce the heat to low and simmer, covered, for 15–18 minutes.

CONTINUE to cook uncovered until the rice has formed a cake that comes loose from the saucepan. Allow to cool. Turn the cake out and dry completely.

FILL a wok one quarter full of oil. Heat the oil to 350°F, or until a piece of bread fries golden brown in 15 seconds when dropped in the oil. Cook the rice cake until it is brown and crisp.

CRISPY RICE

中式薄饼

MANDARIN PANCAKES

THESE THIN PANCAKES ARE ALSO CALLED DUCK PANCAKES AND ARE USED FOR WRAPPING PEKING DUCK (PAGE 134) AND OTHER NORTHERN DISHES, SUCH AS CRISPY SKIN DUCK (PAGE 129), MU SHU PORK (PAGE 156) AND MONGOLIAN LAMB (PAGE 183).

3 1/3 cups all-purpose flour
1 1/4 cups boiling water
1 teaspoon oil
roasted sesame oil

MAKES 24–30

SIFT the flour into a bowl, slowly pour in the boiling water, stirring as you pour, then add the oil and knead into a firm dough. Cover with a damp kitchen towel and set aside for 30 minutes.

TURN the dough out onto a lightly floured surface and knead for 8–10 minutes, or until smooth. Divide the dough into 3 equal portions, roll each portion into a long cylinder, then cut each cylinder into 8 to 10 pieces.

ROLL EACH piece of dough into a ball and press into a flat round with the palm of your hand. Brush one round with a little sesame oil and put another round on top. Using a rolling pin, flatten each pair of rounds into a 6 inch pancake.

HEAT an ungreased wok or frying pan over high heat, then reduce the heat to low and place the pairs of pancakes, one at a time, in the pan. Turn over when brown spots appear on the underside. When the second side is cooked, lift the pancakes out and carefully peel them apart. Fold each pancake in half with the cooked side facing inwards, and set aside under a damp cloth.

JUST BEFORE serving, put the pancakes on a plate in a steamer. Cover and steam over simmering water in a wok for 10 minutes.

TO STORE the pancakes, put them in the fridge for 2 days or in the freezer for several months. Reheat the pancakes either in a steamer for 4–5 minutes or a microwave for 30–40 seconds.

Mandarin pancakes are always rolled and cooked as a pair; the two pancakes are separated by a layer of sesame oil.

BASIC YEAST DOUGH

CHINESE CHEFS USE TWO TYPES OF BREAD DOUGH FOR MAKING STEAMED BREADS, ONE MADE WITH YEAST AS HERE, THE OTHER MADE WITH A YEAST STARTER DOUGH.

This bread dough is twice risen, first with yeast and then with baking powder, which is kneaded into the dough, making it very light and fluffy.

3 tablespoons sugar
1 cup warm water
$1^1/_2$ teaspoons dried yeast
$3^1/_4$ cups all-purpose flour
2 tablespoons oil
$1^1/_2$ teaspoons baking powder

MAKES 1 QUANTITY

DISSOLVE the sugar in the water, then add the yeast. Stir lightly, then set aside for 10 minutes, or until foamy.

SIFT the flour into a bowl and add the yeast mixture and the oil. Using a wooden spoon, mix the ingredients into a rough dough. Turn the mixture out onto a lightly floured surface and knead for 8–10 minutes, or until the dough is smooth and elastic. If it is very sticky, knead in a little more flour—the dough should be soft. Lightly grease a bowl with the oil. Place the dough in the bowl and turn it so that all sides of the dough are coated. Cover the bowl with a damp cloth and set aside to rise in a draft-free place for 3 hours.

UNCOVER the dough, punch it down, and turn it out onto a lightly floured surface. If you are not using the dough right away, cover it with plastic wrap and refrigerate.

WHEN YOU are ready to use the dough, flatten it and make a well in the center. Place the baking powder in the well and gather up the edges to enclose the baking powder. Pinch the edges to seal. Lightly knead the dough for several minutes to evenly incorporate the baking powder, which will activate immediately.

USE the prepared dough as directed.

鸡汤

CHICKEN STOCK

- 3 lb chicken carcasses, necks and feet
- 1 cup Shaoxing rice wine
- 6 slices ginger, smashed with the flat side of a cleaver
- 6 scallions, ends trimmed, smashed with the flat side of a cleaver
- 16 cups water

MAKES 2 1/2 QUARTS

REMOVE ANY excess fat from the chicken, then chop into large pieces and place in a stockpot with the rice wine, ginger, scallions and water and bring to a boil. Reduce the heat and simmer gently for 3 hours, skimming the surface to remove any impurities.

STRAIN through a fine strainer, removing the solids, and skim the surface to remove any fat. If the stock is too weak, reduce it further. Store in the fridge for up to 3 days or freeze in small portions.

CHICKEN AND MEAT STOCK

排骨鸡汤

CHICKEN AND MEAT STOCK

- 1 lb 5 oz chicken carcasses, necks and feet
- 1 lb 5 oz pork spareribs or veal bones
- 4 scallions, each tied into a knot
- 12 slices ginger, smashed with the flat side of a cleaver
- 16 cups water
- 1/3 cup Shaoxing rice wine
- 2 teaspoons salt

MAKES 2 1/2 QUARTS

REMOVE ANY excess fat from the chicken and meat, then chop into large pieces and place in a stockpot with the scallions, ginger and water and bring to a boil. Reduce the heat and simmer gently for 3 1/2–4 hours, skimming the surface to remove any impurities.

STRAIN through a fine strainer, removing the solids, and skim the surface to remove any fat. Return to the pot with the rice wine and salt. Bring to a boil and simmer for 3–4 minutes. Store in the fridge for up to 3 days or freeze in small portions.

VEGETABLE STOCK

VEGETABLE STOCK

- 1 lb fresh soy bean sprouts
- 10 dried Chinese mushrooms
- 6 scallions, each tied into a knot (optional)
- 16 cups water
- 3 tablespoons Shaoxing rice wine
- 2 teaspoons salt

MAKES 2 1/2 QUARTS

DRY-FRY the sprouts in a wok for 3–4 minutes. Place the sprouts, mushrooms, scallions and water in a stockpot and bring to the boil. Reduce the heat and simmer for 1 hour.

STRAIN through a fine strainer, removing the solids (keep the mushrooms for another use). Return to the stockpot with the rice wine and salt. Bring to a boil and simmer for 3–4 minutes. Store in the fridge for up to 3 days or freeze in small portions.

CHICKEN STOCK

SOY AND VINEGAR

SOY, VINEGAR AND CHILI

SOY, CHILI AND SESAME

酱醋调味酱

SOY AND VINEGAR DIPPING SAUCE

SIMPLE DIPPING SAUCES ARE SERVED WITH FOODS SUCH AS STEAMED DUMPLINGS. THE ADDITION OF VINEGAR GIVES A MORE ROUNDED FLAVOR THAN USING JUST SOY SAUCE.

1/2 cup light soy sauce
3 tablespoons Chinese black rice vinegar

MAKES 1 CUP

COMBINE the soy sauce and vinegar with 2 tablespoons water in a small bowl, then divide among individual dipping bowls. This dipping sauce goes well with jiaozi (page 20) or dim sum like siu mai (page 38).

酱醋辣酱

SOY, VINEGAR AND CHILI DIPPING SAUCE

1/2 cup light soy sauce
2 tablespoons Chinese black rice vinegar
2 red chiles, thinly sliced

MAKES 3/4 CUP

COMBINE the soy sauce, vinegar and chiles in a small bowl, then divide among individual dipping bowls. This dipping sauce goes well with jiaozi (page 20) or dim sum like har gau (page 41) or bean curd rolls (page 35).

红醋调味酱

RED VINEGAR DIPPING SAUCE

1/2 cup red rice vinegar
3 tablespoons shredded ginger

MAKES 1 CUP

COMBINE the rice vinegar, 2 1/2 tablespoons water and the ginger in a small bowl, then divide among individual dipping bowls. This dipping sauce goes well with jiaozi (page 20).

酱辣芝麻调味酱

SOY, CHILI AND SESAME DIPPING SAUCE

1/2 cup light soy sauce
1/4 cup chile oil
1 tablespoon roasted sesame oil
1 scallion, finely chopped

MAKES 3/4 CUP

COMBINE the soy sauce, chile oil, sesame oil and scallion in a small bowl, then divide among individual dipping bowls. This dipping sauce goes well with jiaozi (page 20) and steamed breads (page 46).

RED VINEGAR

MAKING GREEN TEA

GREEN TEA is served in glasses so its colour and the leaves themselves can be appreciated. The glasses are warmed, then tea added with a little freshly boiled water (spring water is considered best). The glasses are topped up by pouring in more water from a height, known as flushing, to aerate the water for a better infusion. The tea is drunk very hot and the leaves briefly steeped compared to black teas.

MAKING OOLONG TEA

OOLONG is made here by the *gong fu* method. The cups and pot are warmed, then the leaves are rinsed with boiling water, strained into a jug and topped up with more water. Water is poured over the pot to keep it warm while the tea brews, then when dry, the tea is poured back and forth over tall smelling cups to ensure an even strength. The aroma is taken in from the tall cups after the tea is tipped into small cups to taste.

TEA SEASONS

TEA is seasonal: spring teas are the finest, while winter teas have an enticing aroma but are rare as there is little harvesting. For Dragon Well tea, the first and best quality picking of the year is the *nu'er* (daughter) tea *(left)*. The second is known as *Qing Ming (middle)* as it is picked around the time of that festival in April. The last picking is called *gu yu (right)* and is picked in the season of this name between spring and summer.

TEA HOUSES are popular all over China. Some are a male domain where business is conducted, such as at this one in Yuyuan Bazaar, Shanghai *(top)*, while others, like this one at Wenshu Monastery, Chengdu *(bottom right)*, are family-orientated and allow patrons to sit all day over a constantly refilled cup of tea. Tea houses also offer snacks to accompany the tea, from melon seeds or oranges to more ornate sweet offerings *(bottom left)*.

TEA

TEA HAS BEEN POPULAR IN CHINA SINCE AT LEAST THE SIXTH CENTURY BC, AND IT WAS FROM CHINA THAT TEA TRAVELLED TO JAPAN, EUROPE AND INDIA. INTEGRAL TO FESTIVALS, A SIGN OF HOSPITALITY, A MEDICINE, AND STEEPED IN TRADITION, TEA IS BOTH A DRINK AND A PART OF CHINESE CULTURE ITSELF.

For the Chinese, tea is a drink to be savoured on its own or before or after a meal. The exception is tea with yum cha, which means to 'drink tea' and originated as a few snacks to complement the tea at tea houses, rather than the full meal it often is today. In China, hot water is provided in hotels, waiting rooms and on trains for people to make tea using their own screwtop jar or in a large cup with a lid that can be slid back just enough to drink the tea without the leaves coming too. Carrying a receptacle for tea is not a statement of class or rank, everyone does it.

ORIGINS OF TEA

Tea plants (*Camellia sinensis*) are native to the mountains of Southwest China, and are now grown all over the South, and in the East and North where conditions are favourable. Teas from Yunnan and Fujian are particularly treasured. Tea is made from the two top leaves and bud, picked every 7–10 days to gather the young shoots and to encourage more shoots to sprout, known as a flush. These small leaves are more prized than too large or broken leaves. Fannings (tea dust and broken leaves) are the lowest grades of all.

DRAGON WELL TEA is China's finest green tea, grown around the West Lake of Hangzhou, especially in the village of Longjing (Dragon Well). Here, the Wen family runs a small tea estate producing three pickings a year. The tea buds are hand-picked, then dried by rubbing the leaves around a heated metal basin to arrest any fermentation. The Wen family teas are sold by weight from their house in the village.

VARIETIES OF TEA

Tea is categorized by the different methods of its production:
GREEN an unfermented tea made by firing (drying) fresh leaves in a kind of wok to prevent them oxidizing (fermenting). The tea is usually rolled and twisted to uncurl in boiling water.
OOLONG the leaves are semi-fermented before firing to produce a tea halfway between green and black. The most famous oolong teas are from Fujian and Taiwan.
BLACK a fully fermented tea where the leaves are wilted and bruised by rolling, then fermented and dried.
WHITE a very rare, totally unfermented green tea from Fujian.

Chinese teas can also be categorized by other factors:
BRICK usually pu-er teas from Yunnan compressed into blocks. A piece is sliced off to make tea.
SCENTED tea leaves mixed with scented flowers.
FLOWER petal teas, which are not true teas but tisanes.

BRICK TEA a compressed tea, usually made from Yunnan pu'er, which was originally devised to carry tea easily and was even used as a form of currency. The character on the tea is for wealth.

CLOUD AND MIST (*Yun Wu*) a green tea grown on mountain sides and cliffs, appreciated for its colour and fine clear flavour. It is a legendary 'monkey pick' tea, said to be harvested by monkeys.

IRON GODDESS (*Tie Guan Yin*) a strong, bitter oolong tea, also called Iron Buddha, drunk before and after a meal from a tiny cup. It is often served with Chiu Chow cuisine to balance the rich food.

FLOWER TEA made from chrysanthemum flowers, wolf berries and peppermint sugar, this is not strictly a tea, but is served in tea houses as a medicinal tonic.

QIMEN RED TEA this prized mild, sweet and aromatic black tea from the Huangshan mountains in Anhui is known in the West as Keemun. A gong fu tea, meaning that it is precisely prepared.

LYCHEE TEA made from black tea leaves that are processed with lychee juice, this tea has a fragrant sweet flavour that is very palate cleansing. It is also called lychee red.

DRAGON WELL (*Long Jing*) this fragrant, sweet green tea from Hangzhou in the East is considered the best in China. The leaves are flat, not rolled, and stand up when infused.

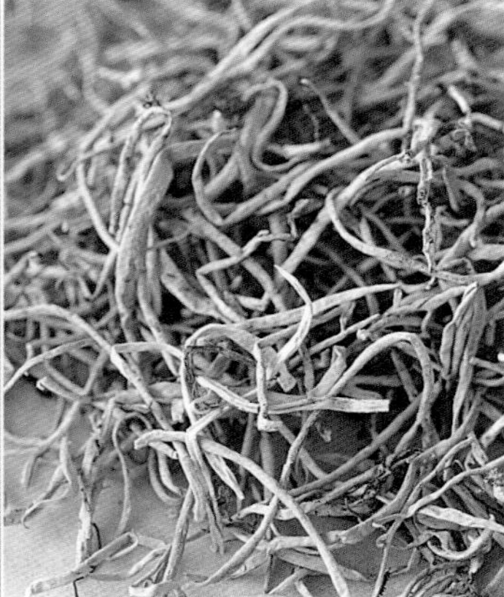

WHITE TEA (*Chai Tou Yu Ming*) this fine white tea is named after a hair ornament. White tea is made from hand-picked buds, dried in the sun to create a silvery tea with a very pure taste.

JASMINE TEA a light, fragrant tea of green or black leaves mixed with jasmine flowers. Jasmine is renowned as a good digestive after a rich meal and contains little caffeine.

CHRYSANTHEMUM TEA a flower tea with a mixture of whole chrysanthemum and tea or just chrysanthemum. It is regarded as cooling and its mild flavour goes well with dim sum.

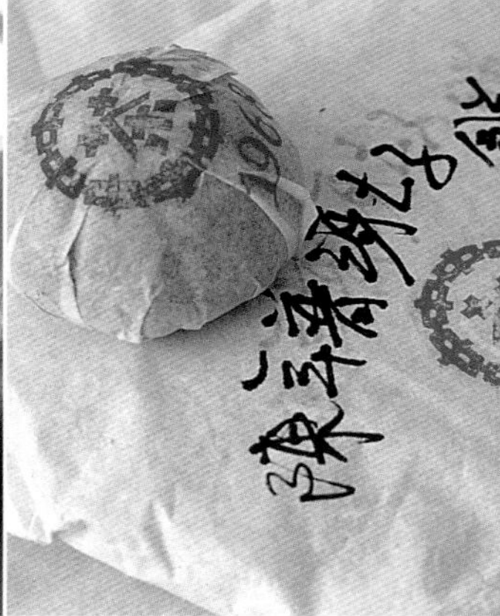

CAKE TEA also known as bowl tea, this is the round form of compressed pu'er. This variety is called gold melon. It symbolizes a blessing and is a gift for a couple's families after their wedding.

PU'ER, or Bou Lei, is a popular black tea from Yunnan that often accompanies dim sum as it is said to aid the digestion of fats (and ease hangovers). Pu'er is sold loose or as a cake or brick.

Chinese chives Garlic chives have a long, flat leaf and are green and very garlicky, or yellow with a milder taste. Flowering chives are round-stemmed with a flower at the top, which can be eaten. Both are used as a vegetable rather than as a herb.

Chinese curry powder A strong and spicy version of five-spice powder, with additional spices including turmeric and coriander which lend the curry flavour.

Chinese ham A salted and smoked ham with a strong flavor and dry flesh. Yunnan and Jinhua hams are the best known, and outside China, Yunnan ham can be bought in cans. You can substitute prosciutto if you can't find it.

Chinese mushrooms The fresh version, found as shiitake mushrooms, is cultivated by the Japanese. The Chinese, however, usually use dried ones, which have a strong flavor and aroma and need to be soaked to reconstitute them before they are used. The soaking liquid can be used to add flavor to dishes. These are widely available.

Chinese pickles These can be made from several types of vegetables, preserved in a clear brine solution or in a soy-based solution, which is called jiang cai. Both can be used where Chinese pickles are called for in a recipe. They are available in packages and jars from Chinese markets.

Chinese sausage There are two kinds of Chinese sausage: a red variety, lap cheong or la chang, which is made from pork and pork fat and dried; and a brown variety, yun cheung or xiang chang, which is made from liver and pork and also dried. Chinese sausages have to be cooked before eating.

Chinese shrimp paste Very pungent pulverized shrimp. Refrigerate after opening.

Chinese spirits Distilled from grains, these vary in strength but generally are stronger than Western spirits. Spirits are used for drinking and cooking and Mou Tai is a common brand. Brandy can be substituted.

Chinese-style pork spareribs These are the shorter, fatter ribs known as pai gwat and are cut into short pieces. If unavailable, use any spareribs but trim off any excess fat.

Chinese turnip Looking like a huge white carrot, this is actually a type of radish and is also called Chinese white radish. It has a crisp, juicy flesh and mild radish flavor. It is also known as mooli, or by the Japanese name daikon, and is widely available.

choy sum A green vegetable with tender pale-green stalks, small yellow flowers and dark-green leaves. It has a mild flavor and is often just blanched and eaten with a simple flavoring like garlic or oyster sauce.

clay pot Also known as a sand pot, these earthenware, lidded pots are used for braised dishes, soups and rice dishes that need to be cooked slowly on the stove. The pots come in different shapes: the squatter ones are for braising and the taller ones for soups and rice. The pots can be fragile and should be heated slowly, preferably with a liquid inside.

cleaver A large, oblong, flat-bladed knife. In China, different cleavers are used for all chopping and cutting, but heavy-duty ones are good for chopping through bones as they are very robust. They can be bought in Chinese markets and at specialty stores.

dang gui A bitter Chinese herb that is a relation of European Angelica and is valued for its medicinal properties. It looks like small bleached pieces of wood, and is generally added to braised dishes and soups. Buy it in Chinese markets or Chinese herb shops.

dried scallops (conpoy) Scallops dried to thick amber disks. They need to be soaked or steamed until soft and are often shredded before use. They have a strong flavor so you don't need many, and as they are expensive they are mostly eaten at banquets.

dried shrimp These are tiny, orange, saltwater shrimp that have been dried in the sun. They come in different sizes and the really small ones have their heads and shells still attached. Dried shrimp need to be soaked in water or rice wine to soften them before use and are used as a seasoning, not as a main ingredient.

dumpling wrappers Used for jiaozi, wheat wrappers, also called Shanghai wrappers or wheat dumpling skins, are white and can be round or square. Egg wrappers for siu mai are yellow and may also be round or square. They are sometimes labeled gow gee wrappers or egg dumpling skins. All are found in the refrigerated section in Chinese markets and good supermarkets and can be frozen until needed.

fermented bean curd A marinated bean curd that is either red, colored with red rice, or white, and may also be flavored with chiles. It is sometimes called preserved bean curd or bean curd cheese and is used as a condiment or flavoring. It can be found in jars in Chinese markets.

five-spice powder A Chinese mixed spice generally made with star anise, cassia, Sichuan pepper, fennel seeds and cloves, which gives a balance of sweet, hot and aromatic flavors. Five-spice may also include cardamom, coriander, dried orange peel and ginger. Used ground together as a powder or as whole spices tied in muslin.

flat cabbage (tat soi) Also known as a rosette cabbage, this is a type of bok choy. It looks like a giant flower with pretty, shiny, dark-green leaves that grow out flat.

gingko nuts These are the nuts of the maidenhair tree. The hard shells are cracked open and the inner nuts soaked to loosen their skins. The nuts are known for their medicinal properties and are one of the eight treasures in dishes like eight-treasure rice. Shelled nuts can be bought in cans in Chinese markets and are easier to use.

glutinous rice A short-grain rice that, unlike other rice, cooks to a sticky mass and is used in dishes where the rice is required to hold together. Glutinous rice is labeled as such and has plump, highly polished and shiny grains. Black or red glutinous rice, used mainly in desserts, is slightly different.

Guilin chili sauce From the southwest of China, this sauce is made from salted, fermented yellow soy beans and chiles. It is used as an ingredient in cooking. If it is unavailable, use a thick chili sauce instead.

hoisin sauce This sauce is made from salted, yellow soy beans, sugar, vinegar, sesame oil, red rice for coloring and spices such as five-spice or star anise. It is generally used as a dipping sauce, for meat glazes or in barbecue marinades.

jujubes Also known as Chinese or red dates, jujubes are an olive-sized dried fruit with a red, wrinkled skin, thought to build strength. They need to be soaked and are used in eight-treasure or tonic-type dishes. They are thought to be lucky because of their red color.

longans From the same family as lychees, these are round with smooth, buff-colored skins, translucent sweet flesh and large brown seeds. Available fresh, canned or dried.

lotus leaves The dried leaves of the lotus, they need to be soaked before use and are used for wrapping up food like sticky rice to hold it together while it is cooking. They are sold in packages in Chinese markets.

lotus root The rhizome of the Chinese lotus, the root looks like a string of three cream-colored sausages, but when cut into it has a beautiful lacy pattern. Available fresh (which must be washed), canned or dried. Use the fresh or canned version as a fresh vegetable and the dried version in braised dishes.

lotus seeds These seeds from the lotus are considered medicinal and are used in eight-treasure dishes as well as being toasted, salted or candied and eaten as a snack. Lotus seeds are also made into a sweet paste to fill buns and pancakes. Fresh and dried lotus seeds are both available and dried seeds need to be soaked before use.

maltose A sweet liquid of malted grains used to coat Peking duck and barbecued meats. It is sold in Chinese markets, but honey can be used instead.

master sauce This is a basic stock of soy sauce, rice wine, rock sugar, scallions, ginger and star anise. Additional ingredients vary according to individual chefs. Meat, poultry or fish is cooked in the stock, then the stock is reserved so it matures, taking on the flavors of everything that is cooked in it. The spices are replenished every few times the sauce is used. Master sauce spices can be bought as a mix, or a ready-made liquid version. Freeze between uses.

Mei Kuei Lu Chiew A fragrant spirit known as Rose Dew Liqueur. Made from sorghum and rose petals. It is used in marinades, but brandy can be used instead.

noodles Egg noodles come fresh and dried in varying thicknesses. In recipes they are interchangeable, so choose a brand that you like and buy the thickness appropriate to the dish you are making. Wheat noodles are also available fresh and dried and are interchangeable in recipes. Rice noodles are made from a paste of ground rice and water and can be bought fresh or as dried rice sticks or vermicelli. The fresh noodles are white and can be bought in a roll.

one-thousand-year-old eggs Also known as one-hundred-year old or century eggs, these are eggs that have been preserved by coating them in a layer of wood ash, slaked lime and then rice husks. The eggs are left to mature for 40 days to give them a blackish-green yolk and amber white. To eat, the coating is scraped off and the shell peeled. These eggs are eaten as an hors d'oeuvre or used to garnish congee.

oyster sauce A fairly recent invention, this is a soy-based sauce flavored with oyster extract. Add to dishes at the end of cooking or use as part of a marinade.

pepper Used as an ingredient rather than as a condiment, most hot dishes were originally flavored with copious quantities of pepper rather than the chiles used now. White pepper is used rather than black.

plum sauce This comes in several varieties, with some brands sweeter than others and some adding chile, ginger or garlic. It is often served with Peking duck rather than the true sauce and is a good dipping sauce.

preserved ginger Ginger pickled in rice vinegar and sugar, which is typically used for sweet-and-sour dishes. Japanese pickled ginger could be used as a substitute.

preserved mustard cabbage Also called Sichuan pickle or preserved vegetables, this is the root of the mustard cabbage preserved in chile and salt. It is available whole and shredded in jars or cans, or vacuum-packed from Chinese markets.

preserved turnip This is Chinese turnip, sliced, shredded or grated, and usually preserved in brine. It has a crunchy texture and needs to be rinsed before using so it is less salty.

red bean paste Made from crushed adzuki beans and sugar, this sweet paste is used in soups and to fill dumplings and pancakes. There is a richer black version and this can be used instead.

rice flour This is finely ground rice, often used to make rice noodles. Glutinous rice flour, used for making sweet things, makes a chewier dough. Obtainable from Chinese markets or supermarkets.

rice vinegar Made from fermented rice, Chinese vinegars are milder than Western ones. Clear rice vinegar is mainly used for pickles and sweet-and-sour dishes. Red rice vinegar is a mild liquid used as a dipping sauce and served with shark's fin soup. Black rice vinegar is used in stews, especially in northern recipes—Chinkiang (Zhenjiang) vinegar is a good label. Rice vinegars can last indefinitely but may lose their aroma, so buy small bottles. If you can't find them, use cider vinegar instead of clear and balsamic instead of black.

rock sugar Yellow rock sugar comes as uneven lumps of sugar, which may need to be further crushed before use if very big. It is a pure sugar that produces a clear syrup and makes sauces it is added to shiny and clear. You can use sugar lumps instead.

salted, fermented black beans Very salty black soy beans that are fermented using the same molds as are used for making soy sauce. Added to dishes as a flavoring, they must be rinsed before use and are often mashed or crushed. They are available in jars or bags from specialist shops. You can also use a black bean sauce made with black beans and garlic.

sea cucumber A slug-like sea creature related to the starfish, available dried or vacuum-packed. When sold dried, it needs to be reconstituted by soaking. It has a gelatinous texture and no flavor .

sesame oil (roasted) Chinese sesame oil is made from roasted white sesame seeds and is a rich amber liquid, unlike the pale unroasted Middle Eastern sesame oil. Buy small bottles as it loses its aroma quickly. It does not fry well as it smokes at a low temperature, but sprinkle it on food as a seasoning or mix it with other oils for stir-frying.

sesame paste Made from ground, toasted white sesame seeds, this is a fairly dry paste. It is more aromatic than tahini, which can be used instead by mixing it with a little Chinese sesame oil. Black sesame paste is used for sweets like New Year's dumplings.

Shaoxing rice wine Made from rice, millet, yeast and Shaoxing's local water, this is aged for at least three years, then bottled either in glass or decorative earthenware bottles. Several varieties are available. As a drink, rice wine is served warm in small cups. Dry sherry is the best substitute.

shark's fin Prized for its texture more than for its flavor, shark's fin is very expensive. Preparing a dried fin takes several days, so using the prepackaged version is much easier as it just needs soaking and then cooking. It looks like very thin dried noodles.

Sichuan (Szechwan) peppercorns Not a true pepper, but the berries of a shrub called the prickly ash. Sichuan pepper, unlike ordinary pepper, has a pungent flavor and the aftertaste, rather than being simply hot, is numbing. The peppercorns should be crushed and dry-roasted to bring out their full flavor.

slab sugar Dark brown sugar with a caramel flavor sold in a slab. Soft brown sugar can be used instead.

soy sauce Made from fermented soy beans, soy sauce comes in two styles: light soy sauce, which is also known as just soy sauce or superior soy sauce, and is used with fish, poultry and vegetables, and dark soy sauce, which is more commonly used with meats. Chinese soy sauce, unlike Japanese, is not used as a condiment except with Cantonese cuisine. As it is not meant to be a dipping sauce, it is best to mix a tablespoon of dark with two tablespoons of light to get a good flavor for a condiment. It does not last forever so buy small bottles and store it in the fridge.

soy beans These are oval, pale green beans. The fresh beans are cooked in their fuzzy pods and served as a snack. The dried beans can be yellow or black, and the yellow ones are used to make soy milk by boiling and then puréeing the beans with water before straining off the milk. Dried beans need to be soaked overnight.

spring roll wrappers Also called spring roll skins, these wrappers are made with egg and are pale or dark yellow. They are found in the refrigerated section of Chinese markets and supermarkets and can be frozen until needed.

star anise An aromatic ingredient in Chinese cooking, this is a star-shaped dried seed pod containing a flat seed in each point. It has a similar flavor and aroma to fennel seed and aniseed. It is used whole in braised dishes or ground into five-spice powder.

steaming A method of cooking food in a moist heat to keep it tender and preserve its flavor. Bamboo steamers fit above a saucepan or wok and a 10 inch steamer is the most useful, although you will need a bigger one for whole fish. Use as many as you need, stacked on top of each other, and reverse them halfway through cooking to ensure the cooking is even. Metal steamers are available, but bamboo ones are preferred in China as they absorb the steam, making the food a little drier.

stir-frying A method of cooking in a wok that only uses a little oil and cooks the food evenly and quickly, retaining its color and texture. Everything to be cooked needs to be prepared beforehand, cut to roughly the same shape, dry and at room temperature. The wok is heated, then the oil added and heated before the ingredients are thrown in. Stir-frying should only take a couple of minutes, the heat should be high and the ingredients continually tossed.

tangerine peel Dried tangerine or orange peel is used as a seasoning. It looks like dark-brown strips of leather with a white underside, and is used mostly in braised dishes or master sauces. It is not soaked first but is added straight to the liquid in the dish. Sold in bags in Chinese markets.

tiger lily buds Sometimes called golden needles, these aren't from tiger lilies but are the unopened flowers from another type of lily. The buds are bought dried and then soaked. They have an earthy flavor and are used mainly in vegetarian dishes.

water chestnuts These are the rhizomes of a plant that grows in paddy fields in China. The nut has a dark-brown shell and a crisp white interior. The raw nuts need to be peeled with a knife and blanched, then stored in water. Canned ones need to be drained and rinsed. Freshly peeled nuts are sometimes available from Chinese markets.

water spinach Called ong choy in Chinese, this vegetable has long, dark-green pointed leaves and long hollow stems. Often cooked with shrimp paste.

wheat starch A powder-like flour made by removing the protein from wheat flour. It is used to make dumpling wrappers.

winter melon A very large dark green gourd or squash that looks like a watermelon. The skin is dark green, often with a white waxy bloom, and the flesh is pale green. You can usually buy pieces of it in Chinese markets.

wok A bowl-shaped cooking vessel that acts as both a frying pan and a saucepan in the Chinese kitchen. Choose one made from carbon steel about 14 inch in diameter. To season it, scrub off the layer of machine oil, then heat with two tablespoons of oil over low heat for several minutes. Rub the inside with paper towels, changing the paper until it comes out clean. The inside will continue to darken as it is used and only water should be used for cleaning. Use a different wok for steaming, as boiling water will strip off the seasoning. A metal spatula (charn) is perfect for moving ingredients around the wok.

won ton wrappers Also called won ton skins, these are square and yellow and slightly larger than dumpling wrappers. They can be found in the refrigerated section in Chinese markets and good supermarkets and can be frozen until needed.

yard-long beans Also called snake or long beans, these are about 16 inches long. The darker green variety has a firmer texture.

yellow bean sauce This is actually brown in color and made from fermented yellow soy beans, which are sweeter and less salty than black beans, mixed with rice wine and dark brown sugar. It varies in flavor and texture (some have whole beans in them) and is sold under different names—crushed yellow beans, brown bean sauce, ground bean sauce and bean sauce. It is mainly used in Sichuan and Hunan cuisine.

INDEX

BIBLIOGRAPHY

Bartlett, Frances and Lai, Ivan. *Hong Kong on a Plate.* Roundhouse Publications (Asia) Ltd, 1997.

Bender, Arnold and David. *Oxford Dictionary of Food and Nutrition.* Oxford University Press, 1995.

Davidson, Alan. *The Oxford Companion to Food.* Oxford University Press, 1999.

Halvorsen, Francine. *The Food and Cooking of China.* John Wiley & Sons, Inc., 1996.

Hom, Ken. *Easy Family Dishes.* BBC Books, 1998.

Hom, Ken. *Ken Hom's Asian Ingredients.* Ten Speed Press, 1996.

Hom, Ken. *The Taste of China.* Pavilion Books Limited, 1990.

Hsiung, Deh-Ta. *The Chinese Kitchen.* Kyle Cathie Limited, 1999.

Hsiung, Deh-Ta. *The Festive Food of China.* Kyle Cathie Limited, 1991.

Hutton, Wendy. *The Food of China.* Periplus Editions (HK) Ltd, 1996.

Lo, Vivienne and Jenny. *150 Recipes from the Teahouse.* Faber and Faber Limited, 1997.

Mowe, Rosalind. *Culinaria: Southeast Asian Specialties.* Könemann, 1999.

Passmore, Jacki. *The Encyclopedia of Asian Food & Cooking.* Doubleday, 1991.

Ross, Rosa Lo San. *Beyond Bok Choy A Cock's Guide to Asian Vegetables.* Artisan, 1996.

Shun Wah, Annette and Aitken, Greg. *Banquet Ten Courses to Harmony.* Doubleday, 1999.

Simonds, Nina. *China's Food, A Traveler's Guide to the Best Restaurants, Dumpling Stalls, Teahouses and Markets in China.* Harper Perennial, 1991.

Simonds, Nina. *Classic Chinese Cuisine.* Houghton Mifflin Company, 1994.

Sinclair, Charles. *International Dictionary of Food and Cooking.* Peter Collin Publishing Ltd, 1998.

Sinclair, Kevin. *China The Beautiful Cookbook.* The Knapp Press, 1987.

Solomon, Charmaine. *Encyclopedia of Asian Food.* William Heinemann, 1996.

Sterling, Richard, Chong, Elizabeth Qin, Lushan Charles. *World Food Hong Kong.* Lonely Planet Publications Pty Ltd, 2001.

Yin-Fei Lo, Eileen. *The Dim Sum Dumpling Book.* Macmillan, 1995.

Yin-Fei Lo, Eileen. *The Chinese Kitchen.* William Morrow and Company, Inc, 1999.

Yiu, Hannah. *Easy Asian Vegetable Cooking.* Oriental Merchant Pty Ltd.

Young, Grace. *The Wisdom of the Chinese Kitchen.* Simon & Schuster Editions, 1999.

THE FOOD OF CHINA

Published by Murdoch Books®

 Published 2001. Reprinted 2002, 2003 (twice).
National Library of Australia Cataloguing-in-Publication Data
Hsiung, Deh-Ta. The food of China. Includes index. ISBN 1 74045 284 4.
1. Cookery, Chinese. I. Simonds, Nina. II. Lowe, Jason. III. Title. 641.5951
A catalogue record of this book is available from the British Library.

Publishing Manager: Kay Halsey
Food Editor: Lulu Grimes
Design Concept: Marylouise Brammer
Designer: Susanne Geppert
Editor: Justine Harding
Photographer: Jason Lowe
Stylist: Sarah de Nardi
Stylist's Assistants: Ross Dobson, Shaun Arantz, Olivia Lowndes
Recipes: Deh-Ta Hsiung, Nina Simonds
Additional Recipes: Wendy Quisumbing
Interpreter: Anna Bryant
Map: Rosanna Vecchio

Publisher: Kay Scarlett
Chief Executive: Juliet Rogers

PRINTED IN CHINA by Leefung-Asco Printers Ltd.
 Murdoch Books® is a subsidiary of Murdoch Magazines Australia Pty Ltd.

Murdoch Books® Australia
GPO Box 1203, Sydney, NSW 1045
Phone: + 61 (0) 2 4352 7000 Fax: + 61 (0) 2 4352 7026

Murdoch Books® UK
Ferry House, 51– 57 Lacy Road, Putney, London SW15 1PR
Phone: + 44 (0) 208 355 1480 Fax: + 44 (0) 208 355 1499

IMPORTANT: Those who might be at risk from the effects of salmonella food poisoning (the elderly, pregnant women, young children and those suffering from immune deficiency diseases) should consult their GP with any concerns about eating raw eggs.

ACKNOWLEDGMENTS

The Publisher wishes to thank the following for all their help in making this book possible:

Bass Hotels and Resorts: Geoffrey Webb, Bradley Moody; Hong Kong Tourist Association: Liam Fitzpatrick, Peter Randall; Oriental Merchant: Hannah Yiu; Chopstix Media: Ian Fenn.

Beijing: Chen Shi, Malan Restaurants, Beijing; Bob Ren, Jerrie Xuan, Crowne Plaza, Beijing; Niu Lihong, Beijing Wangfujing Quanjude Roast Duck Restaurant, Beijing; Li Family Restaurant, Beijing; Lily Wei, Beijing Tourism Bureau; Kaman Ng, Australian Embassy, Beijing. Shanghai: Alex; Maggie Wang, Julie Chan, Crowne Plaza, Shanghai; Mid-lake Pavilion Tea House, Shanghai. Hangzhou: Anne Stackler, Marcel Holman, Kenneth Law, Holiday Inn, Hangzhou; Wen Family Tea, Hangzhou. Chengdu: Valerie Tan, Lakshman T Perera, Willy Schnitzel, Richard Cheng, White Bai, Nancy Lu, Crowne Plaza, Chengdu; Tea House, Wenshu Monastery, Chengdu. Dali: Li-yi He, Mr China's Son, Dali. Kunming: Clark Liu, Holiday Inn, Kunming; Jacky Lee, Yunnan Tea Import and Export Corp., Kunming. Guilin: Tang Jun, Holiday Inn, Guilin. Guangzhou: Ida Chan, Raymond Wong, Holiday Inn City Centre, Guangzhou. Hong Kong: F.C. Tang, W. C. Yip, Ann Wai Pik Wa, Wendy Ko, Lee Kum Kee; Lee King Yin, Luk Yu Tea House, Hong Kong; Johnny Cheung, Ng Long, Wing Wah Noodles, Hong Kong; Tina Jansen, Prudence Mak, Catherine McNabb, Leung Fai Hung, Grand Stanford Inter-Continental, Hong Kong; Chan Janny, City Hall Chinese Restaurant, Hong Kong; So Shing Fung, Kung Wo Bean Curd Factory, Hong Kong.